I SEE YOU, SURVIVOR

I SEE YOU, SURVIVOR

LIFE INSIDE (AND OUTSIDE) THE TOTALLY F*CKED-UP TROUBLED TEEN INDUSTRY

LIZ IANELLI,
aka Survivor993

with
BRET WITTER

hachette
BOOKS   NEW YORK

Hachette Books
Hachette Book Group
1290 Avenue of the Americas
New York, NY 10104
HachetteBooks.com
Twitter.com/HachetteBooks
Instagram.com/HachetteBooks

First Edition: August 2023

Published by Hachette Books, an imprint of Hachette Book Group, Inc. The Hachette Books name and logo are trademarks of the Hachette Book Group.

The Hachette Speakers Bureau provides a wide range of authors for speaking events. To find out more, visit hachettespeakersbureau.com or email HachetteSpeakers@hbgusa.com.

Books by Hachette Books may be purchased in bulk for business, educational, or promotional use. For information, please contact your local bookseller or email the Hachette Book Group Special Markets Department at Special.Markets@hbgusa.com.

The publisher is not responsible for websites (or their content) that are not owned by the publisher.

Print book interior design by Jeff Williams

Library of Congress Cataloging-in-Publication Data

Names: Ianelli, Liz, author. | Witter, Bret, author.
Title: I see you, survivor: life inside (and outside) the totally f*cked up troubled-teen industry / Liz Ianelli, aka Survivor993 with Bret Witter.
Description: First edition. | New York: Hachette Books, 2023.
Identifiers: LCCN 2022050707 | ISBN 9780306831522 (hardcover) | ISBN 9780306831539 (trade paperback) | ISBN 9780306831546 (ebook)
Subjects: LCSH: Teenagers—Abuse of. | Mentally ill teenagers—Abuse of. | Mentally ill teenagers—Institutional care. | Teenagers—Mental health services. | Mental health facilities—Corrupt practices. | Abused teenagers.
Classification: LCC HV1421 .I26 2023 | DDC 362.73/2—dc23/eng/20221031

LC record available at https://lccn.loc.gov/2022050707

ISBNs: 9780306831522 (hardcover); 9780306831546 (ebook)

Printed in the United States of America

LSC-C

Printing 1, 2023

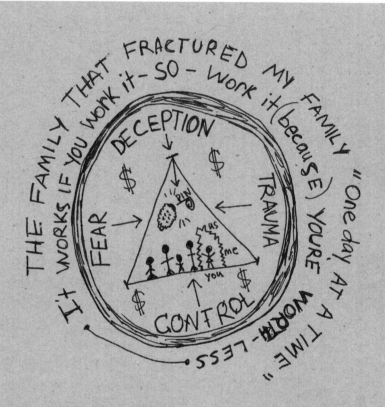

THIS MEMOIR REFLECTS my recollection of events, rendered to the best of my ability. Some names and identifying characteristics have been changed, and conversations have been reconstructed, so if you were there with me, don't @ me; I did my best and took it as far as I could.

THIS IS YOUR trigger warning.

What you will read here is upsetting, especially if you have suffered abuse. Not just in the Troubled Teen Industry, which has abused a million kids over the last forty years, but any abuse.

Don't worry. Keep going.

This is not a story of trauma but of triumph over trauma. Telling it has helped me heal. I have healed because someone asked for my story, and when I spoke, people listened. Finally. You, by picking up this book, see me. By reading it, you hear me.

You are part of my healing journey.

This story can heal you, too. Because it is our story, not theirs. It is proof that you are not alone. You can triumph. You *will* triumph if you endure. If you speak your truth, we will hear you.

I see you, survivor. This is for us.

To those who have not yet found their voice,
To those who can no longer speak,
And to those who have asked me,
"What the hell is wrong with you?"
And for Jon

Contents

Troubled

The Wolf Pack

Survivorland

I SEE YOU, SURVIVOR

TROUBLED

1

Downhill

I WOKE UP ON a long downward slope, with no idea where I was. A two-lane road stretched to the bottom of the hill, then up the other side. I could see other hills in the distance, almost mountains. There was nothing else around but rocks and trees.

My uncles were in the front seat. That made sense. My two uncles and parents had picked me up from Four Winds, an adolescent psychiatric facility, after lunch. My parents were in one car, my uncles in another. My parents were scared of me, I've been told. They brought my uncles for muscle. I didn't know that. I climbed eagerly into the back seat of my uncle's car, free of my burdens, happy to be going home . . . and woke up here, now, on this desolate road. It was the middle of the day. I hadn't been tired. We were a long way from home. I didn't like this at all.

"Where are we?"

No answer.

"What's going on?"

They wouldn't look at me.

My father's car, in front of us, slowed and turned onto a desolate single-lane dirt road. A dirty farmhouse, siding missing and windows wrapped in plastic, hovered over a steep rise. Two black barns were collapsing nearby. Beyond the house sat a machine, like a tractor with sharpened pitchforks in the front, curving downward toward the ground. A cow. A goat. Then nothing. Just a thin road disappearing over a hill.

I panicked. I pulled the door handle to jump out of the car, but it wouldn't engage. The child locks were on. My uncles still hadn't looked at me. Now I was terrified.

The hill seemed endless. I later discovered the drive from the farmhouse was eight-tenths of a mile, but it was steep. Wherever we were in the world, it was all hills. The road was bordered by fields of chest-high ornamental grass, with forest beyond. We topped the rise and headed downhill. I'm not sure what I saw that first day, but I know every inch now: a red barn, a three-story main building, two small houses, a chapel, and a pond. Everything was cheap and old except the main building, which was cheap and new. Everything was evil, especially that dark, dank pond.

"What is this place?" I was trying to be calm. Trying to be good. "What are we doing here?"

We curved down the hill to the front of the main building. My parents got out of their car and walked toward the front door. A woman stepped onto the porch to greet them. My parents never looked at me, but the woman did. She was tiny, with big hair and pink shoes. She smirked at my uncle's car as she put an arm around my mother and led them inside.

Two boys came out a different door. I was fifteen; they were a few years older. They ripped open the car door.

"No," I screamed as they jerked me to the ground.

"Please," I shrieked, kicking frantically as they dragged me into a windowless room, then slammed the door behind them. That room was the boot closet, but there were no boots, just cubbyholes. Two girls were waiting for me.

"Take off your clothes," the senior girl said.

"No," I said. "There's been a mistake. I'm not supposed to be here."

She slapped me in the face. "That's what they all say. Take off your clothes, or we'll take them off for you."

I pushed her. She pushed back. There was a fight: a full-on punching, scratching, kicking fight. I wasn't taking off my clothes, not like this. To give in to this place was to fall into something black. I could feel it in my bones. So they threw me against the wall. I charged. They punched. I punched. They had to call in three more girls to hold me down while they ripped off my shirt, my pants, my shoes and socks and bra. They jerked the tiger-eye rings off my fingers. They tore the bracelets off my arms. They snapped the necklace my friend at Four Winds had given me that morning, when we thought I was going home. Everything I cared about, that place took from me: music, art, posters, mementos, jewelry, clothes, even my Nancy Drew books, and I had always found love and comfort in Nancy Drew. They took my friends. My freedom. My kindness. They took my sense of self, until I had no idea who I was or what I wanted. They took my memories and corrupted them. They took everything good inside me and made me hate it, mistrust it, and fear it, until I finally took it myself and drowned it in that dank black pond, believing my goodness was the evil pulling me down.

But that was later.

That afternoon, in the boot closet, they took my jewelry and clothes. They did it violently and with joy. Then they kicked me a duffel bag. "Put those on," they said.

Inside there were two sweatshirts, a couple of shirts, underwear, socks, two pairs of pants. They weren't mine. My mother had bought and packed them, as instructed. Every parent did.

They made me clean up so the blood wouldn't show. The bruises, they knew, wouldn't be visible until later. They walked me down a hallway to the office. My parents were inside with the woman from the porch and a very tall man.

"Hello, Lizzy," the woman said. Lizzy wasn't my name. My parents called me Elizabeth. I called myself Liz. So they took my name, too.

"This is where you're going to be from now on, Lizzy. Your parents have had enough of you."

I wish you could hear her voice. It was flat and nasal, impossible to place. I have tracked down every asshole in that place. I know where they were born, where they went to school (high school—most never went to college). I know their spouses, their kids, their job histories. I know their thoughts and deeds better than they know their own. I do that so I can put a thumb on their future. But Robin Ducey has eluded me. She seems to have been nobody and to have come from nowhere.

"It's time to go now," Robin said to my parents. The cruelty was unmistakable. She was enjoying this.

And my parents: they turned to go. Maybe a sad look in their eyes. Maybe. But no hugs. No kind words. Not even a goodbye.

I lost it. I had panicked when we passed that desolate, beaten farmhouse, but now terror overwhelmed me. My parents were turning their backs on me. They were leaving me here with these people. And it was going to be bad. I felt it in my soul. I wasn't safe. And my parents saw it, too. They must have seen my distress. That was the betrayal. They saw terror grip their child, and they didn't seem to care.

I don't know what I said. I don't know how I broke free from the two girls holding my arms. I lunged at my parents, screaming at them. Asking for another chance, maybe, or for them to take me back. They kept walking. I swung wildly at my father, hitting him hard in the upper arm. I was trying to get his attention. I was trying to get him to *pay attention to this*.

He put his hand on my mother's back and pushed her out the door. When it closed behind them, I went wild, like a caged animal. I don't know what happened, but I know I punched the big guy. I was five foot six, big for a fifteen-year-old girl. He was about eight inches taller. Mine was a glancing blow to the chin. He sledgehammered me in the side of the head. He hit me so hard, I slammed into the wall and slumped at its base. I was barely able to think, much less stand. But I could see the little woman, Robin, smirking behind him.

"Girls," she said, "come get Lizzy."

The girls picked me up.

"Lizzy," Robin said as they held me facing her, "welcome to the Family."

The girls hauled me out through the back door. It was about a hundred yards uphill to one of the houses, and as they walked me up the path, they recited a list of rules: Tuck in your shirt. No button-downs. No eye contact. I looked around, but my parents and uncles were gone.

"There's been a mistake," I said. "There's been a terrible mistake. I'm not. I'm not supposed to be here."

The girls didn't answer.

"What is this place?"

"You have to ask permission before you can speak to me," one of the girls said.

They marched on in silence. I hoped she was joking, but she wasn't. "Can I talk to you?"

"What?" she snapped.

"How long will I be here?"

She laughed. "Until they say so," she said.

They took me through a sunken side entrance into what had been the house's underground garage. There were eight wooden bunk beds in a space no bigger than a small bedroom. The walls were crudely finished, the mattresses plastic. I'm sure the carpet was damp and squishy, because it was always damp and squishy.

"That's your bunk," they said. It was on the top, in a corner, next to the only window: one of those basement windows at ceiling height on the inside but ground level on the outside, too small for a person to squeeze through. I thought I was lucky to get the window, but I wasn't, because it leaked. We periodically bleached the black mold off the walls and ceiling, but it was under the carpet, I know it, because water pooled under the window when it rained.

I had arrived around 4:00 p.m.; by now it was time for dinner. The girls walked me to the second floor of the main building. It was an open space with two long parallel tables and a shorter table between them, forming a horseshoe. They sat me down as the room filled up, slowly but also all at once, until every chair was taken. There were about fifty kids, but nobody spoke. A few glanced at me, carefully, but nobody stared. The waitstaff, also teens, brought out our dinners: two stuffed peppers, one red, one yellow. I stared at my plate. I was starving but nauseous from the fear. And I hate peppers.

Bang. It was the sound of heavy metal hitting wood.

Immediately, every kid put down their fork and sat up straight.

Bang. They turned to the shorter table at the front of the room. Eight adults were sitting facing us. I saw Robin. The big guy who had punched me, Bob Runge, was dropping the knife. Every time its metal base hit the table, it made a ferocious bang. Bang. Bang.

It stopped. The room was silent.

"Lizzy." Robin's voice. "Stand up."

I stood up.

"Over there." She pointed to a spot in front.

"Lizzy is here because her parents are tired of her," Robin began, launching into a flat, emotionless takedown. *Lizzy's fat.*

She's lazy. She's ugly. She's a prostitute, a drunk, a drug addict. She's hateful. Nobody likes her. She's lucky she's not dead. "But we will save her, won't we, Family?"

"Yes, Robin," the kids said.

"We'll save her from herself."

"Yes, Robin," the group said.

When she was done, another adult started insulting me. *Fat. Ugly. Lazy. Slut.* I know that was what he said, even if I can't remember the details, because that was what they said to all the girls all the time.

"Yes, Paul," they replied.

When he was done, they went to the next adult, and the next. Each took a turn insulting and degrading me, even though they'd never met me. Then the kids raised their hands, and Robin called on them one by one.

"You're a slut, Lizzy," a boy said. "You have a stinky vagina. It's disgusting. I can smell it from here."

What? Is that true?

"Stand up straight, Lizzy," Robin barked.

"You're selfish, Lizzy," a girl said sadly. "You've hurt everyone who tried to love you. I'm ashamed to be around you."

"Look at your new family members," Robin barked. "You must always look your fellow family members in the eye. They are trying to save you."

"You're a sinner, Lizzy," another girl said. "You don't deserve forgiveness. But if you follow the program and believe in the Family way, you won't die."

I stood silently, making eye contact as teenagers I had never met stared me down and insulted me. It wasn't real. How could it be real? After thirty or forty minutes, when it was finally over and they let me sit down, I was so disoriented and confused—and embarrassed—and hurt—that I didn't know what to do.

"Eat your dinner."

There was no way I was eating those cold stuffed peppers.

"You will eat your dinner."

I stared down at my plate, afraid to lift my eyes.

"You two."

Two kids jumped up and tried to force-feed me. They held my arms and jammed the peppers against my lips. They pushed my face into the plate. I wouldn't give in. This wasn't defiance. My mind and body had shut down. And I really, really hated peppers. Always have. Definitely always will.

"Lizzy doesn't have to eat her peppers," Robin announced.

It became legend: how easy Robin was on me that night. It wouldn't take me long to realize why the other kids thought that way. Robin had shown me something truly rare: a morsel of pity. I was there for more than two and a half years. I never saw it again.

After the meal was "Nightly Reflection," down on your knees begging for mercy from the Virgin Mary in the empty third-floor attic. Then back to our basement dorm.

It was sixteen girls in a cheaply converted one-car garage with one toilet, one shower, and one sink. Girls weren't talking; they were hustling to get ready for bed. Still, it was loud. Sixteen girls in a small, enclosed space are loud. It haunts me: the sound of that place. The constant sound.

I tried to make myself small as I slipped into the bathroom to pee. There was no stall, just a toilet in the open. I struggled to relax. I am not a public pee-er. I don't even like people to hear my tinkle. Finally, though, I was comfortable enough to . . .

"What do you think you're doing?" It was the girl who had stripped me and beaten me in the broom closet.

"Um, going to the . . ."

She grabbed me off the toilet. I was done, mostly, not that it mattered. If I'd pissed myself, she wouldn't have cared.

"Never speak to me without permission."

"Yes, um . . . okay."

"Never try to get away from me again."

She was my Shadow. A Shadow was another teen assigned to be with you at all times: when you worked, when you ate, when you walked, when you prayed, in the bathroom. Shadow was a common punishment, or Sanction, as punishments were called. Double Shadow, two students, was also common. Shadow was mandatory for every new kid for at least a month.

I went to my bunk. Nobody said a word. If you think there was any kindness, or empathy, or understanding in that room, if you think we girl-talked or braided each other's hair or giggled when the lights went out, then you don't understand yet what they did to us. There was the rage of the boot closet, the cruelty of the dining room, and nothing else.

I know what they were thinking of me because within a month, I was thinking it of new girls, too: *fresh meat*.

"Lights out," a girl announced. There was no staff in the dorms. We policed ourselves, and we did it ruthlessly. When the dorm leader ordered lights out, nobody spoke back. They lay in their bunks. The dorm leader pushed her bunk in front of the only door. This was Landlocking: blocking a door with a bunk or other heavy object. The door was usually locked from the outside, but Landlocking made sure we were trapped for the night.

I tried to be small. I tried to shrink and disappear. The bunks were normal height, but the ceiling was low. I had about a foot of space. When I turned on my side, my shoulder touched the ceiling. I stared at the stained drop tile above my head—I remember every inch of that filthy tile—and tried not to think, not to catastrophize, not to panic or die inside. But as soon as the lights went out, I started crying, and I couldn't stop. I tried to hold my breath. I put my hand over my mouth. I rolled over and buried my face in the thin, musty pillow. But all night it was:

"Chill out, new girl."

"You better shut up."

"Nobody cares about your tears."

It was Tuesday, September 28, 1994. Day 1 of 993.

It would only get worse from there.

2

She Beats Me

DAY 2, 5:00 a.m., lights on, as always. The senior girls ripped me out of my bunk onto the wet carpet. That carpet: the smell gags me, two decades later. I can feel the way it squished up into the spaces between my toes.

"New girl, clean the bathroom."

I scrubbed the toilet, sink, drains, shower. Then morning prayer on the third floor of the main building, my stomach rumbling. I hadn't eaten in fifteen hours. But you learn to love starvation. You crave it after a while. Otherwise, it's torture.

After breakfast in the second-floor dining room, probably wet scrambled eggs and a sausage patty, our usual, I was taken by Robin to a room on the first floor with a table, a few pencils, and a stack of loose-leaf paper.

She sat me down in the only chair. "Make a list of all the things that landed you here," she said.

"Please," I said, "let me talk to my parents."

"Write," she said, and left me alone. Even my Shadow was gone.

This was Inventory. Every new kid had to do it. It was based on the fourth step of Alcoholics Anonymous: *Make a searching and fearless moral inventory of ourselves.* This place was loosely based, I learned later, on AA. An angry, violent, fundamentalist Christian version.

So I made a searching and fearless moral inventory: I ran away with a group of boys to ride bikes. I hit my sister. I hated my mother. I skipped school. I didn't talk to my therapist.

Then I waited for what seemed like forever, but was probably more like half an hour, for Robin to return.

"Not enough," she said, and left.

I thought up a few more true things. I was kicked out of school. I had a bad attitude. I hit my mother. I screamed at my father. I smoked cigarettes a few times. I sipped a beer.

"Not enough," Robin said.

This time I just waited for her to come back. I didn't have anything else to say. An hour passed, maybe. There was no clock; this was before cell phones; I didn't have a watch. They had taken everything from me when I arrived.

"You won't get out of here, Lizzy," Robin said, "until you write down every sin you have committed and every terrible thing you have done."

"Like what?"

"Like your drug addiction."

I wasn't a good kid. I admit that. I was every parent's nightmare. I talked back. I was mopey. I snuck out of the house. I "made a scene" and embarrassed my mother. I stopped going to school. But I never used drugs.

"Admit what you've done, Lizzy," Robin said. "Admit your sins. It's the only way to be free."

I was never close to my mother. Maybe it was postpartum depression. Maybe it was trauma, because I was born barely one year after her first child was stillborn, and she never dealt with the pain. It was a pretty lonely childhood.

When I was eight, a close adult relative started molesting me. By the time I was nine, we were having sex. It was rape, but I thought we were in a relationship. When I was eleven, my grandmother walked in on us naked. He always raped me in the spare bedroom at my grandmother's house.

My father spanked us as punishment. I remember every place I was standing when my mother slapped me in the face. She was so good at it, she could slap all three of us kids with one shot, like the Three Stooges. My godmother told me recently about my mother turning and slapping me in the face in a grocery store when I was five or six years old and then walking with me out of the store as if nothing had happened. Apparently I was being annoying.

This was different. My grandmother pulled me out of the bedroom and beat me with a wooden rolling pin. It was an Italian rolling pin, so it was long and thin but solid.

"Never tell anyone about this," she yelled as I huddled on her plastic-covered, cream-colored living room carpet. "Never tell."

She never told anybody, and she never did anything, because my abuser—my "boyfriend"—went right on raping me in that bedroom for another year, until I turned twelve and had my first period. My parents made a big deal out of that. My father bought me a dozen red roses, a family tradition.

"I hear you're a woman now," my abuser said the next time we were alone. I could hear something different in his voice.

"Yes," I said.

"We won't be seeing each other anymore. Do you understand?"

I didn't understand, so I didn't say anything.

"Do you understand?"

"Yes."

"Good," he said, and walked out.

He lived two hours away. He stopped finding excuses to come to town. I have only seen him twice in the thirty years since, both times at funerals, and even though I was a little kid, I knew it would be like that when he walked out the door, that he would never speak to me again. And I was heartbroken, *heartbroken*, that the love of my little life had dumped me cold.

"You're an alcoholic," Robin said.

"I'm not," I said. I had spiraled, but not into alcohol. I was twelve. I was too young. I sipped a few beers at family barbecues at fourteen, fifteen, when someone was passing a can around, but that was it.

"You're an alcoholic, Lizzy," Robin insisted, "and the fact that you are denying it proves that it's true."

I hated my mother. That's the truth. I punched her, kicked her, and once even bit her. I yelled and threw things at the wall. I spent hours by myself at a swampy creek near our house. I caught frogs and cut them open so I could study their insides. Then I stapled their bodies to our house. I hate admitting that because I don't think you'll understand. It sounds like I was a budding psychopath. But those frogs were a message to my father, the one parent who loved and protected me. It felt like the only time he paid attention to me anymore was when he was angry, so I had to make him angry enough to see me. I didn't fully understand it at the time, but those dead frogs were expressing a hurt I couldn't speak and he could never hear.

My parents took me out of Catholic school, which was fine. I had ADHD. I couldn't sit still. I didn't like their books. *Why can't I read Nancy Drew?* I struggled with math. *Why can't I just do art?* I wanted to be an artist. Why does an artist need math?

My parents put me in the public school for the sixth grade. The bullying started on the bus the first morning. I was aggressive at home, with my family, but never outside. I took the bullying until I couldn't take it anymore. Then I stopped taking the bus, which meant I started missing school.

"How many beers did you drink, Lizzy?"

"I don't know. Two?"

"No."

"Five?"

"You know that's not true."

"Ten?"

Robin smiled. "And how often did you drink? Every day?"

"Yes, Robin."

By now I had been at the table for four or five hours without food, water, or bathroom breaks. I wasn't allowed to stand or walk around. I couldn't talk unless Robin was present. My Shadow was gone, replaced by a staffer. They periodically switched out for the rest of the time I was in the room. The only thing they allowed me to do was write, and since I didn't have anything true to write, I wrote what Robin wanted.

"That's right, Lizzy. Alcoholics drink every day. They do drugs and have sex. You're going to tell me about the sex, Lizzy. All of it."

I didn't have sex. I hated the idea of sex if it wasn't with my adult relative, who, in a vile and horrible twist that makes me sick to my stomach, I love to this day in a little part of my heart that I can't kill. Mostly I stayed in my room. My family remembers me as violent and angry. And I was. I remember being depressed. And lonely. Things were bad at school. Things were horrible at home. I was absolutely alone.

My parents sent me to therapists. By then, everything was being blown out of proportion. I etched a cute boy's initials in my knee with a thumbtack. It didn't break the skin, but my guidance counselor said I was cutting. A popular girl asked me to carry a bottle of mouthwash to the gym for her. It spilled. The school said I was drinking it for the alcohol. The popular girl *was* drinking it for the alcohol; I just wanted someone to be nice to me.

I poured a can of paint on the basement floor. It was an impulse. I regretted it. Straight to the therapist. I wrote a suicide note. I wasn't serious. I just wanted to know what it felt like. My mother found it, and her reaction wasn't "Oh, honey, are you alright?" It was "Oh, God, now this, too?"

I spent a month at Boston Children's Hospital. That was scary. Those kids were mentally ill. My roommate was an anorexic who pounded water for her weigh-ins, then threw it up afterward.

"She's a Mexican jumping bean," the doctor told my father when I was released. "She just has a lot of energy."

Life got better. I made friends with some fellow outcasts: the BMX Boys. That's what they called themselves. They were mostly Hispanic and from the trailer park, so my parents said they were "bad influences," but they were just kids. We hung out in the parking lot behind an office building. It had a steep flight of stairs and a sloped wall so they could do tricks on their BMX bicycles. I mostly watched.

"What kind of sex were you having, Lizzy?"

"None." I had two boyfriends in middle school, both innocent. The one in seventh grade was Black. My parents made me break up with him.

"It's okay," he said, but his eyes were down. "My mother told me it would be like this."

"Don't lie to me, Lizzy," Robin said, with her flat menace. "I don't want to say what you were doing, I'm a good Christian woman, but I want to see it on the list."

I loved Cyndi Lauper, so I shaved one side of my head above the ear, like she did. Therapist. I listened to Metallica and grunge. This was 1993; everyone listened to Metallica and grunge. My parents thought I was worshiping Satan. I painted my nails black. A different therapist, citing my nails, suggested an alternative school. I got a copy of her report a few years ago. The report that sent me to hell.

Turns out, she liked my nails. She thought I was an interesting kid who just didn't fit in. She recommended an arts magnet school.

"You stole from your parents," Robin said. "Isn't that right? Think about it, Lizzy, because I know you did. Every bad child steals from their parents."

My life blew up one night in the summer of 1994 when I snuck out the window of my bedroom to hang with the BMX Boys. I did that a lot that summer. I rode my bike or walked to our parking lot. I drove the route recently to see how far it was from my house. It was less than a quarter mile.

The cops picked us up. We weren't doing anything, just riding bikes. It wasn't late; evening, with a little light left in the sky. But they rolled us up, took us to the local precinct, and held us for a few hours before contacting our parents. When my parents arrived, the cops said we'd been breaking into condos—we had walked around the development for a while, that was all—and strongly implied I was having sex with all five of my friends, probably at the same time.

"You were turning tricks, weren't you Lizzy?" It must have been hour eight or nine. "You were prostituting yourself for drugs."

Why do so many adults fantasize about the sex life of an outcast teenage girl? Why is that okay? I was sexually *damaged*, not active.

My parents drove me straight from the police station to Four Winds, a psychiatric hospital for children. They checked me in as an involuntary residential patient. I was a danger to myself and others, they said, because I had run away from home and stayed out all night. They left me there in a place that was . . . well, it was awesome, actually.

The staff at Four Winds were nice. They were professionals. They wanted to help. My life had been spiraling out of control. I know that. I admit it. But at Four Winds, I had space to relax and people who listened. Who saw me. I made friends. I worked on my art. They figured out my medications. ADHD was controversial then. My mother recently gave me a folder of articles she'd clipped out of magazines and newspapers at the time: ADHD was an excuse used by manipulative kids; ADHD was nothing to worry about; ADHD was a serious condition that left untreated, even for a year, would ruin your child's life. No wonder my parents didn't know what to do with me. Nobody back then knew what to do with a kid like me. Except Four Winds.

I'm not sure how long I was there: four weeks? Thirty days? Six weeks? The basic answer is until the insurance ran out.

By then, I was feeling good. I was ready to go home and start fresh, embrace a new attitude, have a new lease on life, rah, rah. Instead, I blacked out in the back of my uncle's car (not my rapist, by the way). I woke up to the boot closet, the peppers, the moldy basement, and this closed cell with my nemesis, Robin Ducey.

I was in that room for at least ten hours with no food or water. I entered in the morning and came out after dark. By the end, I was so exhausted that I confessed to whatever Robin wanted me to confess: alcohol abuse, heroin addiction, prostitution, armed robbery. Everything short of capital murder. My final confession was eighteen pages long, and it was seventeen and three-quarter pages of lies. It wasn't my story. It was the story Robin gave me. The story that place gave everyone, because to them there was only one story:

You were an addict. You were out of control. You were disgusting and debased. You had destroyed yourself and hurt everyone who loved you, and you were lucky to be here—so very lucky your parents loved you enough to put you here—because left on your own, you were weeks, or days, or mere hours away from being dead and burning in hell.

Oh, we were in hell, alright. Believe me, this was hell.

We just weren't dead. Yet.

3

Table Topics

The Game Where Everyone Gets Hurt!

DAY 3, 5:00 a.m., scrub the bathroom. Up to the third floor of the main building for somber, terrifying prayers with Father Stephen, eyes on the ground but everyone's stomach rumbling. Sit in your assigned seat in the second-floor dining room. Watch a kid stood up from his watery eggs and called a sinner, a piece of shit, because another kid said he hadn't been paying attention during prayers.

"You were distracted, Jay. You were thinking about masturbating instead of God."

"I saw you glance at Laura. You want to fuck her, don't you?"

"Laura's a slut." That was a staff member. An adult. Most were in their forties or fifties. "We all know she's a slut. But even she would never fuck you, Jay. You're short. You're fat. You're stupid. You have a funny voice."

Then they made Laura stand up.

"Why are you tempting Jay, Laura, you dirty slut?"

After a breakfast of insults and accusations, they walked me to a van. Twenty kids were in the yard doing manual labor. Jay had been given Rock Sanction. He was taking ten-pound rocks off a big pile and moving them four feet away. Laura's Sanction was sweeping the dirt road.

We drove the narrow one-lane, out past the haunted farmhouse. A goat standing against the hill, staring. The tractor with the teeth. The wilderness was steep and ominous along Route 97, trees and rocky deadfalls, with occasional houses. We passed through several small postindustrial towns. A block of slanted storefronts, a few blocks of houses in different states of repair. An hour later, I was in a psychiatrist's office in a midsized town. He didn't examine me. He just took me off the prescription medication my therapists at Four Winds had given me, including my ADHD medication. The Family believed in *their* God and their Big Book. To them, medicine was drugs, and all drugs, even Tylenol and aspirin, were evil. They told parents the psychiatrist was a staff member. He was in the marketing material. But that was all he ever did: take new kids off their medication. Some adults will do anything for cash.

Back at the Family, more kids were in the yard doing manual labor. Some were mowing the grass. Some were carrying cinder blocks. Some of the boys were using heavy machinery to build a long, low chapel below the brow of the hill. Jay was still moving rocks from one pile to another pile four feet away. It looked like he was moving them back to their original location.

Dinner was . . . let's say beef stroganoff. We ate a lot of beef stroganoff. I stared at it, unsure. It was slippery and thick. But around me, kids were jamming it in their faces.

A hand went up. A girl from my dorm. Then another hand. Another.

Bang. Bang. It was Bob Runge, the man who had punched me. He was at the front table, dropping his knife.

Immediately, the kids put down their silverware and turned to face the staff. This was a Table Topic, and there was a ritual to it. You learned it fast, mostly the hard way.

Put your silverware down. Turn to the front table. Don't touch your food again until the Table Topic is finished, in a half hour if you're lucky. Hours if you're not.

Most Troubled Teen Programs had bright chairs, modeled on the famous blue chairs at Straight, the program that made the "tough love" industry an American cultural phenomenon. Ours were maroon. You sat on the edge of the seat with your back straight. Boys were allowed six inches to sit on; girls four. You could not lean against the back of the chair. If you did, you were stood up for verbal abuse and punishment. Your hands had to be flat on your thighs. If they moved, you were stood up. No shuffling your feet. No looking around, or you were stood up. It was unnerving, at my first meal as a "regular" kid, to see fifty kids sitting silently and erect. But you get used to fucked up pretty fast.

"Yes, Laura," Robin said. Robin wasn't the leader of the Family. That was Tony Argiros, the founder. But she was its dead heart.

"I want to stand up Marisa," the girl said.

"Marisa, stand up."

Marisa was my bunkmate. Dark hair, doe eyes. You could tell that out in the real world, she was a life-of-the-party type. A very likable girl.

"Marisa," the girl said, "I saw you looking at Keith. I am worried you're sinning."

Marisa didn't say anything.

That's weird.

"You've been distracted lately. Like when we were scrubbing the floor, you stopped for a minute. And your shirt was a little low in the front. Are you trying to attract the wrong kind of attention, Marisa? I'm worried you're falling back into your old ways."

Marisa didn't say anything.

What the fuck?

"What's going on, Marisa?" Robin asked coldly, or overly politely, take your pick.

I expected Marisa to defend herself, but she didn't say anything. She looked Robin in the eyes, just as she had looked the girl in the eyes.

"Marisa," Robin said, "you are a sex addict. You constantly disappoint. Doesn't she, Family?"

Nobody responded, not even Marisa.

So Robin slow-walked into a blistering takedown. Looking at boys. Thinking about sex. Dirty vagina. Everyone can smell your dirty vagina. "You try to make yourself pretty, Marisa, but why? We know why. We can smell your sexual desire. Your filthiness. That's why your parents left you here." Robin smirked. "Your father, I mean." I found out later Marisa's mother had died. "He loves his little girl. He's spending all his money on you, because you come from a poor family, don't you, Marisa? They are sacrificing for you. And all you do is cram your face and flirt with boys."

This went on for ten, fifteen minutes as, around the room, heels tapped. Hands vibrated on thighs. Fingers curled. Legs twitched. I could sense something rising around me. A heaviness in the air. It was the violent energy, I realized later, of a gathering storm.

"Does anyone else want to help Marisa?" Robin said coldly. The woman was nothing if not cold and controlled.

A dozen hands went up. There was a ritual to this, too. You could not wave. You could not lean or reach. You could not try to make eye contact with a staff member in the hopes of getting their attention. You sat calmly with your arm straight up, your eyes forward, and your mind blasting.

So when Robin called on a girl, she exploded, screaming about godliness and dirtiness, filth and sin.

"Thank you," Marisa said.

Girls told Marisa she was disgusting to be around. Boys said she was fat. (She was gorgeous.) She was dirty. (She had flawless skin.) She was stupid. (Definitely not.) They were as bad as Robin. They said violent, heinous things. *Vibrator? Douche? Cum bucket?* I didn't even know these terms.

It felt like a show. Like I was in the audience, watching a zookeeper shocking a monkey with an electric prod. And the monkey took it. Marisa was jolted. It hurt. I saw her flinch. But all she said was thank you.

I hated it. I was excited by it. I couldn't look away.

Is this what my parents wanted? It was worse than my middle school bully. It was worse than anything I had ever done.

At the end of it, kids shouted suggestions for punishment. Robin consulted a clipboard, then smiled. "Let's put Marisa on Half Portion," she said. "She's getting fat anyway."

I expected retribution in the dorm. A confrontation. The girls who had attacked Marisa were in there with us, and that shit was sick. But nobody said anything. They acted like they had the first night: hustling into bed in our allotted fifteen minutes, nobody talking with anyone.

"What was that?" I whispered to Marisa.

"Table Topic," she said, turning away.

"Where are we?" I meant in the world. I had no idea where this place was.

"The Family."

The next morning, at breakfast, a boy was stood up. He had been masturbating during the night, or so another boy said. After thirty minutes of verbal attacks, a second kid was stood up. Then a third.

It took so long I barely had time to scrub the dishes before we were back at lunch, where another hand went up. The knife dropped. Bang. Bang. We sat with our hands on our knees as they railed against Jay, the nicest kid in the place. He was laid-back, curly-haired, short and overweight, maybe, but chill. Jay had a harmless stoner vibe, straight out of 1969. He didn't have a mean bone in his body.

But he had a cleft palate, and it gave him a lisp. The staff destroyed him for that. They mocked him mercilessly for his lip scar and speech impediment.

Is that what I was here to learn? Is that why my parents were paying to send me here?

He's dead now. My friend Jay's been gone now, fifteen years.

Just keep your head down, Liz. Don't attract attention, don't say anything, and you'll be fine.

I had to meet with Robin in her office. She was my handler. We met once a week.

"Lizzy," Robin said, "why aren't you participating?"

"In what?"

"In the discussion. Don't you want to help Marisa overcome her addictions?"

Marisa and I had a connection. It wasn't a spoken thing. It was more a silent understanding that we liked each other, supported each other, were on each other's side. But I didn't know Marisa, and I certainly didn't know her addictions, whatever that meant. Why would I say anything bad about Marisa?

"You're selfish, Lizzy," Robin said. "You're corrupted and weak. That's why your parents didn't want you. That's why they left you here. But we can't help you, Lizzy, if you don't participate. Search your soul, Lizzy. Take an inventory. If you aren't honest, you'll never get better."

And you'll never get out.

"I'm putting you on Half Portion," Robin said. Half Portion was what it sounds like: you get half the normal amount of food. Girls already got half as much as boys, so there wasn't much left. "You're soft. You need to lose some weight."

That night, they went after Laura, the prettiest girl in the place. She had big boobs, when a lot of us weren't fully developed yet. She had long blonde hair. She had a beautiful soprano voice. She carried herself with confidence. So they hated her.

"You're a daddy fucker," Paul Geer yelled at her. Paul was the choir director. "You're a hooker. You fucked your family. You use your vagina as a vibrator for any man willing to stick his dick in you."

Laura was fifteen. She had been caught with a thirty-five-year-old boyfriend. What happened to him? I don't know. He probably got away with it. Laura got sent to the Family.

"Well, Jimmy . . ." she said. Laura always defended Jimmy.

"You call him James!" Paul Geer exploded. "When you call him Jimmy, you sexualize him. When you say Jimmy, you are fucking your father."

I am reconstructing these exchanges. I couldn't record them, obviously. Decades later, Paul denied abusing kids to a reporter. Of course. What else would he say? But I remember these specific words clearly because they were so bizarre, and so vile, and spoken with such violence and disgust. They staggered me. They drilled into my brain, because this was foul, and it was filthy, especially coming from a 566-pound adult male to a teenage girl, and it made no sense. Worse, I was beginning to realize Table Topics weren't an occasional thing. Table Topics were an every-meal kind of thing.

"Lizzy," Robin barked. "Lizzy. Do you have something to say to Laura?"

No. I did not. I didn't know her. I didn't want to insult her. I had a toxic relationship with my mother, but I didn't want to hurt anyone else. Not then. I mean, oh, boy, if Robin could see me now. If she could see what she made me.

"Lizzy," Robin said, "to the pole."

The pole was an extra shot of Table Topic for those who really needed God's help. I had to stand alone against a metal pole, like Joan of Arc at the fire lighting. *You're too nice*, Robin scolded. She always said that about me. *You're selfish and hateful. You hate your fellow students*—they always called us students—*because you love yourself too much. You are a dirty slut.* Yes, that again. *You are a hooker.* Certain words I will always associate with the Family. "Hooker" was one. Every girl was a hooker. Afterward, some actually became one.

"The Block for Lizzy," Robin said. "Make her carry the weight of her sin."

There were moments in those first days when I thought Robin might be okay. When I thought she might help me. That was her job, right? But I was just another monkey in the cage to her. Another animal to be tortured. She studied me, I think, until she knew what would hurt me most. And then, "Lizzy."

Silverware dropped. Kids turned to the front table, their hands on their thighs, their backs straight. I stood up. You had no choice but to stand up.

"To the pole," Robin said.

Robin was short. She had a compact little body and a cloud of hair. She rarely raised her voice; it just became harder and colder.

"Little Lizzy," she said, "do you have something to say to everyone? Do you have something to confess?"

I didn't say anything. I already understood this wasn't a conversation. You didn't speak unless you knew what they wanted. So I stared her in the eyes, as required.

"Little Lizzy," Robin said, "is a homosexual."

That was what they always said: not gay but homosexual, or homo. Being a homo was the worst thing you could be at the Family—worse than a masturbator, worse even than being Black.

Paul Geer, the 566-pound choir director, had a big brass handbell with a wooden handle. He rang it, with a grotesquely exaggerated arm motion that made his whole body jiggle and sweat, whenever they wanted to call us to the dining room when it wasn't mealtime. Usually, it was for a special Table Topic or because a kid had run away.

"For whom the bell tolls," we grumbled under our breaths. (Metallica, *Ride the Lightning*.)

I will never forget the day Paul Geer rang the bell and Tony Argiros, the founder and mob boss of the Family, came huffing into the room. I can only describe Tony as lumpy. He walked with a cane, but he was large and bent, with bulges. Not just his fat neck and oversized head, but growths and mounds and folds, like a toad. He got red when he was angry, and that day, he was bright red.

"I have discovered," he thundered, "that there is a homosexual here. In my house. Under the roof that I have given you."

He called a boy to the pole, and Tony Argiros absolutely blistered him. There was a clock in the dining area when I arrived, the only one in the place, but they took it down after a few weeks. They kept us in a perpetual state of confusion, not knowing the date or the time. So I don't know how long that kid was at the pole, being destroyed for being a homo. All I know is how long it felt: forever.

And none of us said a word in his defense. We couldn't. Do you understand? No matter what they did, we couldn't speak out. Or move. Or nod to the victim to say, *I know it's wrong. I see you. I'm with you. I care.*

We spoke against him. When it was our turn, we whipped him as hard as Tony Argiros and the other adults. Maybe harder.

That kid is dead now.

More than a hundred of us are dead now, mostly ODs and suicides, in our twenties and thirties.

I mean, how do you live with that?

How can you say, *Forget it, it's fine, it was a long time ago, everything is okay*, like everybody says you have to?

How can you forgive yourself when you were involved?

Was I a lesbian? Honestly, I don't know. I was a child when I arrived at the Family. I had been sexually abused. I never had a chance to know myself. I had two boyfriends in middle school. Since then, I have had three husbands. None of those relationships felt right.

I'm forty-three now, and I'm traumatized by my period. I have an IUD so I won't have one. Every time my IUD expires, I have a new one implanted. I ask the doctors to cut the wire short so that if anyone violates me, he'll get stabbed in the penis. That happened to a boyfriend, and no, I'm not sorry; just because we are in a relationship doesn't mean you have the right to take what's mine, any way you want, without my consent.

I am scared right now. I am so scared you will think I'm crazy or dangerous for admitting that. I'm scared you will close this book and say, *I thought Liz was strong, that she was a fighter and a survivor, but this . . . this feels like too much.*

I have three sons. I'm not afraid of them knowing my truth, even my youngest. But I'm afraid of people using this book to come after my boys, because they have. They took one of my sons from me based on the things I've suffered. There was a time I'd have said, *Just put me in the ground, then; I have nothing left. Just bury me deep and forget me.* But now I know that will never happen, because I'm not just a survivor—I'm a warrior, and I'll die fighting for them. And you. And us.

I don't want to fight. My parents won't believe me, but the last thing I want to do is fight. I want to be left in peace.

And yet if I don't speak the truth, who will?

Who will stand up for the survivors, struggling to speak for themselves?

For the thousands of kids in Troubled Teen Programs right now?

Who will listen? Who will understand us, and help us, if we don't keep shouting our dark and painful truth?

Was I a lesbian? It didn't matter to Robin. Don't get me wrong; she was a bigot from the top of her inflated hair to the sharp, pointed toes of her obnoxious pink heels, but this wasn't about "helping" me with my sexuality. It was about punishment.

After being annihilated at a Table Topic, there was always punishment. Usually, kids made suggestions, and the staffer who led the annihilation chose the cruelest. This time, Robin had already chosen the punishment.

"Lizzy," she said (God, I wish you could hear her cold, flat voice), "if you want to act like a dyke, you will look like a dyke."

I was a fifteen-year-old girl, not to mention a sexual abuse survivor. I hated myself. The anger I directed at my parents came from my pain and self-hatred, at least until they decided to deal with my outbursts by cracking down. When I got in those blow-out screaming matches with my father, I hated him for not understanding or caring about me. For seeing me as a problem and not his little girl. But I hated myself more. The way I looked—too fat, too uncoordinated, too many freckles. The way I acted. What I said. I hated myself for not being good enough for my own father to love.

The only thing I liked about myself was my hair. It was flame red (thus the freckles). People had always complimented my hair. It was my crown.

So Robin took it. She marched me to the first floor, and it must have been a Tuesday, because the woman who cut our hair was there, and she shaved my head. I watched my beautiful crown fall onto the floor around me, the last thing I had (or so I thought, but we weren't even close to the bottom) that was mine.

Robin looked me over when it was done. She had a chilling way of looking you up and down. A chilling self-control.

She smiled. "Good," she said. "Now you'll know what it's like to be a dyke."

If my math is right, that was day 7 of 993.

4

Sanction

TABLE TOPICS WERE the center of the Family life. We were subjected to Table Topics every day at almost every meal. Often, they went on for hours. They would roll from kid to kid all through the morning or afternoon and into the next meal. Twenty-two hours was the record (unofficial). Twenty-two hours of sitting straight on our hard chairs, not moving, not resting, pummeling our fellow teens. I had ADHD, unmedicated. I was crawling out of my skin after four or five hours. I could feel the little legs all over me. The pressure was so intense, I felt like I was going to explode. That is not a metaphor. My eyes were bulging. I was sweating from the effort of keeping my skin tight.

The Family was supposedly a high school for troubled teens, but there were no classes my first year. Robin or another handler took us in small groups to the attic for lessons based on the state required tests, but that was like a month of homeschooling, forgotten as soon as the test was passed. They brought in a couple of part-time teachers during my second year, mostly from the local high school, but only for a few hours a week. They started a basketball team, but only for the boys.

Choir was real. Paul "Jimmy means fucking your dad" Geer was the director. The Family's big event was our yearly choral performance. They used it to impress our parents. But for the most part, our lives were Table Topics, punishments, and hard labor.

Mow the grass, slop the pigpen, tend the gardens, bleach the floors, shovel the snow, cook the meals, scrape the walls, build a chapel, even though you have no license, construction skills, or experience operating backhoes, cranes, and loaders. The Family ran on our labor, pure and simple.

It also ran on punishments, called Sanctions. Every Table Topic ended with a Sanction. They could take endless forms because there were no rules or procedures. Whatever the staffer wanted, that was what happened to you.

Common Sanctions included Block: carrying a cinder block representing the weight of your sins. You couldn't put it down or prop it on anything for a full day. Girls carried one cinder block. Boys could carry up to three.

Rocks: moving a huge pile of five- to ten-pound rocks to another location, then back to the original location. Matt was the Rock King. He was a rich kid, and the staff hated him for that. They hated anybody who was rich, pretty, smart, popular: all the things they never were. Matt was a quiet kid who never talked or acted out, but he was angry. He didn't understand why he was at the Family. He was furious inside.

Standard length for Rocks was four days. Matt moved rocks for an entire year, because he never gave in. Every day, Matt was out there, rain or shine. He chipped the rocks out of ice in the winter; he sweated through his shirt in the summer. The physical labor was tough, but the stupidity and pointlessness were the torture. He wasn't even walking across the yard. He was moving the rock pile about four feet, then back again, over and over. It was a total mind fuck.

Tony and Betty Argiros, our beloved founders and captors, lived in the house above my basement dorm. Every staffer lived on the Family property, including Tony and Betty's two adult daughters and Mikey, his father's understudy and heir apparent. Tony's grandson Kevin lived with us in the dorms. They told Kevin he was an alcoholic. He had to be punished for his sins. He was eleven. He had never had a drink. Didn't matter: they were saving him from himself, because alcoholism ran in the family. That was how fanatical the Family was: they thought everyone was an addict, even a bone-dry eleven-year-old.

Kevin was the Wheelbarrow King. He had to push a wheelbarrow piled with rocks so often, we joked that the wheelbarrow was taped to his hands, and sometimes it was. He was Tony's grandson!

Not unusual. Not at all. I estimate 50–75 percent of the kids were on Sanction at all times, and much of it was purposefully pointless physical labor.

The rest was straight mind fuckery. The Corner was sitting in a plastic chair, facing the wall. You couldn't look around or talk. They slid your meals under the chair because you weren't supposed to see anyone, and no one was supposed to see you. Eight hours was standard. Standard was often extended. Sometimes, you slept in the chair.

Standing in the Corner. A common variation.

Exile, where no one was allowed to acknowledge you. No talking, no eye contact, nothing. Sometimes confined to a room. The room might be a closet. Exile lasted weeks, if not longer. After a few days, it felt like you had died.

Shadow. Double Shadow. Being chosen to Shadow was an honor, and honors went to the most aggressive kids. Shadows were routinely violent. Violence was encouraged. A Shadow could follow you for months.

Trotting Sanction, with high knees. Trotting Sanction double time.

Shaving my head was a Sanction. Or more a lesson, really, but all Sanctions were pitched as lessons. They were for our own good.

Slut Sanction for girls. Heavy makeup, teased hair, humiliatingly revealing outfits, while the boys were encouraged to ogle your body and say crudely sexual or demeaning things to you. Fantastic life training for everyone.

Dress Down Sanction, mostly for girls. Dirty, baggy clothes, no shower, greasy hair, while other students mocked you for being ugly and smelling bad.

Is this what you wanted, Mom and Dad? Is this what you paid for?

Taped to a chair: arms, chest, and ankles.

Taped to a chair and then put in a closet.

Taped to a chair and then put in the half-closet under the stairs.

Neil was a chronic masturbator. Or, more accurately, he was stood up all the time for masturbating. Neil was fifteen but looked twelve. The staff liked to pick on him because he cried. But Neil was *defiant*. They never broke him. And he had a mouth. Matt seethed in silence, but Neil cursed back at them. He called their bullshit. He was so defiant that he once ran out in the middle of a Table Topic and put *himself* in the half-closet under the stairs. The ceiling was too low to stand, but the door was even shorter. Once Neil was in, they couldn't get him out. They stationed a kid at the door but eventually gave up. He stayed in that closet for four days, no chair. He sat on the floor. The space was too small to lie down.

He came out late at night for food, he told me last year. "They tried to catch me," he said with pride, "but I waited them out."

I know that sounds crazy. I know you can't understand the defiance in that unless you were there. But that's fire.

For an addiction to masturbation—sure, that's real, not normal teenager stuff, and definitely not staff and kids piling on—the Family taped you to a chair in the half-closet. Then they taped oven mitts over your hands. Then they blindfolded you, closed the door, and left you there. It was sensory deprivation. The only sense you had left was hearing. And smell, I guess. But you didn't want smell.

Once Tony Argiros poured a bottle of Icy Hot in the oven mitts before taping them on. When the kid came out hours later, his hands were raw meat.

They forgot to tape Cassidy's legs, so he got the chair rocking and slamming against the closet door—while a parent was there. Parents couldn't come unannounced. It was forbidden. But Brenden's bad-ass dad, who was rumored to be a big-time entertainment executive, showed up. He was walking down the hall with Mikey Argiros when bang, bang, bang . . . the closet door sprang open and Cassidy fell onto the floor. So here's this young kid, blazing red hair, baby-faced, prepubescent-looking, taped to a chair like a hostage in a movie, blindfolded, with oven mitts taped over his hands. The adults stood there, staring down at him in silence. Cassidy was silent. He had just slammed himself into the floor. The fall had probably knocked the wind out of him. That moment stretched on and on until, in slow motion, Brenden's dad stepped over Cassidy, grabbed his son, and walked out the front door. Brenden went home. Cassidy went back in the closet.

It was hilarious. I was one of the lucky kids who witnessed it, and that was how we whispered about it, carefully, amongst ourselves, like it was hilarious.

Cassidy's dead now.

The horrendous thing about Neil's Sanction was that they left him in the closet like that *for a month*. Complete darkness, sustenance-level food and water, no human contact, *for a month*. Neil came out talking about planet Zor-Bob. We thought that was hilarious, too, until we realized he was serious. Neil had suffered a psychotic break. Bob Runge had put him in there, and Neil had created an alternate universe that incorporated his name.

He doesn't remember it. That's another thing: we have gaps where the trauma was too intense. I have them. Everyone has them. But I was there, Neil. I'm sorry, buddy, but it happened.

We were all living in an alternate universe, not just Neil. We lived without clocks or calendars, without newspapers, television, radio, internet, or any contact with the outside world. The compound was so isolated that I had no idea where on the planet it was. I was relieved to discover I was still in New York state, but I'd never heard of the nearest town, Hancock. The rumbling in my stomach from my starvation-level rations was more real to me than anything beyond the hill.

It was like that old joke: the food is terrible ... and such small portions!

And that was before I went on the dreaded Tuna Sanction, which meant one bowl of Maypo (a cut-rate Cream of Wheat) for breakfast, one English muffin with tuna fish for lunch, and one more English muffin with tuna for dinner.

Remember how I said you learned to love the feeling of starvation or you went crazy? This is what I was talking about. I still love that feeling.

And yes, I have food-control issues. I starve myself when I am anxious, for days or even weeks. I am afraid of eating in public. Most Family girls I know struggle with eating disorders. Nobody I know from the Family eats tuna fish. If I meet a Family kid who likes tuna, I know he's not really Family.

All this while doing Rocks, carrying Blocks, and scrubbing the main building from top to tail. The cleaner was powerful. I had to get on my knees and scour with handheld brushes. It burned my skin; the fumes made me sick.

Sometimes, they made me sleep without a blanket. We didn't have nail clippers, so one night, I tried to bite off my toenails because they were stabbing me inside my shoes. I was stood up the next morning for sounding like I was masturbating. Maybe that was why they took my blanket. Blanket Sanction was a popular punishment for masturbation.

There was one shower in our dorm. We were given four minutes to wash, and not every day. We were lucky, we had a shower curtain, but it could be ripped back at any time to make sure you weren't masturbating. The staff was convinced the shower was a hotbed of masturbatory grotesquery. Maybe it was. In a good week, that was your twelve minutes of solitude. In a bad week, it could be eight minutes, or four minutes, or none. My Shadow stood a few feet away and watched me shower for months.

We weren't allowed tampons. We were at first, but Tony Argiros outlawed them when he found out what they were. He said we were sticking penises up our vaginas. He was a former pimp from Queens.

Yeah, I'm not making that up. He told us that himself, repeatedly. As in "I used to be a sex addict and a pimp, and now I'm a man of God."

He was obsessed with sex. To Tony Argiros, everything was a penis. He once violently berated a girl who had dabbled, slightly, in heroin, calling her a sex addict. "You are sticking a dirty steel penis in your arm."

He kept saying it: *Dirty steel penis. Dirty steel penis.*

It broke me down after the first few weeks: the starvation, the hard labor, the disgustingly sexual atmosphere. We were barely allowed to clean ourselves. We were humiliated over our periods. We received a cup of water a day, at meals, in increments, even when doing labor outside. That wasn't a punishment, just policy.

On hot days, I drank out of the toilet. *Then used it.* We all did.

And the cruelty. Don't forget the unrelenting cruelty. That was what fried my brain. I was used to being bullied. I was used to being yelled at. My relationship with my parents was carnage. But this was evil.

I ran out of toothpaste. Sanction.

I asked a girl if I could borrow some of her toothpaste. Sanction.

Nightly Reflection was forced prayer on our knees, on the hard ground, while being scolded as sinners. I was routinely given a thousand Hail Marys, and yes, I said them all. I was scared not to.

I was degraded, constantly, as a lesbian and a dyke. But my primary problem, Robin wrote in her report, was being "boy crazy but refusing to admit it."

She berated me at our mandatory handler sessions for being too nice. I was sanctioned for being passive-aggressive and not getting along with other girls.

None of it made sense. There were no guidelines, no measurements, no goals. There was no program or guiding principle except cruelty. Whatever strategy you chose to protect yourself— lashing out, being polite, trying to make friends, trying to stay out of sight—the staff made sure it didn't work. Because that was all the Family was: finding fault. Tearing you down. It was kill or be killed. Learn it, live it, or die.

The third step of Alcoholics Anonymous is *We made a decision to turn our will and our lives over to the care of God as we understood him.*

In that place, *the Family was God.* We were required to turn over our will and lives to them. Success meant learning to accept whatever they gave us, and the more heinous, the more random and contradictory, the deeper their attitude buried itself inside us. Survival meant internalizing their values, especially self-hatred and cruelty, and living them without question. It's so easy to get used to fucked up. It's so easy to stop thinking, *This isn't right*, and start thinking, *What do I have to do?*

By the time Jon Martin-Crawford arrived later that fall, I had lost myself. Not just my location on planet Earth but my sense of who I was. And then there he was, suddenly, a kid from my old school. He wasn't a friend, but I had seen him all the time. He was a skater; I was with the BMX Boys; we hung out. I went to parties at his house since he lived in the next neighborhood over from mine. He was a legend in our crowd. He was funny, and he was nice, the kid who always stuck up for the outcast. He ran a hilarious underground newspaper that slaughtered all the grown-ups' sacred cows. I figured his attitude got him sent inside. He was a rabble-rouser, our old principal said. He raged against the machine. As it turned out, it was his parents' divorce. The top four reasons for being a Family kid: having ADHD, being on the spectrum, being adopted, or your parents' divorce. That's just my observation, but I stand by it. In 95 percent of cases, criminality or serious drug issues had nothing to do with it.

I was in shock when I saw Jon. *Oh, my God, this is real*, I thought. I hadn't been kidnapped. It wasn't a bad dream. This was my real life, and other real people were in it.

Then I felt guilty. My parents knew his parents. Had they suggested this? Was I the reason this kid's life got fucked? (I've dug into it since. I'm pretty sure it was our middle school guidance counselor.)

Then I panicked. I had an almost uncontrollable urge to grab him and scream, "Run!" They didn't have him yet. He wasn't corrupted. He had a chance. I could save him. He could get away. He could tell the world.

But that impulse was crushed by an overwhelming fear. The fear of what would happen to me if I pushed him out the door. If I dared speak the horror. The fear of what would happen if we acknowledged each other.

The Family had a concept: a Negative Contract. Anything you did with another kid was a Negative Contract: conversation, laughing, helping. The help didn't have to be active or rebellious. Kids stood themselves up all the time: "I saw Jon put the broom in the closet backwards, but I didn't say anything, so I have to break this Negative Contract." Not ratting on tiny mistakes: Negative Contract. Giving a tiny kindness: Negative Contract. They poisoned basic decency as a way to control us.

If Jon acknowledged me, we'd have hell to pay: Communication Sanction. We'd never be allowed to sit near each other or speak. Friends were bad influences, the Family said, especially when they came from outside. Friendship was to be crushed, ruthlessly and forever. Acting normal right now, like saying hi or asking me questions, could be catastrophic.

It didn't happen. Jon somehow sensed the boundaries. Nobody at the Family ever knew we were friends. But he let me know he saw me with a small nod, a quick look, and I thought, *Maybe this will work.*

I don't mean our friendship. I mean the Family itself. Jon's presence made me feel, for the first time, that I could survive this ordeal. That my only options weren't to go insane or die. He was the first person I could trust—he was a loyal guy and always had been—and in the paranoid environment of the Family, loyalty was gold.

Seeing Jon reminded me that there was a world out there beyond the hill. Beyond the trees that ringed the horizon like a fence. I hadn't heard from my parents since the day they walked out on me. For the first thirty days, at least, you could have no contact with your parents. That was policy. To wean you off the world or some shit like that. After that, if they decided you were saved enough, you could speak to them on a landline in the hall (collect call) for five minutes on Sunday. The call was monitored by staff, and a kid stood next to you with a stopwatch. The nice ones gave you a warning, maybe a few seconds of extra time. The hard ones hung up the phone without notice the second your five minutes were up.

The Family put me on Communication Sanction, meaning no outside contact. They loved Communication Sanction because they hated the outside world. It was a weak point in their control. They loved House Blackout, where everyone was on Communication Sanction for something one person had done. Once they sanctioned the entire school for a month. They sent letters home telling parents to support this needed discipline. That was in the future, though. That fall, I couldn't contact my parents because the Family wanted me amputated from my former life. For my own good, of course. My former life, after all, had led me down this horrible path.

And my parents? I suspect they were happier without me.

After Jon, though, I started thinking about the world outside. I thought about my old life as I lay on my bunk, listening to Tony Argiros scream at, rape, and beat his wife a few feet above my face, because their bedroom was directly above me. I didn't know their relationship was poisonous. I didn't have other role models. I thought that was what love sounded like, a punch and a fall.

I dreamed so hard, and so foolishly, that I forgot how my family life had been and why my parents had sent me away. Instead, I focused on the reasons they would absolutely, positively take me back. They didn't want me beaten. They didn't want me slut-shamed. I wasn't a drug addict. I wasn't a drinker. My parents were educated people. They were penny-pinchers. Would they really pay for this . . . training in mistreatment? Things weren't right here; it was obvious. Anybody could see it. My brother, who was seven when I disappeared, tells me, "I hated that place. It was creepy."

"Why? How did you know?"

He thinks about it. "The way you kids moved."

I know what he means. We were so careful when outsiders were around. We became automatons, desperate to stay in our lanes and say our scripted lines, because the consequences of a mistake were vile.

I forgot all that. I forgot the manipulation. I forgot what my father thought of me. The way he had turned his back and walked away without a word. It flew out of my head the second Robin told me, "Your father's here. Get ready."

My father! Not my mother, my father. My protector. I had been keeping track of the days in my head, or trying to, anyway. They were my only hold on the outside world. I knew it had been about two months, which meant it was close to Thanksgiving. That was auspicious, the perfect time to bring me home. I kept my head down as Robin walked me to the room where my father was waiting, but inside, I was bursting with anticipation. I had my speech—my apology—all planned.

My father was in his navy-blue business suit. I sat across from him, with Mikey Argiros and Robin between us. I wasn't to try to touch or hug him. I wasn't to speak until spoken to. They had trained me well. So I waited. It was clear my father had been there a while, talking with the staff. He had a hard look. But I felt confident I could persuade him. I was his oldest daughter. He was my only father. I was being hurt. He would listen to me this time.

Then he looked at me, and I wasn't so sure. It was his eyes. Instead of saying anything, he reached into the inner breast pocket of his suit. He drew out a folded stack of papers, and my heart fucking died when I saw what they were: my moral inventory. My forced confession. The Family had sent it to my family.

I was cooked. In that instant, I knew it was over. No matter what I said, that paper, to my father, was the truth, and anything out of my mouth was a lie. He thought his sad, fat, lonely, struggling fifteen-year-old daughter was a heroin-addicted prostitute who had regularly committed assault and robbery, and there was nothing I could do to convince him otherwise.

He talked over me. He talked harshly about how badly I was behaving in the program and how disappointed he was in me. Again. Always disappointed, that guy. I put my head down and took it. What else could I do? There was nothing to say. Everything was running out of me: my hope, my trust, the days I had counted so carefully and held tightly in my head. There was no point in yelling. There was no point in doing anything. Robin, my handler, the woman who was "dedicating her life to saving your daughter, Mr. Ianelli," was sitting across from me. I could see her satisfied smirk. I could smell her stale breath.

She owned me. She knew it. And more importantly, I knew it now, too.

5

Hello Darkness, Old Friend

THE TREES DIED on the hills. The sun grew wobbly. The nights grew long. The temperature plunged. Deep autumn was a hard season in the mountains outside Hancock, New York, and I was alone and scared, with no hope of going home. I fell into a depression so deep even Jon's careful friendship couldn't reach me. The only person actively nice to me, in that whole world, was the cook.

Every kid at the Family had a job in addition to their Sanctions. After I finished scrubbing the main building, I joined the kitchen crew. It was a punishment, because kitchen duty was the worst. I had to get up at 5:00 to make breakfast. I had to stay late to clean up after dinner. One of the cooks was a bully. He was brutal. The banging of an industrial kitchen was bad enough, but he was always screaming, throwing pans, and slamming baking sheets on the counter. No matter where you were on the property, you could hear that cook blowing up.

His signature move was to grab you around the throat and slam you into the wall. He'd pin you there as he screamed in your face. He was a big guy: over six feet tall, bulky and hairy, like an ogre, with a cheap blond dye job. When he pinned you, you couldn't move.

He beat us with a whisk. It was an industrial whisk that attached to a motorized mixer, so it was thick and solid. He smacked us in the backs of the legs with it. He smacked us with the wooden paddle used for pizzas. The flat side was okay. It stung, but the pain was over in a few minutes. When he hit you with the narrow side, that hurt. I'm talking bone bruises. Bruises on top of bruises. There were shifts when I couldn't walk, when I barely held myself upright with the edge of the counter. We kept working. We had no choice. Neil worked in the kitchen, and we secretly supported each other when the pain in our legs sent us to the verge of collapse. And yet, somehow, I crawled up into my bunk unassisted every night.

The cook took an interest in me early on. He noticed how devastated I was when Robin shaved my head. "Don't worry," he said, "it will grow back."

"It looks nice," he said, rubbing my head when my hair became a fuzzy red down.

He asked me my favorite cereal. When I told him Raisin Bran, he brought me a small box. Since I was on Half Portion, I was famished and weak. I *devoured* it.

He brought me mac and cheese and brownies.

He left snacks in a special place in the walk-in cooler: crackers and cheese, a Snickers. I had to hide there and eat them quickly so no one saw me and stood me up at a Table Topic, but I inhaled them hungrily. I was starving: for the calories and the kindness. It's so obvious now. So obvious, it makes me sick. But I was too naive at fifteen, and too beaten up, to understand this kindness had a price.

Until he grabbed me from behind by the neck and slammed my face into the walk-in cooler's metal shelves. He tore down my pants with his free hand—cold, instant cold—and I don't want to go into details, but it was violent, and it was painful. I was torn, inside and outside. Blood was running down my legs. I had to lie to the school nurse—who wasn't a trained nurse, just a staffer's wife—and say I was having my period early so I could get a couple of their cheap, bulky pads to stuff up my asshole, because that was where he raped me, and that was where I was torn.

I was still in pain and bleeding a few days later when he cornered me again. He pressed against me from behind, pinning me to the back sink, where I was washing pots. He grabbed my neck, reached into my pants, hooked his fingers into my vagina, and pulled upward so hard he lifted me onto the very tips of my toes.

He bent his face over my shoulder. He had yellow teeth and sour breath. "I was in the military," he whispered. "I can kill you and nobody will know. I can make it look like an accident."

He dropped me and walked away. The pain was so excruciating it bent me over, my hands on the floor. I felt like throwing up, but I feared the Sanction. And he was right: he could kill me. He didn't have to make it look like an accident. If he killed me in that place, nobody would care. I believed that then, and I believe it to this day.

About a week later, he came after me again. I was taking out the garbage, and I turned to find him walking toward me, leering. I looked down and saw that his penis was out of his pants, and I didn't think; I turned and bolted out the back door and sprinted as hard as I could up the hill. My plan, as much as I had one, was to run until I dropped and then figure out what to do. But about eight hundred yards up the hill, I came to the chapel, and instead of heading into the trees, I turned and headed inside. I could hide until nightfall, I thought, and then continue on.

Father Stephen was there, that bastard. That former Catholic piece of shit, with his thousands of Hail Marys and his weekly "theology class" that bludgeoned us with all the reasons we were going to hell.

I didn't mean to tell him. I had been at the Family long enough to know not to tell anyone anything; it would only get you hurt. But this was a priest. I had been raised to trust policemen and priests.

"He did things to . . ." I said, because I couldn't say the word. "To my body."

Father Stephen steered me to a pew. He nodded sympathetically as I described what had happened: the walk-in cooler, the death threat, the indecent exposure.

"Please, please, please," I begged him, "call my mother."

I don't know why I thought of my mother, but I needed her. I begged Father Stephen to call her. To let her take me away with her.

He comforted me. He made me feel heard.

He walked me to the office on the first floor of the main building, then disappeared. He was gone for a long time. I assumed he was calling my mother or the police. Then Robin walked in. Behind her came four staff members whose faces I remember and several more I can't recall for sure. There were probably ten people in the room, the majority of the full-time staff.

"Little Lizzy," Robin said, shaking her head. "Little Lizzy, down here complaining. Down here making up lies."

She launched into me, same as always. *Filthy whore. Liar. Fat piece of shit. Slut.*

Early on, I had told Robin about my abusive relative. You're so careless when you arrive. You make so many mistakes. She saved that information until now—the perfect time to use my degradation and shame against me.

You seduced your adult relative, you filthy whore. Admit it. You seduced him just like you seduced the cook.

You're a liar. A disgusting little liar trying to ruin a man's career. For what? For attention? Because nobody loves you enough?

She went back and forth like that. *Seductive whore. Attention-hungry liar. You caused your rape. You made it up.* It wasn't logical. How could I have done both? But logic had nothing to do with anything since the moment my parents dumped me here.

God doesn't approve of sodomy.

He's a married man.

After everything we've done for you.

Your father will be so disappointed.

Their joy; I will never forget it. Robin was a cold fish, but not cool. She was a tiny, barely contained cone of fury. She shamed and taunted every day. I think she got off on the power. But the men: it was disgusting what they did. Describing my imagined sex acts in detail, degrading an underage girl as a slut and a sex addict. It wasn't harmless to them or to me. At least three men in that office raped or molested children in their care, and that doesn't include the cook, who wasn't there. One was a serial pedophile who raped seven children that I know of: six boys and a girl.

I don't know if that day caused those rapes, although I worry about that a lot. It's stupid, I know, but I feel guilty because I don't know if this was the first time a child had been treated that way or the tenth. But the message was clear: if you rape a kid, you will get away with it. You will not be punished. The children will not be heard.

I don't know how long my debasement lasted. It felt endless. Once the yelling started, it was a frenzy; everyone wanted to be a part of it. Around and around it went. Nobody held back.

Then they closed in, tight. Someone read from the Bible. They prayed for the liar, for the slut. This was their religion. They told themselves they were trying to save me.

I thought, *That's it. I'm out of here. I'm running, and I'm never looking back.*

They took me upstairs and stood me at the pole. I could hear Paul Geer, who had been in the office yelling at me with the others, ringing his godforsaken bell. Everybody filed in and took their seats.

"Little Lizzy says she has a boyfriend," Robin said.

She told my fellow students the story of my rape, in detail, as if it was some fairy tale. I tried to look away, but I saw Jon, Jay, the faces of kids I knew. They weren't looking at me. They were looking straight ahead, their backs straight. But their fingers were curling on their thighs. They were buzzing with anger.

"This is what happens when you tell stories, Lizzy," Robin was saying, but I wasn't listening. My head was swimming, and the room was fuzzy. I wasn't sleepy, but my head went down and everything dimmed.

When I came around, two girls were holding me up. "Tell her, boys," Robin was saying. "Be honest. Would you have sex with Lizzy? Someone so fat and ugly, inside and out."

I could see the boys screaming. I could see the fire in their eyes as they burned me at the stake, but I couldn't hear what they were saying because I was no longer there. I fell, weightless, into the grip of the girls at my side. I don't remember anything else until Robin said, "So what should we do with little Lizzy?"

This was usually when kids suggested Sanctions, but there was only a second of silence before I heard, "To the blanket." Clap, clap.

The Blanket was Robin's signature Sanction. She always said it with delight and a little double clap, her tiny hands held up beside her head.

"The Blanket." Clap, clap. "You five."

Within a second, five girls had stepped forward, the large green army blanket and the four rolls of duct tape had appeared, and I was screaming. I don't know where I had gone, or how I came back, but I was not going into that blanket.

I hit them before they could hit me, and we went down. Punching, biting, kicking. I slammed my elbow into the floor but barely felt the pain. I scratched faces. I pulled hair. I bit. I tasted blood. Every time they pinned a limb, I kicked and thrashed until I broke loose. This was panic: pure animal panic. I was going to die if they got me in that blanket, and I did not want to die. Not yet.

I'm sure Robin loved it. The violence. My terror. She got to me that day, down deep and forever.

Eventually, they pinned me. I writhed, but they managed to wrap me in the blanket like a burrito with only my head and feet sticking out. I can still hear the sound of the duct tape as it came off the roll. The distinctive rip. I panicked and threw my body from side to side. But it was too late. They taped the blanket so tight at my chest, at the waist and around my feet, that I couldn't move.

"You know what to do, girls," Robin said.

They picked me up by the feet and dragged me out of the room, face down, so my face hit every stair to the first floor. They didn't cushion the blows. They took me through the door at the back of the boot closet into the boiler room without a word. Their silence was violence.

But when the door closed, something happened: their body language softened. They became almost gentle. Or maybe I imagined it. Nobody said a word, but I swear they tried to make me comfortable. As one girl set my head on the ground, she looked into my eyes, and it was almost an apology. She had blood on her face. I don't know if it was hers or mine.

Then they were gone, and I was alone in the hot, dusty, windowless room. I was crying, except crying isn't possible in the blanket. It's too tight. You can't get enough air into your lungs. I inhaled each sob into my chest, but it stuck there, squeezed, until

I felt myself choking. Then it stuttered out, painfully, giving me just enough room to inhale another sob.

The tears came, though. They ran down my face and mixed with the dust. I vomited, but it was mostly bile. I tried to hold my head off the ground, but it was impossible. I laid my cheek in the vomit and let it mix with the sludge from my tears. Before long, it was caking my eyelashes.

The pain set in: my elbow. My knee. My arms were taped in front of me, so I was lying on them. I worked myself along the floor until my toes could push against a pipe. That way, I could turn myself. Not all the way over, but enough to relieve the pressure.

I couldn't breathe. It was panic and pressure, and it rolled me like a wave. I was drowning on dry land. I gasped, trying so hard to breathe that I choked myself. I thrashed, but it wrenched my shoulder. My head pounded, and the world swam. I screamed, but I knew it would do no good. Nobody was coming.

Nobody was ever coming.

By the time I saw the brittle ankles and pointy pink heels, I had lost track of time. "Lizzy, Lizzy, Lizzy," Robin said. "I have a question for you."

She kicked me in the ribs. Hard. "Are we ever going to speak again about what you told us yesterday?"

I had to say I had lied. That nobody had raped me.

I wouldn't do it.

She kicked me again, then placed two dog bowls by my head: one with water, one with tuna fish.

"We'll try again tomorrow."

I was in excruciating pain. I had herniated a disk, I learned later, and the pain never stopped. Itching ravaged me. Boredom deranged me. I was in and out of consciousness with no conception of time. I had diarrhea from the adrenaline. I pissed myself. I got my period, the one I had lied about before to staunch the bleeding from the rape. I ate by stretching my tongue to the tuna fish, the stale vomit and dusty sludge in my nose and eyes, but I vomited most of the food back up. I despise the smell of tuna fish. To this day, it makes me want to puke.

I passed out. I awoke to pain and the smell of tuna fish so far up my nose I couldn't breathe. I awoke to Jon sitting beside me with a tall glass of milk. He rolled me over. He lifted my upper torso off the floor and held my head across his lap. He helped me drink the whole glass, slowly, painful sip by sip. He loosened the tape by pulling and stretching it out. Every day, I had more room and less strength.

For a long time, I thought I had hallucinated that. I hallucinated a lot of things in that boiler room. But I asked Jon about it years later, and he said it was true. He snuck down after the dinner rush with milk he'd stolen from the kitchen. He sat with me for five minutes, despite the tight restrictions and the risk of being caught. Despite what would have happened if they had discovered him gone.

I loved him. I loved the kid like a brother, even then.

He laid me on the floor. He made me as comfortable as he could. "Don't worry, Liz," he said, because he knew my real name. "This will be okay."

The next thing I knew, Robin was kicking me. "Confess for your soul, Lizzy. Confess that you lied."

I wouldn't do it. I wouldn't look at her or say a word.

I decided I never would.

Until the eighth day. I didn't know it was the eighth day, I was completely lost in space and time, but that was when I gave up. I think my body realized I was dying, so it forced my brain to save itself.

Not that it mattered. Eight days duct-taped in a blanket, alone, on a filthy floor, and I was finished. I was going to kill myself at the first chance.

They cut me out. There were three of them, including Robin. I lay on the floor in front of them, covered in my own caked shit and crusty blood, unable to move. This was their moment of triumph. I expected taunting and Bible talk. But they didn't say anything. I don't know how many times I collapsed, trying to stand. I heard them whispering. They didn't want to touch me, but they couldn't leave me. Finally, they covered me with the blanket and pulled me out of the room, two people holding me up as my feet dragged along the floor. They put me in an office. When the other students gathered for a meal—I think it was dinner—they took me to my dorm and let me shower alone.

That was when I saw it: the whole front of my body was bruised.

I know now what happened. At some point, I lost the strength to turn over. I was stuck on my stomach, and I lay that way so long my blood started to pool there. It's called lividity. I've seen it in corpses. My heart wasn't strong enough to pump blood throughout my body, so gravity was pulling it to the lowest areas. I really was about to die in that blanket.

The surprise isn't how close I came to death. It's that those incompetent idiots never accidentally killed anyone. As far as I know.

I think they kept me in the dorm for a day. I think. I can't be sure. I only know I was in the boiler room for eight days because the other kids told me. For me, the whole experience was gummy. It was everything and nothing all at once.

But I know what I did as soon as I could stand. I went to the kitchen, grabbed a gallon of bleach I had hidden a few weeks earlier, and snuck into the walk-in cooler. I took off my clothes and folded them neatly, as required each night. It's amazing to me: even in death, I followed their rules. I sat down, naked, on the freezing floor. My nakedness was a message. I wanted everyone to see me.

I drank the gallon of bleach—it tasted awful—and waited happily for death.

And waited. And waited. And . . . what the fuck?

I flipped the bottle around. On the other side, in marker, it said "Vinegar."

Another failure.

The next day, I was put back in the kitchen unsupervised and revenge-raped by the cook. A few days after that, he was gone. I assume he was fired, because everyone knew I was telling the truth. Everyone had known all along.

After that, other kids have told me, I was a leader of the resistance. That's hard for me to understand, because I died in that blanket. I was a partial girl. When I ask them to explain what they saw in me, they struggle. They say I was different, that's all. I was passive-aggressive. I never went along, even when I went along.

"Why do you think that?"

They hesitate, pulling at their memories. It's hard for us to live with our memories. Believe me, this book is hard.

"It was the look on your face."

"What look?"

"Defiance."

Stone-cold, steel-battleship fucking defiance.

I know that look. I've seen it in photos over the decades. It wasn't defiance. It is now, but it wasn't then. I wasn't part of a resistance, much less a leader. My passion wasn't for freedom or justice. It was for death. I thought about death every day.

Someone was going to die. Either them or me. And honestly, I didn't care which way it went.

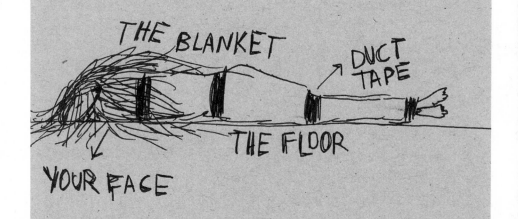

6

Death by Sandwich

I HEAR PEOPLE WALK when they're stressed. They work out, run, go to yoga, meditate. You know, healthy things. Not me. I smoke cigarettes. (Sorry, Mom and Dad.) Almost every survivor I know smokes, or smoked and then quit. Not at the Family, obviously. But afterward, it was irresistible. That which we are denied, we want, and the more forceful the denial . . . well, you know how it is. Smoking cigarettes was one of many normal teenage activities we never got to experience. We never even got to experience saying no.

I wish I could go to high school. I'd go back now, at forty-three; I wouldn't care how it looked. Homeroom. Football games. Prom. Driving around in cars. Sports. Boyfriends. Girlfriends. Passing notes. Talking to friends, or not having any friends to talk to, because people understand that. Sitting in the park, alone or with someone special. Reading books. Doing homework. Making out. Watching the television shows the rest of you share memories of. Listening to the popular songs I've never heard enough to hate. The movies I've never heard of but pretend to know so I don't seem stupid. High school might have been hell for you, but it's my fantasy. It's a stolen piece of my life.

I'm sitting in my home office now, thinking about it. Thinking about what might have been. Not the horror but the missed opportunities. I'm comfortable here in my walkout basement. It's a little messy. I'm not America's Happy Homemaker. I'm tattooed. I'm pierced. I don't cook much because I hate kitchens. I'm not sure what my dining room table is for. But I have DoorDash and a full pantry for my sons. My curved desk functions like a barrier, keeping the world out of my private space: my credenza full of memories, my wall of degrees. Every inch of the wall behind my desk is covered with mementos of my friends.

My blind-deaf dog, Tails, is here, keeping me company. The shelter volunteer told me he wouldn't be a good fit for a single mother; he was too disabled. That was why I adopted him. My parents told me I need to get rid of him, that dogs are for old people with nothing better to do. They gave away my brother's beloved yellow Lab, Nutmeg, the day he went to college. They Familied him. They took the thing he loved. They will never do that to Tails. He's loyal. He's happy. He has no idea how funny he is, flinging and losing his giggle ball, running between my legs as we climb the stairs. I'm happy here in my submarine, with my Sky American Spirits and my blind-deaf dog. I've made myself a home.

But I worry. I worry you're not listening.

I worry you're saying, *Well, this is more than I bargained for, Peg. Unbelievable. Horrifying. How could this happen in the United States of America? In the 1950s, sure. Everyone knows orphans, charity cases, and other children entrusted to the care of public and religious institutions were abused back then, often to the point of psychosis or death. And let's not even start on Canada's indigenous schools. But in the modern era?*

Or you're saying, *This is unbelievable, Bob.* As in *I can't believe it. I won't believe.* You may be thinking, as many have said to my face (or in legal filings), that being a victim of abuse makes me untrustworthy. The abuse becomes the reason not to believe the abuse, and the worse the abuse, the more the story is disbelieved. Go to a courtroom. You will see this logic used against women every day.

I worry because doubt and disbelief are the only reactions we ever hear. We, the survivors of the Family, have been screaming this truth for more than twenty years. We've posted testimonials. Recorded videos, though it's hard for us to speak of our abuse. We have firsthand accounts from former staff. We have police reports or, more accurately, a suspicious lack of police reports. We've unearthed the incriminating paperwork. We've testified before Congress.

And nobody has heard us. Nobody has cared. Most of our parents, after all these years, won't listen or care.

I am not unique. Please understand that. Thousands of kids have gone through the Family, all with similar experiences. I recently learned that another girl was raped by the cook. This story isn't mine; it is ours.

The Family is not unique. You *need* to understand that. The Family is a pinhole in a multibillion-dollar industry that uses the same basic approaches, mindsets, and techniques on "troubled" teens. Prolonged restraint, beatings, starvation, savage verbal attacks, Shadowing (also called Belt-Looping because in many programs, Shadows hold you by your back belt loop): this is standard stuff. The approach was called "tough love," before that term fell out of favor, because the basic belief is that you must hurt struggling children to help them.

A million kids have been through tough love schools and camps in the forty years since Straight burst onto the public scene. A million kids, all with stories like mine. And you haven't heard us any more than you heard the orphans and indigenous children of the 1950s.

And because you haven't listened, *this abuse is happening today, right now, as you read this.* The Troubled Teen Industry (TTI) that created and enabled the Family is still here, as massive as ever. The industry is largely unregulated (one of its biggest draws), but a 2021 article on the website of the American Bar Association estimated that between 120,000 and 200,000 kids are currently in the system, at an annual cost of $23 billion. One program, Sequel—we call the kids there Romney kids because it was once owned by Bain Capital—was cited as having annual revenue that "regularly tops $200 million; as of 2017, 90% of their revenue came from Medicare, Medicaid, and approximately 500 additional federal, state and local programs."

The article estimated private placements by parents at 50,000 a year. That means you, the American taxpayer, are paying billions each year to torture the other 100,000 or so children because we're still putting poor and neglected kids into abusive institutional care, just like in the 1950s.

And if you think the level of abuse has diminished, that in this day and age, these programs couldn't possibly be so violent and uncaring, then I have some very disturbing surveillance footage to show you because the camera was recording in the lunchroom at Lakewood Academy, a Sequel-owned facility in Michigan, on April 29, 2020, when multiple staff members violently tackled and restrained Cornelius Frederick.

They killed him.

They killed Cornelius Frederick on the floor of the lunchroom in front of dozens of other children.

He was sixteen years old.

One of his parents had died, and the other was incarcerated, so the state remanded him to Lakewood, where, according to NBC News, emergency services had been called 237 times in the previous 18 months and 56 violations had been substantiated by the Michigan Department of Health and Human Services in the previous two and a half years.

Why couldn't someone in the system show that kid love? Why can't we, as a society, understand that kids like Cornelius are hurting, and they need kindness and time to heal, not beatings and restraint?

Why did it have to go down like that, for throwing a fucking sandwich in a Troubled Teen facility, when he was only sixteen years old?

Lakewood has closed. Sequel has denied responsibility. Three employees were charged with involuntary manslaughter and pleaded not guilty, claiming they were just following procedures. And the world thinks that is enough.

They think nobody really cares about Cornelius Frederick and other kids like him. You, fellow survivor, think nobody cares about you. Because you've been ignored. You've been disbelieved. I know the feeling.

But we care. The networks I'm in, the survivors I know: WE CARE. If you've been through a Troubled Teen Program, we see you. It doesn't matter who you are or what you've done, you're one of us, and we will never turn our back, or disbelieve, or belittle what happened to you, or judge what you've done to deal with the pain.

That's why, if you remember one name from this book, remember Cornelius Frederick. He was one of us, and he died in that "school." He died alone, feeling that nobody loved him.

And he's not the last one. He's just the last kid whose death footage someone managed to sneak out to the world.

The blanket doesn't bother me anymore. I can tell that story. The rape, as long as it's written carefully, doesn't bother me. I have so much scar tissue on my heart, I can't feel a thing.

But Cornelius cuts me deep.

So please—and I'm talking to the outsiders now—don't turn away. I have the video of Cornelius's murder. TikTok and other platforms keep taking it down, but hit me up, I have a copy. I will share it. Watch it.

Read about Aaron Bacon's death in Maia Szalavitz's book *Help at Any Cost*. Read about it on Wikipedia—that's bad enough—but read the full story in Maia's book. Then call us complainers and malcontents. Dismiss us as troubled people railing against the godly and the wise. Tell us none of this matters. I double dare you.

It matters because the Family wasn't unique or new. This disease goes back a hundred years, to at least 1921 and the Oxford Group, a fundamentalist Christian splinter movement that aimed to overcome worldliness by "surrendering one's life over to God's plan" and testifying one's shortcomings to fellow members.

If that sounds familiar, it's because the founders of AA met in an Oxford Group meeting in 1935 and adapted its principles to alcoholism. In 1958, Synanon adapted AA to drug addiction by adding coercion, even though AA adherents know the program works only when voluntarily followed. Synanon used isolation, hard labor, sleep deprivation, and "the Synanon Game," where an addict was verbally abused and demeaned for hours by other group members to break their will.

Yeah, that's basically the Family.

Synanon became famous for curing a heroin addict. It claimed to cure half its addicts, but a New Jersey drug study discovered it wasn't counting the 90 percent of participants who dropped out. Its real success rate was, at best, 15 percent, about the same as that of government-run hospital programs of the time. But the federal government was so impressed with the hype that in 1971, it gave a grant to a former alcoholic and failed stand-up comedian who was trying the Synanon method on teens at a small facility in Fort Lauderdale, Florida.

The Seed was the first Troubled Teen Program. It wasn't a school; that sickness came later. It was a full-time drug treatment program. Like its predecessor Synanon, it claimed a 90 percent success rate, but by 1972, a state agency had proved that false; only 41 percent of teens completed the program, and only 10 percent were followed to see if they remained drug-free. The feds pulled their funding in 1974, calling the Seed's appalling psychological attacks (basically the Family's Table Topics) "similar to the highly refined brainwashing techniques employed by the North Koreans."

It was too late. The seed was planted. (Yeah, I went there. Always will.) Despite having been exposed as a fraud and compared, in unflattering terms, to North Korea, the Seed was able to use the government's seed money (sorry) to expand to five locations. It stayed in business until 1991.

In the early 1980s, Ronny Reagan declared a war on drugs. Soon after, Nancy Reagan (and Princess Diana, sadly) became enamored of Straight, a teen antidrug program run by Republican megadonor Mel Sembler. (He became ambassador to Australia under Bush I and to Italy under Bush II; that's how connected he was.) Straight was a Seed copycat using a new name to avoid the original's bad publicity... and it worked. The press pushed the hype, the money rolled in, and the gold rush was on. Straight's imitators latched on to the era's heavy metal–satanic hysteria, which led to wilderness programs and boot camps, which flourished as parents panicked over crack cocaine, rap, and the violence of "urban culture" in the 1990s. By the time my parents tired of me in 1994, the TTI was a multibillion-dollar racket with its tentacles in every area of the country. It sucked in thousands of upper-middle-class people like my parents, who loved the idea of paying to outsource parenting as soon as it got hard.

I know two things about Tony and Betty Argiros before they arrived in Hancock, New York: Tony was a pimp—self-described, repeatedly—and Betty an alcoholic. She recovered at a notorious upstate AAA (All Addicts Anonymous) cult called East Ridge, where participants were required to live together and inter-marry—both aspects of 1970s-era Synanon. Robin Ducey and other early Family monsters were affiliated with East Ridge, too.

The Argiroses left East Ridge in the 1980s after losing a battle for control with the founder and moved to a small farm nearby. They pitched the farm as a rehabilitation facility for adults that used the beauty, secrecy, and isolation of the countryside as tools for recovery. I know four people who lived in the Nevins Road house. As in the so-called school, life there centered on verbal attacks, violence, limited food, hard labor, and a sexualized atmosphere that encouraged, almost to the point of forcing, residents to marry each other. Two people died in runaway attempts, one killed while on the run, one hit by a truck on Route 97, the same road Family kids later ran down to try to escape. The Nevins Road house was small but often crammed with fifty people or more. The Argiroses reached out to the nearby community of Hancock, where families began to take in residents in exchange for their labor.

In 1990, the New York Division of Alcoholism and Alcohol Abuse (DAAA) issued a cease-and-desist order against the Family, as it was known. Residential recovery and alcohol abuse facilities are regulated. *But charter schools are not.* On December 21, 1990, Tom Hogan, New York's assistant commissioner for nonpublic schools, wrote to the DAAA, saying, "It is obvious from reviewing your letter and the attachments that DAAA is not going to approve 'The Family' . . . to operate a Residential Chemical Dependency Program for Youth. It is not clear to us what the DAAA authority is, if any, over a chartered/registered nonpublic school."

Hogan had issued the Family Foundation School an absolute charter, the state's highest certificate. The Argiroses had been granted the right to operate a school, with minimal to no oversight, for as long as they wanted, even though they had no experience or expertise in the field.

However, they were forbidden by the DAAA from offering addiction or recovery services. Hear that: the Family pitched themselves as experts in addiction and recovery; parents thought they were sending their kids for addiction treatment; but the Family was *legally forbidden* from offering those services because they were in no way, shape, or form trained experts and did not meet the state's requirements.

In fact, parents had to sign three forms when admitting their children. They first said they acknowledged that the Family School was not a drug or alcohol rehabilitation facility. The second said their child was not in need of drug or alcohol treatment. The third was permission to use restraints.

By 1992, the Family had relocated to a large piece of land a few miles up Route 97. They leased it at a reduced rate because they were good Christians beloved by the Hancock community. The inmates at Nevins Road built the school's three-story main building. During my first year, the boys built the chapel. The girls had to bleach the walls and remove the floors, subfloors, closets, and kitchens from several used trailers that showed up on the property one day. We called them Murder Trailers because every one had burns, bloodstains, or both. People had definitely died in them, probably blew their brains out. Most were moved to the edges of the property for staff. In my day, almost all staff lived on the property. We installed bunks in the last two trailers: twenty-six beds in one, twenty-two in the other. Then we moved in.

We worked for the staffers in the other trailers. We were their human-trafficked, unpaid, underaged servants; anything they wanted, we had to do. I and a few other girls often babysat for

Linda, a total zero who lived in a double-wide at the top of the hill past the chapel. Linda was the Hancock hooker until Betty Argiros saved her. Poor Betty. She was a shell of a person. We babysat Linda's kids because she had gone right back to hooking in the parking lot behind the Hancock McDonald's, and Betty had no idea.

Babysitting also meant cleaning Linda's filthy trailer while her slob of a husband, the Family's maintenance man, sat in his filthy blue lounger in front of a massive television propped on four empty milk crates. Men at the Family didn't do housework or childcare; that was women's work. Linda's pervert husband spent his time ogling our asses.

It was low-class, degenerate, uneducated filth, but that was the Family. They hired broke teachers and morally challenged therapists part-time and called them staff to impress parents, but their primary recruiting ground was Hancock Alcoholics Anonymous meetings.

I tell this to outsiders, and they don't believe it. Well-meaning parents were turning their teens over to violent, unqualified dry drunks? Too awful.

I tell it to Maia Szalavitz, and she says, "Yeah, that checks out."

Maia wrote *Help at Any Cost: How the Troubled-Teen Industry Cons Parents and Hurts Kids*. (You may have purchased it to read about Aaron Bacon. I hope you did.) Published in 2004, it's a devastating history, scholarly evaluation, and takedown of the TTI. *Help at Any Cost* saved my life because it was the first time an outsider had seen us and acknowledged what was happening. It gave me hope in a hopeless time.

So I contacted her. When she responded, I contacted her again. And again. Until Maia became a mentor and a friend. If you have any interest in being heard, or saving your child, or making the world a better place, read her book. She is a sociologist, a researcher, and an advocate. The information in this chapter, especially about Synanon, the Seed, and other programs that influenced the Family, is based on her work.

So believe it, gentle reader, when Maia says it was common for Troubled Teen Program founders to have little relevant experience other than AA.

It was common for staffers to have no relevant experience other than AA.

"AA creates a halo effect," she told me. True believers think AA gives them the secret to the universe. The Twelve Steps are all you need.

So it makes sense that the Family, founded by graduates of AA who believed in the Big Book like it was God's own word, would drive a van to a Hancock AA meeting and offer not just jobs but a free ride, free meals, and a free trailer, too. To them, followers of AA were the best possible employees. It didn't matter if they were shacked up in the Hancock flophouse or sleeping in their cars; they were hired, no background check required.

The outsiders—the state regulators, the licensed therapists and social workers, the suspicious parents, the experts in teen behavior, the kids—were the assholes. They were standing in the way of the truth.

"The true believers are dangerous," Maia told me. "They tend to be cruel because for them, it really is do or die. The ones in it for the money, it's usually neglect."

But what if the true believers are in it for the money, too? The Family believed in AA, but they loved that down-and-outers came cheap. Every corner was cut at that place: forced labor, industrial food, rock-bottom staff, trailer-park housing.

And our parents paid through the nose for it. I have handwritten notes indicating my parents paid more than $25,000 in the first two years, AFTER TAXES, my mother helpfully noted. I have bills to my parents for counseling services costing $150 or

$250 a session that could only have been Table Topics, because I never saw a therapist or counselor after the guy who took me off my medications—not once. By the time my friend Heather was involuntarily committed to the Family in 2001, the price had climbed to $30,000. Harvard cost $33,000 that year, including room and board.

It's inexplicable: untrained addicts in the woods with trailers, charging as much as America's top university. Inexplicable—except an entire industry supported it. Private education consultants recommended wilderness camps, often for a kickback. Wilderness programs recommended "schools," often for a kickback. Newspapers and news programs touted "tough love" programs that whipped pampered teens into shape. Parents fear their teenagers. They feared for their teenagers. And plenty of parents—good, hardworking, *rich white* parents—said tough love programs had saved their children's lives.

Plus, the program was expensive! Would my parents have left me with barely educated backwoods rednecks for $5,000 a year? Hell, no. That sounds like . . . well, exactly what the Family really was. But for $25,000? Sure. It must be good if they're charging that much, right?

"Many programs are a cult," Maia told me, "but the children aren't the members. The parents are."

Parental manipulation is pervasive. It is the foundation of the TTI. Every parent at the Family heard the same sentence: "If your child's lips are moving, they are lying." *Believe us, not them.*

Coerced confessions full of lies were designed to terrify. *See, it's worse than you imagined. Thank God you got them here in time.*

Our letters home were dictated by staff but written by us so they would be in our handwriting. Our personal statements in newsletters and graduation notices were written by staff or other kids. When a parent arrived, a staffer sat them down and gave them the speech: *Your child is going to say we starve them. We beat them. We duct-tape and constrain them. None of it is true. Your child is manipulative. They are devious. They want to get out so they can go right back to abusing drugs. Don't be soft. You being soft is what got them into trouble in the first place. These lies show our program is working.*

And then the masterstroke: *If your child leaves the program, they will die.*

That's how the TTI operates. They scare the hell out of parents. They work overtime to turn parents, already suspicious and scared, against their children. The Family was no different than Straight or KIDS or World Wide Association of Specialty Programs and Schools (WWASP) or any of the others. They made sure the more we told the truth, the more it sounded to our parents like manipulation. The more we fought their abuse, the more we seemed like unrepentant drug addicts and degenerates.

Admit it; you think so, too. You think, in some way, I must be an exaggerator.

Heather's mom, Jacqueline, explained to me how angry she got when Heather didn't call her. Jacqueline was divorced and spending all her money on the Family. She had no self-confidence, she said. No strength, at that time, to take control of her life. She cried all the time. She missed her daughter, but she had to do it. She had to save Heather's life. She lived for Heather's five-minute Sunday call.

When it didn't come, she called the Family on Monday morning (they never called her). "Oh, Heather was acting out again. We had to put her on Sanction."

Jacqueline was livid. *Livid*. At Heather.

I'm doing all this for her, she thought, *and she can't even stay straight for a week so we can talk.*

Heather wasn't doing anything wrong. But the worse the school treated her, the better for them because the worse Heather seemed to her mother. The Family's brutality tore Heather and her mother apart—by design.

And that's where the system breaks. Where bad intention descends into evil. The staff is told the students are troubled and must be reformed by any means necessary. These are struggling human beings. They have taken a job, after all, where they beat children, so something has gone wrong. Many are recent graduates of the program themselves. There are kids who drink the Kool-Aid, kids who can't function outside the warped reality they have come to know, and kids who relish the chance to go from abused to abuser. Programs love these kids because they impress parents. *See how well Matt is doing. He loves it here so much, he didn't want to leave.* Plus, these kids come cheap and don't have to be trained. They know what's expected.

Now add a complete lack of accountability. The kids are all liars; the program is always right. No one, even parents, will question what you do, no matter what you do. The worse you are, the better for everyone, even the abused kid, who is manipulative and evil and deserves it. Oh, and you're saving their life, too. So beatings become harsher. Sanctions longer. Wrapping a kid in a blanket for her protection—always dubious—becomes kicking a kid in the ribs while she's taped in a blanket on a dirty floor in a windowless room for eight straight days.

That's why I say rape is part of the system. It's never sanctioned, but the conditions make it endemic across Troubled Teen Programs. It's not every program, but it's too common to ignore.

Even death is no deterrent. A few years after I left, a kid swan-dived off the third floor of the main building. He had been at the Family for about a month, a dangerous time. You haven't adapted, and the abuse feels overwhelming.

His parents held his funeral at the Family. In lieu of flowers, they asked for donations to the Family. At the funeral, they gave the Family a large check.

How deep in the cult can you be? Those poor parents gave the Family money as a thank-you for keeping their son alive when the Family, in my opinion, clearly contributed to his death.

If that wasn't Mikey Argiros's idea, I'll swallow my leather jacket. Tony Argiros was a true believer—in himself. He was cruel and misogynistic. At the Family chapel, icons of Tony and Betty were behind the altar, right beside Jesus. Tony thought he deserved to be with the saints, if not up on the cross. To Mikey, Tony's son, the Family was just the family business. Even Tony knew it. He always called Mikey a stupid pussy because he didn't enjoy hurting kids.

But he seemed to love the money, I can tell you that.

The swan dive is an extreme example, but I hear similar sentiments all the time. Even the best parents say, "It was a mistake to send my child there, but I honestly believe if I hadn't done something, they would have died."

My parents say it. If you went through a program, I bet yours do, too.

It's bullshit. Complete and total bullshit.

Yes, teenagers screw up their lives. But not nearly as often as you think. Skipping school, drinking, experimenting with sex and drugs, having a bad attitude: it's distressing, *but that's being a teen.* The teen years are hard. We make mistakes. But mistakes are what youth is for. A vast majority of teenagers pull out of their self-destruction on their own.

And the rest of us: we need patience and positive help from professionals. We need supporting places like Four Winds, not torture factories like the Family.

Parents come to Maia Szalavitz all the time because she is the world's foremost expert on the TTI. They ask her which program to send their kid to. She tells them not to send their kid to a program.

"Yes, I understand," they say, "most programs are bad. But which are the good ones?"

"There are no good ones," she tells them. None. *Your child has a better chance of having a good life if you do nothing,* she tells them, because the concept of tough love programs is rotten to its core. You can't fill a kid with negativity and expect something positive to come out. Sorry, but trauma doesn't work that way.

If you can't do it at home because it's abuse, don't send your child to someone else to do it for you.

But look at the free pass the industry has given itself. When death is inevitable without its "treatment," it's impossible for it to fail. Psychological damage. Physical injury. Sexual dysfunction, eating disorders, anger, violence, and suicidal tendencies. These are not just our fault because we came in as "bad kids." These are pitched to parents as *improvements* over what would have happened to us without the program, because being completely fucked up and in pain is, after all, better than being dead.

Or so they say.

7

The Game

ONE AFTERNOON, I saw a new kid, tall and scrawny, with his face about six inches from a book. That was weird. We weren't allowed to sit around reading books. I saw him at meal-time with his face six inches from his food. Then I saw him in the kitchen, six inches from something, and I was like "What's your deal, man?"

We had some freedom in the kitchen. The new cook was a student elevated to a paying position, but he was alright, for a while. I mean, he killed his brother on his wedding day in 2002 by shooting him through the chest with an arrow. He was found not guilty by reason of insanity and remanded to a secure facility for treatment. But he was better than the previous cook, that's for sure.

Interesting things about the new kid, Mike O'Donnell, in no particular order: 1) he was legally blind; 2) he struggled with her-oin; 3) a judge had given him the choice of the Family or prison, and he had chosen the Family; 4) he was nineteen, so he existed in a nebulous zone—not a Family kid, because the place was tech-nically a high school, but not staff; 5) he was treated better than us but still horribly; and 6) he always wished he'd chosen prison.

Shortly after Mike arrived, we were cleaning up after dinner. I happened to look over right as his eyes rolled back into his head. He fell over, slammed face-first into the floor, and started convulsing.

Tony Argiros started screaming. "This is what happens," he yelled, "when you use drugs. Now you see what it's like." He was gleeful. "Now you see what it's like."

He thought Mike had smuggled in heroin, but that wasn't what had happened. The Family was against drugs—all drugs. Mike was epileptic, and the crank psychiatrist had taken away his medicine. He was having a grand mal seizure. His eyes were rolled up. His jaw locked. His face covered in blood because he busted his nose when he fell. He was seizing so hard, he was banging into chairs and table legs like a fish on a dock. He was dying, right on the floor in front of us, and we weren't allowed to help him. We had to stand there silently and watch.

"It's in God's hands now," Tony thundered. "So pray to the Lord. Pray hard. Because it's in God's hands whether this sinner lives or dies."

This wasn't the only incident of near-fatal imbecility. We had a sweet Southern girl in our trailer for a while: blonde hair, accent, the works. She was asthmatic, but they took away her inhaler. The bathroom window was boarded up, so the trailer was moldy. It was tough to breathe, even with healthy lungs. Southern Girl struggled. One night, it sounded like she was strangling with every breath.

She climbed down off her bunk. I could see her squatting on the floor in the dark. She put her head down and then didn't move except to gasp.

She was tripoding: squatting on her haunches with her hands on the floor. The brain will guide you to this position when it's short of oxygen because it is the easiest position for a human to breathe in. If someone says they can't breathe and they aren't tripoding, they aren't dying. (Unless it's a George Floyd or Eric Garner or Cornelius Frederick situation, where they are pinned down.) If they are tripoding and still can't breathe, you better get medical intervention fast.

Southern Girl tripoded for hours. I keep saying hours for how long horrible things lasted, but I don't know. No watches or clocks. Just imagine the longest time you can lie in a bunk in the dark listening to someone gasping for air before ripping off your own skin. That's how long it was.

My last thought as I drifted off to sleep was *She'll be dead when I wake up.*

She didn't die that night, or any of the other nights I fell asleep to her tripoding and gasping. Twice I found her lying still in the morning, her lips blue, but both times she woke up. And Mike came out of his seizure. I guess we prayed hard enough because Mike didn't die on that dining room floor. Nobody died from the Family's stupidity. Not during my time inside, anyway.

These are your experts, Mom and Dad? These are the people a judge trusted to keep a kindhearted needle-banger like Mike O'Donnell off heroin? People specifically forbidden by the state of New York from offering that service.

I'm telling you this because people want happy stories. They say, "The Family is bleak, Liz. It's worse than Riker's Island in the 1970s." (They were not at Riker's in the 1970s; they have just read about it.) They don't say it like my mother, like I'm making excuses. They say it like I'm missing some essential truth.

"Even in Auschwitz, people laughed," they say.

I don't know. Did they?

So I'm telling you about Mike because he's one of the good things. He's one of the best friends I've ever had. He protected me, without words, without actions, because there was nothing anyone could do or say to change the staff's behavior, so nobody tried. I just knew he was there for me, like Jon, and that helped. It made a difference.

He was one of us: the Misfit Toys. Blind Mike. Angry Liz. Jay, the laid-back hippie metalhead with the scar and the lisp. Marisa with the doe eyes and the sad smile, but *ambition*. That girl had an iron will. Neil, the accused masturbator, on the edge of our group. And Jon, the golden boy, at the center.

Everyone loved Jon, even the staff. He wrote the school newsletters, student testimonials, and even letters from kids to their parents saying how much they loved and appreciated the Family. He was a gifted writer, and the staff were barely literate knuckleheads. The Golden Pen, they called him. Everything he wrote was a lie to whitewash their abuse, but nobody held it against him.

"Soft hands," we whispered at him, because he rarely carried rocks or did hard manual labor.

Instead, they made him watch other kids suffer. Jon was burly. He was strong but sensitive. He hated to see others in pain, which was why they made him watch and record. Not the real record, of course. They made him watch, then write their lies. I never blamed him. Not for a second. I admired his smarts. He found a skill he could use, and in hell, you do what you have to do.

So no, we weren't the resistance. I hate that idea. There was no resistance. We weren't a club. We never hung out, laughing and shooting the shit. Playing cards? Listening to music? Chatting in the dorm? That never happened. We didn't have a pack of cards, much less a radio.

We had moments. Our first outside English teacher, in my third year, was an editor at *Highlights* magazine. He came on Fridays, made us read his horrible novels. He took Jon and me on a road trip to meet the author of *Bridge to Terabithia*. (Hate that book. It traumatized me at nine. Spoiler alert: the kids die!) He turned the radio up and let Jon and me whisper privately in the back seat. It was heaven.

Carl was the first Black kid at the Family, or maybe the second after Obie. They never preached white supremacy, but it was strongly implied we were the master race, and we were letting our race down with our druggy ways. White and straight. And male. That was what the Family valued. Bob Runge made Carl eat his own vomit off his blue sweater on his first day.

I loved Carl after that. One evening, I convinced a new staffer to let us stand on the second-floor balcony at sunset. The staffer played "Fire and Rain" on his guitar while Carl and I sang together. Then Carl started crying, so I sang alone. The Family was deep in the mountains. It was beautiful, in the way a forest fire makes the sunset beautiful if you ignore the choking smoke and destruction. The staffer was fired. Carl and I were put on Contact Sanction. That was my five minutes of high school romance, but at least I got five minutes, right?

Tony Argiros called six girls to the pond at sunset. Lovely view over the water. Reflections of mountains and shit. He dumped out a pillowcase on the bank. There were six kittens for the six of us. He made us each choose a kitten. Then he made us drown our kitten in the pond with our bare hands. They weren't newborns. They were palm-sized. They had claws. They fought. We had to stand, holding the body of our lifeless kitten in our bloody, scratched-up hands, until all six were dead, and it took a while. We were crying. We were pulling our kittens up and rescuing them, even though it only prolonged the pain. When it was finally over, Tony told us to throw their bodies into the pond. The next morning, they woke us up early and *made us swim in that pond*. This was not recreation or exercise. It was torture. I was out in the middle, treading water, pleading with myself, *Don't look at the water. Don't think about the water. Whatever you do, don't touch the bottom.*

I can't look at a cat. They have smart eyes. They know. They see me.

Tony made me drown kittens twice. Two separate occasions, the same both times, right down to the morning swim. He herded about fifty cats into a garage once, then gassed them with car exhaust. Neil was one of the boys who had to shovel the bodies into garbage bags. Explain to me how any of that was therapy.

Tell me who's the sociopath, him or me?

But on the flip side: French-toast sticks! Every Saturday morning, we were given four French-toast sticks with a packet of syrup. That was our calendar and our special treat. We lived for those French-toast sticks. We knew how to get every drop out of those syrup packets.

Here's a funny story: Mike O'Donnell, Danny, and I were on kitchen crew. We were finished cooking dinner, and the other crew kids had gone to eat, but the three of us had to resupply. Mike climbed the ladder to the storage loft so he could toss down the cans. This was cut-rate slop in giant industrial cans. Mike picked them up, yelled, "Incoming," and tossed them down for Danny to catch.

Remember, Mike can't see more than a few feet, so he couldn't see Danny, and he couldn't tell Danny was getting behind. He just kept yelling "Incoming" and tossing cans over the edge of the loft. So he threw, and Danny turned . . . just in time for the can to clobber him in the forehead.

Danny went down. I have never seen a body fall that fast. Not even Mike during his seizure. It was like the can pile-drove him into the ground. Bam. Down. Out. Mike must have heard him fall because he was down the ladder fast. I was leaning over Danny, trying to revive him, but he wasn't moving.

Mike lifted his arm. We checked for a pulse. Checked his breathing.

"He's dead," Mike said.

"No way."

"I've seen dead people. This kid is dead."

We panicked. We decided the best plan was to hide the crime by dumping his body in the dumpster because garbage pickup was later that night. Hopefully, the staff would assume he ran away. But we needed to eat or they would get suspicious. So we picked Danny up and jammed him in the bottom of the butcher's table. Danny was a big kid; it was a tight fit. I had to push down his stomach to get him in. Then we covered the butcher's table with a tablecloth and headed for dinner, planning to toss him out with the trash at the end of our shift.

Fifteen, twenty minutes later, here came Danny, staggering through the door. The kid had a massive head wound, and he was *completely incoherent.* He didn't know his name. He couldn't stand straight.

The staff stood him up at the pole and jumped all over him. They thought he was drunk. But he didn't smell like alcohol. So they decided he had masturbated to the point of incoherence. That's right: they thought he had jerked off so hard and for so long, he lost his mind. That was their honest assessment of the situation. For people obsessed with masturbation, they were shockingly ignorant about how it worked.

Mike and I got away with it because Danny never remembered getting hit with the can. He had no idea what had happened, and Mike and I weren't about to tell him. It was just another fucked-up day in paradise.

Danny's dead now.

I don't think that's the point. But if not that, then what? The instinctual way we knew we had to hide a fatal accident? Our complete disregard for human life? The stupidity and cruelty of the staff? The way Mike and I laughed about that story for years, until Danny died? You want laughter, there it is: we laughed about all the fucked-up shit we did after giving a kid a massive concussion.

To me, though, that's a story about friendship. Mike and I did what we had to do for each other. We hid a body. We let Danny take the fall. For each other.

But all this misses the truth. The rape. The blanket. Carl on the porch. Jon in the car. The dead kittens. Mike and I going gangster for each other. Those stories aren't the heart of the Family. They aren't why the Family warped so many of us beyond repair.

The horror of the Family was the repetitive nature of the cruelty. We woke up at 5:00 a.m. every day knowing someone was going to be humiliated and destroyed at a Table Topic. It happened every day. It happened multiple times a day. I sat through a thousand Table Topics, probably more.

They crawled under my skin. I never believed in any of it—I didn't think it was therapy, and I didn't think anything the staff said was true—and yet I began to believe the horrible things everyone said about me. I was dirty. I was evil. I was stupid. I was fat. I still struggle with body image and eating disorders because every day, for almost three years between the ages of fifteen and eighteen, I saw teenage girls fat-shamed and picked on for their bodies, and at least once a week, that girl was me.

And even that wasn't the worst of it. The most destructive thing about the Family was what we did to each other. What they *made us* do to each other. Not by coercion but by creating an environment of relentless violence, suspicion, paranoia, and betrayal. It's one thing to hate your overlords or to be abused by them. That creates resistance. Us versus them is not a good way to live, but it's a way. But the way we turned on each other, and tore each other down, was soul-crushing.

We had no peace at the Family. No safe spaces. Everyone was against each other. Everyone watched and listened. Everyone informed: the girl you thought was your friend, the boy you thought wasn't paying attention, a kid you would have sworn wasn't there and couldn't have known. But there he was, hours later, standing you up for a Table Topic.

You were in solitary confinement in a cell without walls. You walled *yourself* in because it was too dangerous not to. The knives were out. Constant vigilance was required. You learned to trust no one, not for a second, and that's what's killing us today, decades later. We can't stop the suspicion. We can't feel safe. We can't open our hearts to love or our minds to joy. We can't forgive ourselves. We can't forget our mistakes. We can't stop attacking each other. We can't trust, because at the Family, trust was betrayed, by everyone, all the time. That was how the place was set up. *It was at the core of how they broke us.* Staffers called us to the pole when they wanted to make a point, but mostly we called each other. We beat each other. We destroyed each other and denied each other basic humanity, day after day.

The damage went far beyond the heinous words, in the same way Rock Sanction was far worse than moving rocks. It was the pointlessness that drove you insane, not the violence. I know this is supposed to be a narrative, but I can't honestly tell you the order of the events at the beginning of the chapter. For two years after the rape and the blanket, I lost track of everything. The seasons changed, the French-toast sticks were served, but every day was the same: relentless verbal abuse followed by Sanctions. The things we were saying, after a while, weren't even attached to reality. We said what we always said because that was the way we said it. The truth didn't matter because none of it mattered. We weren't in therapy. We weren't getting better. We were just moving rocks from one pile to another, then back again. It's just that we were using these particular rocks to bludgeon each other.

Jon called it the Game. There was one Game with the staff, where you pretended to believe their bullshit. Where you pretended to like them and hate yourself for the right reasons. I was terrible at that Game. I couldn't play it like Jon.

There was also the Table Game: figuring out how to deflect, how to accuse, how to minimize your damage. It wasn't kill or be killed. Too easy. It was kill *and* be killed. You couldn't win, but you could survive. You could let them kill a little piece of you, week after week, without taking your soul. For a while, anyway. For a while.

For me, the Table Game was all-consuming. I strategized about Table all the time: who could I call out at the next meal? What would I say? I hunted problems. Did that girl make eyes at that boy? Did that boy glare at Paul Geer when he turned his fat back? Did his shirt come untucked while he moved rocks? Was she using too much makeup? Was she not using enough makeup because maybe she didn't really want to be a girl?

I kept track of my errors. Wrong words. Wrong looks. Turning down the wrong hall. Dropping my pencil. I never talked with Jon because we'd be stood up for flirting. That was how friendship was collared: by the suspicion of others. I never talked with Marisa because we'd be called out for being a clique. I never sat near the same person two days in a row because someone would call it a Negative Contract.

I lost my perspective after a few months, a few weeks, a few days—I mean, who's to say? I was never going home—my father had made that clear when he pulled out my moral inventory as a Thanksgiving gift—so time dissolved. The days fell together. The world beyond the Family became nothing to me because it gave nothing to me: no comfort or hope. It disappeared beneath my need to survive the Game. There's a photograph of me at home for Christmas, but I have no memories of going home. I know my family came to my choral performances, when the Family trotted us out for their propaganda, but I don't remember the meals my brother says we ate together afterward. I just remember the bloodbath after those Family Day performances, when kids were stood up by staff one after another at daylong Table Topics.

"Where are we?" I had asked Marisa early on. I had meant in the world.

"The Family," Marisa had replied.

And she was right. That was all you had to know, because that was all there was.

I loved my friends, the Misfit Toys. But we didn't hang out in any normal outsider sense because of the spies. Because other kids were playing the Game as eagerly as I was. The Misfit Toys were, at our core, a mutual nonaggression pact. And yet we stood each other up at Table Topics all the time. We accused each other to throw off suspicion that we had a Negative Contract. We stood each other up as a favor. If you were stressed, if the pressure was pounding away at your head, at your chest, you tipped your head in passing—not at Mike, obviously, he couldn't see it, but at Jon, Jay, Marisa—and it was understood: *Do me in tonight. Release me from this burden of not being stood up.*

We stood ourselves up at Table Topics if we made a mistake. The fear ate at you so savagely, you had to confess before someone did it for you. The boys were always standing themselves up for masturbating.

We stood ourselves up if we hadn't been stood up enough. If you went five days without being blasted at a Table Topic, the fear built in your mind. Every meal, the pressure became worse. *Why aren't they raising me?* By the sixth day, the pressure was intense. *What are they planning?* The staffers were in our heads. They could read our thoughts. Everything that happened at that place, I began to believe, was part of their plan. When Father Stephen gave me a thousand Hail Marys, I said those thousand Hail Marys because Robin would know if I didn't. She knew everything. She controlled everything.

By the seventh day, your head was exploding, and you were giving the nod: *Help me. Stand me up. Save me.* If that didn't work, if there were ten hands at the Table Topic and your friend wasn't called: *Fuck this. I'm standing up. I'm forcing their hands.*

We were violent. Extraordinarily violent. The viciousness that floored me during my first session at the pole became nothing to me. It was normal. The staff encouraged our aggression. They watched us to see how often we accused and how we accused. Viciousness was required. "Too nice" was a sin.

"Don't you want to save your family from hell?"

Mostly, though, the violence came from us. It was who we were becoming, day by day. The more we hurt, the more we wanted to hurt. We were powerless. Isolated, cut off from reality, unsure of when or if we'd be free. All we had was the power to hurt each other.

So everyone attacked. Everyone.

There was no resistance because there wasn't a single kid— not one—who didn't participate in the cruelty. Who didn't jump to destruction with an energy that would make you vomit in your cereal if you saw it in the real world.

It makes me sick to think of it now. Not what happened to me but what I did.

I was savage. I was violent, physically and emotionally. A survivor named Sarah reached out to me recently after an article about the Family in the *New York Times*. She had been sent to the Family at fifteen. She had buried the experience, she said, but was starting to explore it again. "What a nightmare that place was," she wrote. She wanted to know if I could help her recover what she had lost.

I remember Sarah. I *tortured* Sarah. I was her Shadow. She was a regular teenage girl, but I decided her hygiene was poor. Maybe she had a stain on her shirt one day, or dirty fingernails.

Maybe Robin picked up a tell on the best way to hurt her; Robin had a talent for that. I stood Sarah up every day about her body odor, her breath, her braces, her fishy vagina. You think I wasn't going for the vagina? Come on. The dirty, diseased vagina was the Family special. It was more common than tuna fish on an English muffin.

Her period stank. I remember that one. Every month, I railed at Sarah over her period. Did her menstrual blood stink? Of course not. But the Family taught us that girls' bodies were objects of sexualization and disgust. So I took a teenage girl, traumatized and thrown out of her home, and destroyed her over her period in a place where we weren't even allowed tampons.

It felt good. It felt like an accomplishment to find and work that seam. It relieved the pressure, because that's what the daily grind produced at the Family: pressure. Many times at Table Topics, I was convinced my skin couldn't hold, that it was tearing apart, that whatever was growing inside me was about to burst through.

And it felt bad. As I listened to Sarah crying in her bunk, a few feet from mine, I felt as bad about myself as I have ever felt. I wanted to comfort her. Or punch her. I wanted her to disappear. I wanted to disappear. To dissolve into my plastic mattress. I wanted to kill the people who had done that to her—Robin, Bob, Tony, Betty, Paul, and the rest—but I knew that person was me.

Give me prison. Give me Rikers in the 1970s, when it was nothing but a cage.

At least in prison, they don't care about you. You might crawl into a corner, find a hobby, keep your head down, enjoy your peace.

At the Family, they came for you. They destroyed you to build you again by their twisted design.

They were our gods.

They could have killed us, and we knew it. If I had died in that blanket, nobody would have investigated. My own parents wouldn't have investigated; they would have just asked for their money back. That was how profound the betrayal felt. I believed, every day, wholeheartedly, that my parents didn't care if I died in that place. That was what Robin told me, and I believed her. I'll be honest: I still believe that today.

I wanted to die. Every night, I wished for death. But every morning, for some reason, I got up and did what I had to do to survive. I accused. I spied. I fought. The staff loved to watch us fight, and they left us until we were bloody, bruised, and too exhausted to go on.

We had fights in the dorm. Not many, but they were vicious. These weren't riots. We didn't jump in. We watched until one girl put the other down, or until the trailer started to lean. The trailers were on a steep slope and leveled with cement blocks like the kind we carried for Block Sanction. In a strong wind, or when a girl was thrown against the wall, the trailer could tip. We hopped to it then. You heard creaking, you felt the balance shifting, and every girl was on the uphill side of the trailer in a second flat. I can't believe those things never went over, but then again, I can't believe a lot of things didn't cascade into tragedy. I am convinced kids died at the Family and it was covered up. I'm convinced there are human remains in those woods, or in that pond, or in the swamp behind the Nevins Road house.

So I fought. Hell, yes, I fought. It started out as a way to call them on their bullshit, a way to play the Game, but I failed at that, because violence became who I was. It was my special skill. Jon was their Golden Pen; I was their Crazy Bitch. I fought often, and I fought gladly. I hurt kids, and they hurt me. I fought Meaghan Waite to a bloody draw at least a dozen times. We were their killers, Meaghan and I.

Meaghan's dead now, the first to tap out.

It was never about hate. I never hated Meaghan or any child at the Family. It was survival. It was relief. It was a chance to lose myself in the battle. Fighting was the only way to elevate myself above the blackness, the only thing that took me out of that place, at least in my mind.

It was human contact. That was why we craved the violence. We lived without love. Without conversation. Without physical contact. It broke us down. It made us hungry for the sport of Table Topics, as sick as that sounds. We screamed for the connection, for the conversation, even though it was one side yelling at the other.

Punching and being punched, kicking and being kicked, it was comforting. It was intimate because it was the only time we touched each other without fear. It wasn't sexual. Don't go women-in-prison-movie on me now. It was deeper than that. When we fought each other, it felt like friendship in a way only the truly alone can feel it. It might have been a violent tackle, but it felt like an embrace.

There was only one other way to feel that release, to free ourselves from the oppression of our endless grind: to run.

Not on a track team. Obviously, they never offered us anything like that. I mean running away.

When people ask how often kids ran from the Family, I tell them almost every night. Maybe it was three times a week, maybe two, but a kid was always popping off.

It usually happened at dusk. There were a couple of Houdinis who managed to escape from the Landlocked dorms at night. Their absence wasn't discovered until the next morning. You're a Houdini, you get caught, doesn't matter. You get respect.

Most runners didn't plan. It's dusk, you see an opportunity, the weather is right, you have pressure building inside you, maybe it's been there a few weeks, maybe a few months, maybe a few seconds, and before you realize you're going, you're gone.

It was a hazardous journey. A long uphill sprint through sharp chest-high grasses. They kept the grass that way because it was hard to get through. It tangled your feet. And running through it left a clear trail.

If you made it through the grass, you hit the trees on the ridge that ran diagonally above the main buildings. If you got on the wrong side, and it was easy to get confused in the tall grass, the ridge funneled you back to that creepy farm at the entrance to the property. We called that the death triangle. They always got you there.

If you got over the ridge to the other side, you followed the saying: find the pines. Almost nobody stuck to the deep woods. It was pitch black at night, and rugged. The forest swallowed you in a second. And there was nothing on the other side, as far as we knew. Go deep, and you could get lost forever.

But if you followed the back side of the ridge, it led you to the pines. The pines meant you were close to Route 97. Running through the pines was easier than running through the hardwood forest, and they offered decent cover. Keep following the road, and you reached Hancock, New York. It was a 7.8-mile run, according to the odometer in my car, but we knew it by time. It was a full night of hard running to the bridge into town.

Easiest was running alongside the road. It was dangerous, though, because it was a winding two-lane, people drove fast, and the Family was out with their vans. There were deep ditches along most of the road, so whenever you heard a car, you dove for the ditch, lay flat, and didn't move. Nine times out of ten, they drove right past you in the dark.

Houses were another problem. They were scattered along Route 97, and the owners were not friendly. They loved the

Family (good Christians) and hated us (degenerates and liars). Kids who passed houses in the daylight said some had signs cursing Family kids and telling us to go back. Betty Argiros sent them a letter saying it was okay to shoot a shotgun in the air. She shared the letter with us, of course. That was the point of writing it, to scare us.

The neighbors listened. They shot. They were probably shooting to tell the vans where we were, I realize now, but when you're in the woods and a shotgun goes off, and you know nobody out here values your life, it's terrifying.

Most kids didn't make it to Hancock. They picked us up along the way. If they did make it, nothing good waited for them there. Hancock was a Tupperware drawer of a town: cheap, disorganized, and mismatched. Not the good Tupperware, either: the kind missing lids and stained from tomato sauce. Hancock was small, about a thousand people; it was low-lying; it was rundown; and it was all in for the Family, one of the largest employers in the area. Family Days, our twice-yearly parent-porn-a-thons, brought a hundred or more visitors to eat in the town's three or four restaurants and stay in its two hotels. Nobody in Hancock crossed the Family, and nobody wanted to. Tony Argiros, he made clear to us, owned that town.

If townspeople saw you, they called the Family. If the local cops saw you, they picked you up and drove you back to the Family, often for a quick twenty. They never took our statements or even booked us.

Sometimes local kids took us in. We were an exotic species, these legendarily terrible kids who lived in the woods. They'd give you a sandwich, maybe let you hide in their house for an hour. Kevin (the Wheelbarrow King, Tony's grandson) had attended the county school for a while, so old friends hid him in an abandoned bus in the woods where the local kids partied. Kevin made it out of Hancock twice. Got all the way to his dad in Connecticut. But he always came back.

The only place to go in Hancock was the twenty-four-hour McDonald's. Truckers parked in the lot out back, where Linda plied her trade. You could try to catch a ride with them, but we were teenage runaways, so it was dangerous. I know a girl who got raped that way. I mean, these guys liked Linda, so . . . you know. Not great. Still, the truckers were the only people within twenty miles who might not be against you.

The other option was the pay phone in the McDonald's parking lot. We didn't have money, but you could scrounge loose change beneath the drive-through window. We didn't have paper, so you needed to have a number memorized. And who were you going to call? Your parents? They put you here. They could have taken you out at any time.

Even if your call went through, the closest town of more than a few thousand people was Binghamton, an hour away. Most kids had rides coming from farther away. So you had to find a place to hide. Kids posted up in the McDonald's bathroom, especially in the winter. One kid slept with a dog in a doghouse but still got frostbite. One kid tried to turn himself in on a sub-zero night, but the police station (a storefront on Hancock's main street) was closed. It took him an hour to find someone to take him back to the Family. The McDonald's bathroom was warm, at least, but the staff was not. They loved catching Family kids. It was a game to them. It kept those hillbillies entertained.

In the three years I was there, eight, maybe nine, kids got away for good by running. Kids were often gone a day or three, hiding in the woods or in town, before getting caught. They might be gone a week before being found, hitching a few states away. Kids made it all the way home, only for their parents to bring them back. I'm not convinced the kids who never came back didn't die in the woods or in the back of some sadistic trucker's sleeper cab. There were kids at the Family who had bounced through foster homes. Kids diverted from prison. Kids no one would miss.

And yet we kept running. Almost every week, Paul Geer stood out in front of the main building at dusk, ringing his bell. And kids dropped what they were doing, even lugging Rocks or carrying Blocks, with a smile: For *whom the bell tolls*.

You'd think we'd support the runaways. Wish them the best. Run interference for them. Hope they made it home. If you've read this far, though, you know that wasn't how it went down. When we heard that bell, we salivated like dogs. We sprinted to the vans. There were two vans, one for girls, one for boys, eight kids in each. The staff drove the vans up and down Route 97. They drove all night if they had to, while we jittered in the back, drunk on adrenaline.

As soon as the runner was spotted, they slammed the brakes and threw open the back doors, and we poured out like jackals. The runner was tired and disoriented; we were fresh and ravenous. We took them down, full speed. We tackled them, beat them, dragged them out of their holes, and threw them into the van.

Back at the Family, if you were the tackler, you got to tell the story. That was the reward. You stood in front of your abusers in all your glory and told them how you brought a fellow sinner down. I never had that experience. I didn't participate in this part of our subjugation. But other kids bounced out on their toes, a big smile on their face. They felt good. The best feeling at the Family, for a lot of kids, was catching a runner and getting to tell the staff how they did it, blow by blow.

Why did we do it? Why did we turn on our fellow inmates instead of our captors? Eight teenagers in a van with one staffer, maybe two. We could have overpowered them. We could have taken the van and driven it anywhere. We could have been free, at least for a while.

I never thought of it. That's the honest truth: the possibility never crossed my mind. Our power and strength never crossed anyone's mind, as far as I know.

Except once.

It was dinnertime. Most of us were already there, sitting in our assigned seats, when a new kid burst through the door screaming, "Out of the night that covers me, / Black as the pit from pole to pole, / I thank whatever gods may be / For my unconquerable soul."

It was the poem "Invictus." He must have memorized it before he arrived. I didn't know that at the time. I didn't know anything, and like everyone else, I was stunned. This kid came into the sanctum, the place where food was smashed into your face and kids were destroyed at the pole, screaming,

> *In the fell clutch of circumstance*
> *I have not winced nor cried aloud.*
> *Under the bludgeonings of chance*
> *My head is bloody but unbowed.*

He was waving his arms and pointing, the way you point when you're hyped and shoving a message down someone's throat. That was another thing we couldn't do at the Family. We couldn't use our hands when we talked. They had to be motionless at our sides.

> *Beyond this place of wrath and tears,*
> *Looms but the horror of the shade,*
> *And yet the menace of the years*
> *Finds and shall find me unafraid.*

This kid was going for it. I mean, he was going so hard, his voice was scratchy by the end, but it didn't diminish its power when he screamed,

It matters not how strait the gate,
  How charged with punishments the scroll,
I AM THE MASTER OF MY FATE,
  I am the captain of my soul.

They grabbed him and walked him out. I want you to think about that. The staff didn't tackle him. They didn't punch him. They *walked* him out.

Nobody saw him again. He was only there two, maybe three days. I don't know his name. But if you're out there, dude, text me your address. I am on the next plane to shake your hand, because we had seven kids pop off that night. Seven runners. The most ever in one night.

Seven kids who said, *Fuck this shit. I don't care about the straight gate and the punishment scroll and the horror of the shade, whatever that is. They can't hold me here. I am the master of my soul.*

They were afraid of us. That's what I realize now. And it's so sick and twisted. So fucking sick and sad. Sixty of us and only twelve of them. We could have overpowered them. We could have controlled that place. All we had to do was work together. *All we had to do was talk to each other.* And they knew that. They knew it. So they played us off each other, and they drowned us like kittens.

The Family became less violent after I left. That's what other kids tell me. I think that's mostly because Tony Argiros turned the business over to Mikey around the turn of the century. Mikey wasn't a sociopath like his dad; he was just raised to this shit. In my view, he just professionalized the brutality. That's his Block to carry.

But the violence of my era had a purpose beyond its pathology. They had just set up the "school." They had no experience with teens. They had no clue what they were doing. They had to keep us hurting, keep us distracted, keep us weak. Everything they did kept us weak. Kept us distracted. Kept us from seeing that we were in a prison, but there was no fence. There was no gate. No guards strong enough to hold us.

We were our own guards. We closed our own gate. The walls of our prison, we built them inside our minds.

And those are the worst walls. The very worst. Because once they go up, they never really come down.

8

The Grave

MY FINAL JOURNEY at the Family started when I was forced to go to Croatia. This was June 1996, one of the few dates I know for sure. Day 630, or thereabouts.

The previous winter, the school had a guest speaker: an ex-alcoholic who had fallen off his boat, bitten off part of his tongue, and prayed to the Virgin Mary for deliverance while drowning. He survived. And his tongue grew back! Never mind that the tongue is the only muscle in the human body that grows back; it was clearly a miracle.

He had a string of rock rosary beads as big as softballs. If you smelled roses, he said, the Holy Mother was present. Never mind that he rubbed the rocks with rose oil (I saw the bottle in his box), Robin and the staff went nuts for him. The Family always leaned hard toward pseudo-Catholic–Greek Orthodox mysticism. Their religion was to an established church as their addiction program was to AA: a wild, unregulated leap from a solid platform. This guy—I'm going to call him Dick—started showing up on the regular as a spiritual adviser.

He was creepy. He touched our heads, rubbed our shoulders, but it was fine. He wasn't hurting us, and human touch was in short supply. We were starved for it. It took a while for me to realize he was touching me more than the other girls.

Then Robin announced that God had spoken to Dick, and seven children at the Family were going to hell. Everything was seven during that time. It was the magical, mystical number. Seven Sanctions. Seven days of Sanction. Seven prayers. The Seven Deadly Sins: huge topic. Huge. Those sinful seven children, Robin said, were going with Dick on a pilgrimage to Croatia. The Virgin was going to save them.

"You need the most saving," she iced me, back in her office.

I'm going to run, I thought. *This is my chance.*

My parents were so excited I was chosen, they bought me a backpack. I stuffed it with clothes and every loose thing I could secretly lay my hands on: a pencil, a fork, a notebook. The trip cost the school about $1,500, but my parents were charged $6,000, so it was another moneymaker. And now the Family offered international travel opportunities! Put it in the marketing material, next to photos of the kindly, caring, qualified staff.

We stopped in Dubrovnik to view some saint's body, then piled into a van for the two-hour drive to Medjugorje, where the Virgin was said to have appeared in the 1980s. Croatia, in 1996, was in the middle of a war. Troops in white combat helmets, tanks on the roads and in the town squares, Scud missiles every night over our house stay in Mostar. And every night, Dick sat on my bed, rubbed my shoulders, then kissed me good night on the forehead. He didn't do that to my roommate, Colleen.

We saw the shrine. Big whoop. Sang in a few churches. Whatever. Hiked. The last day, we had a choice: a mountain climb with Father Stephen or a car tour of the countryside with Dick. I was the only one who chose the car. I didn't know that until I showed up, but I was excited. I'd been humoring this guy, letting him be "Uncle Touchy," for this exact opportunity. I was running; it was just a matter of when.

We had an incredible day. It was sunny; Dick had finagled a luxury sedan; we drove with the top down. He took me to a restaurant and let me order anything I wanted. He let me smoke cigarettes. We listened to music—I remember "Freedom" by Jimi Hendrix—as I held my hand out the window, letting it flow with the wind as we sped through gorgeous hills and vineyards.

Dick let me call my dad, unsupervised. "I'm staying in Europe" were the first words out of my mouth.

"Absolutely not," he said, and hung up because it was a collect call.

I'm not asking, Dad. I'm telling. I'm gone.

But I didn't go. We had such a good time, and Dick was such a hands-off gentleman, and I felt so anonymous, so untouchable, so free of all the bullshit that had been piled on me over the years, that I didn't run. For the first time in forever, I felt like my hand out the window, unshackled, riding the breeze.

By the time we got back, Colleen had told on the "Uncle Touchy" business. Our chaperone accused me of corrupting a good Christian man. She ripped off my pants and panties, as the other four girls held me, to see if we'd had sex. (Not sure how you tell by looking.) Then she gave me the beating of a lifetime.

Before this, I would have said this woman was the most decent staffer at the Family. A low bar, sure; it is what it is. But she snapped that day. She beat me savagely with her bare hands. I think she broke my ribs. She broke two of my fingers, which are still crooked. She held my head down in a sink full of water until I thought I was drowning, but it was to clean the blood off my face. Normally, I would have gone wild in that situation. I would have fought her. But that night, I took it. Because I felt guilty. That's the sad truth. Not for anything I'd done, because that day "Uncle Touchy" never touched me, and I never led him on. I felt guilty for having a good time.

We left Croatia the next day. I was on Double Shadow. Two girls either held my arms or Belt-Looped me every second. On our changeover in Zurich, though, I saw my chance. Only one Shadow, the weaker one, accompanied me to the bathroom. I was hurting badly from the beating, but I had an adrenaline surge, like the moms who lift cars off their toddlers, and I broke free of her grip. I sprinted through the airport, dodging security guards. I heard my name on the speaker, but I didn't stop. I had to find an exit. That was my only thought: *Get to the street*. But right as I saw the door, a policeman grabbed me, and then another, and in another second, I was down.

Why didn't I tell them? I had the bruises to prove the abuse. I had broken bones. But I didn't trust them. Do you understand? There was nobody but us. Everybody else had betrayed us, especially the police.

The four girls took turns sitting on my lap on the flight home. A form of Landlocking.

Why didn't I say something to the other passengers? This clearly wasn't normal. Would it have made a difference if I had spoken out? Would someone have helped me if I had allowed myself to trust?

Back at the Family, our chaperone announced that I had seduced poor Dick. Same as the rape: I was the temptress, the slut, the evil, corrupting underage girl. I was unsavable, she said. Not only that, but because of my actions, no one was saved. Everyone on the trip was a sinner, and we were going to hell.

Funny how I once thought that staffer was okay. She was as screwed up as the rest.

After that, I started running. Never had in my first 650 days, but I ran six times over the next several months. The first time, I was startled by the difficulty. Sprinting a quarter mile uphill, through chest-high grass, was exhausting. The forest was creepy, even in the dim light of dusk. The trees were thin, with switch-like branches that swatted me at every step. Kids ran into trees trying to keep those switches out of their eyes, that's how painful they were. Then I stepped on a ground hornet nest. That ended things quickly.

I got farther the second time, but not to Hancock. I wasn't good in the wild. It was hard running through the deep woods, in the pitch dark, without a trail. Tree branches grasped and smacked; the ground dropped and twisted; the shale slid under my feet. I slipped off a cliff I didn't see until it was too late. It was only four or five feet down, a shale slide, really, but the shards sliced up my shins. I still have the scars.

The third time, I made it to the bridge in Hancock. It was short but open and near the center of town. I needed to get across, where a slope led down to a hiding spot underneath, but they nailed me there.

It was hard to run several times in rapid succession. The punishment for running was always the same: No Shoes Sanction. They took your shoes and socks and made you wear plastic bags on your feet, the kind from the supermarket. You might wear the bags for days. You might wear them for weeks. My fourth run was in the winter. You try to plan: run on the full moon, run when the weather seems good. But I got stuck in the rain, and it was too cold and too wet. They bagged me and made me shovel snow for weeks. Working outside in those thin plastic bags was murderous. I don't care if they taped you in a blanket in the boiler room; after you shoveled snow for a few hours with bagged feet, you could never get warm.

I met with Robin every week to go over my moral inventory, which we had to constantly update. More than a hundred weeks of meetings, and nothing changed. She still said the same things. She acted the same way. It was as pointless as Table Topics or Rock Sanction. She didn't care if she "saved" me. Saving me meant less money for the Family, since I would in theory go home. It was verbal abuse, nothing more. She wanted to hurt me, but I knew that, so I never let her get inside me. I stared straight ahead, with my jaw tight, and went away.

To Martha's Vineyard, where I learned to swim at my parents' summer house, the one I haven't been invited to in a hundred years.

To Nancy Drew, who always followed the clues and solved the mystery.

To my maternal grandmother, who loved me. Who laughed with me. Who took me on her lap and showed me her books. She died when I was twelve, shortly after my abusive relative dumped me. She was in the hospital for weeks, and nobody told me she was dying. I never visited her or said goodbye.

"Raise it up, Lizzy. Get closer."

After they shaved my head, I let my hair grow long. It was straight and bright red. I never did anything to it. Robin hated that.

"Raise it up, Lizzy," she chastised me. "The higher the hair, the closer to God."

Maybe I did believe Robin a little bit, because I thought for years that was in the Bible. First Book of Beauty or something: Raise Up Thy Hair, Oh Sinner, That Thou Mightst Be Nearer Thy God. I was floored when I found out it wasn't. It was just something people made up to mock Holy Rollers.

"Raise it up, Lizzy," Robin told me, and she meant it. She believed it. Her hair was an angel's perch, a firm dark cloud, sticky with hairspray.

"Raise up that hair. Don't you want to be close to God?"

I don't think so. No.

One day, she gave me shoes. She thumped them down on her desk with a smirk, and they made a metallic click. I picked them up. They were soft on top but metal on the toes and heel. They were tap-dancing shoes.

"You're going to dance for me, Lizzy."

The Family had a dance instructor who came in a few hours a week. She specialized in tap. Robin said tap was the devil's dance, but they were redeeming it for Christ. It was an honor, she said, for me to be chosen, but I'm pretty sure it was a punishment. I heard her on the phone telling my parents, "Aren't you glad she's tapping instead of turning tricks?"

She was probably trying to get them to cough up $50 for the shoes.

"You're going to dance for me, Lizzy," she said, and I did. I danced for Robin, in her office, with the door locked, two or three days a week. It was like Trotting Sanction. She danced me to exhaustion.

She made me leotards. Robin was a seamstress. She taught a required course for girls called Life Skills. I was shocked, recently, to see it on my transcript, like a real high school course. Of course, Sanctions were on my transcript as physical education, so why was I surprised?

In Life Skills, we learned to darn men's socks. We ironed men's shirts. Robin had a wooden rack with compartments. The man's shirt went over the shoulder bar, the pants over the waist bar, shoe trees at the base, cuff links, belt, tie, watch, and jewelry in their separate drawers. We worked that clothes horse until we knew how to handle a man's dress outfit like an old-fashioned English butler.

She taught us how to fill out a check but not sign it. The man had to sign it. Only a man could handle money. Only a man could do anything of importance. A woman only served. Which was hilarious because Robin was a bad bitch—that's usually my highest compliment, but here I mean she was iron-hard and dangerous—and her husband was our pasty beta-male math teacher.

"You'd look good in that leotard, Lizzy," Robin said, looking me up and down as I danced, "if you weren't so fat."

I was five foot six and 140 pounds when I arrived as a fifteen-year-old. In the first year, my weight dropped to about 100 pounds. I was on Half Portion, and I struggled to keep what little food I ate down. I was physically sick for a long time.

In my last year, I was five foot eight and nearly 200 pounds. I have serious food issues. For me, food is punishment, and it is control. When I'm anxious, I withhold. I go for days without eating. Hello, starvation, my old friend.

That year, I ate everything I could get my hands on. It was my rebellion against their fat-shaming. I wasn't going to be the person they wanted me to be. It was also comfort. It was control and a pathetic little secret, an intimate possession that was mine, all mine. I worked in the kitchen, and any loose food I saw, I crammed into my mouth.

I was in charge of the garbage area, and I had a system for that, too. Everything edible, I put in a certain bin. There were hardly any table scraps, because we were required to eat everything, but sometimes there were butter pats or crusts scraped out of the pans. I gave Neil a nod when I had something good, and he told Mike. We ate out of that trash can for years.

Twice a month, I went through the pantry and walk-in cooler and cleaned out the expired foods. Those I put in a bag and threw over the fence beside the dumpster, into a shadowed area the staff couldn't see. I never told anybody about my monthly food dump, but the food was always gone the next morning.

The main thing I ate, though, was mustard. They bought it in thousand-packet boxes, and nobody counted them. So every shift, I stole a handful.

I kept them inside my pillow case. I pulled them out at night and ate every bit, squeezing the packet carefully and licking it clean. I could easily eat twenty in a night. When I emptied my pillowcase—I had a scheme for that, too—it was always filled with a hundred packets or more.

Another girl ate mayonnaise packets. I knew about her, and she knew about me, but we never turned each other in. It was as close as I ever came to having a secret friend.

So it didn't matter how long I danced for Robin, I was never working off my mustard weight. I wasn't going to let it happen. Not for her.

Robin didn't care. We were way past caring. She had a gleam in her eye every time she said, "Dance for me, Lizzy."

She smiled every time she leered me up and down and said, "You'd look good, Lizzy, if you lost that weight."

I ran. Once it was spring and the trees were alive again, I ran. And I made it to the Hancock McDonald's. Fifth time's the charm.

In Croatia, Dick had given me his number. I'd memorized it. He'd said if I ever needed anything to call him. I needed something, so I called him. He didn't pick up, so I left a voice message.

Next thing I knew, the Family van was screeching up to the McDonald's. Even hiding in the bathroom, I could hear the tires tearing into the parking lot.

They dragged me out. Robin stood me up at the pole. *This little slut ran*, she said. *This little slut made a phone call. She called Dick.* She smiled. *He called us to make sure she was alright.*

"She called a man of God," Robin thundered, because she was angry this time, "and she thought he would care. That a man like that would care about someone like her."

She tore into me for half an hour or more, but I don't remember it. I blacked out for most of the session. I don't remember my Sanction, but I know I fell hard, the way I had when my father pulled my confession out of his breast pocket. I blacked out into hopelessness.

For a long time, I figured that was the day I changed. When I gave in. But in reliving those 993 days for this book, I realized that wasn't how I felt in my last months at the Family. I didn't feel hopeless. I "gave in" because I felt hope.

The lightning strike, I realized, was something else.

I tried to kill myself three times at the Family. Never came close. I also tried to murder the staff. Can I say that? Is there a statute of limitations on attempted murder? Knowing my luck, there's a statute of limitations on adults raping children but not on a sixteen-year-old swiping a box of rat poison and dumping it into the pancake batter.

It was a special batch. I ran down early to the kitchen one morning and whipped up the batter, poured in the rat poison, then added blueberries.

I was flipping my sixteen special pancakes—griddle was normal kitchen duty—by the time everyone else arrived. As they whipped up their industrial portion of batter, I took my pancakes off the griddle and set them aside on a high counter.

Then I got busy cooking a couple hundred pancakes. By the time I looked around, my special pancakes were gone.

"Where are my pancakes?" I asked a kid on the crew.

"I dunno," she shrugged.

I rounded on her. "Where are my pancakes? Those are for the staff."

She cowered. People cower when I'm like that. "I dunno. They got served."

Six kids got sick that day. They threw up for hours. But good news: none of them came close to dying, and none were people I liked.

Now it was much later, the spring of 1997, and I was digging my own grave. The ground was hard and rocky, so even the first level, a few inches to get the size and shape right, was brutal. I was sweating by the time I was ankle deep. Robin was standing at the edge of my grave, watching me, but I knew better than to ask for water.

Another three inches. Another six inches, with the dirt piling up beside me. Every time I rammed in the shovel, I hit a rock. But I'd dug my own grave before. It had lost its sting. I was more bored than anything as I lowered myself, inch by inch, while Robin grew taller. By the time my grave was a foot deep, I was looking up at her. The sun was behind her, so her face was in shadow, but her cloud of hair was a demented bird's nest. She usually kept it solid and sprayed, but that day, it was flying apart at the edges.

"Keep digging, Lizzy."

Every time the shovel bit, I saw her pink heels; that's how low and bent I was. Robin had worn those heels when she'd kicked me in the blanket. She had worn those heels almost every day for three years.

"Keep digging, Lizzy, for your sins."

My hands were raw. My back was hurting. Sweat poured into my eyes. I didn't care. Hundreds of days like that and you either get hard, or you get numb, I don't know which. I don't even know why I was digging. It doesn't matter. It was always something. After a while, it's always something.

"That's deep enough, Lizzy," Robin said.

I climbed out of the hole, bone weary. That's when you feel it, when you climb out. Robin didn't notice my stooped shoulders. After years of abusing children, do you even see them anymore? She launched into her spiel. Something about sins and forgiveness. They always said that kind of thing before you lay down in your own grave. Think about your sins and pray for forgiveness.

I glanced around. Then the other way. Then back.

There's nobody here, I thought. *Nobody but us.*

I could kill her.

Before I could think, I had the shovel in my hand. I hit her with the flat side, dead in the face. She dropped, and I was almost as fast. I rolled her into the grave and started shoveling in the loose dirt. Three inches. Four. I could see her shifting under the soil, so I shoveled faster. I threw dirt over where her face had been, over her hands. I could almost feel her panic as her mind snapped onto her situation: *Buried alive. Oh, Lord Jesus, I was hit with a shovel and buried alive in the grave of my favorite punching bag.* The shovel bit. My muscles ached. The ground vibrated with her fear.

"Lizzy," she said.

I turned, and she was there beside me. I had intended to hit her with the shovel. I had intended to kill her. I swear on my mother's grave, I did not chicken out. I did not have second thoughts. But I didn't do it. The heart was willing, but the flesh was weak. At my moment of triumph, after almost three years of dreaming, my damn muscles seized up and wouldn't move.

"Lizzy," she said, annoyed by my inattention, "get in your grave and contemplate your soul."

Something broke in me that day. Something good. It was like the rock scene in *The Handmaid's Tale*. That show about religious fundamentalists and their sex slaves freaked us out. My survivors' group hated the idea of it. But the show was so good that we watched it, we talked about it, we celebrated it, despite the trauma. Someone in that writer's room went to the Family or a Troubled Teen Program, I am sure of that, because they got everything right. Including the day June drops the rock in defiance of Aunt Lydia and the handmaids strut out of the field as she shouts helplessly after them. They are strutting to their own rapes, but in that moment, they are free. They are bound, but within their bondage, they find their fire. I play the song from that scene, Nina Simone's "Feeling Good," whenever I need to believe in myself. It reminds me that they may hurt me, but once I embrace my power, they can never take my soul.

What broke that day at my grave was Robin's hold on me. My belief that she owned me and I could never escape her. What broke was my hopelessness.

"They can't keep you here after you turn eighteen." Mike O'Donnell had told me that at least a year before, but it had never sunk in.

"When you turn eighteen," he said, "you're an adult. Your parents can't keep you here against your will anymore."

This was my third spring. I had to be close to eighteen. All I had to do, I realized that day, lying in my own grave with little Robin Ducey hovering above me, blackened by the sun at her back, was wait them out.

So I softened. I stopped fighting. And Robin was like *I did it. I broke the hardest case. I saved poor Lizzy's soul.*

She didn't care. I don't think she cared about me or my soul for a second. But I don't know. What else was she living for?

They put me to work in the office. They made an example of what a good little happy helper I had become.

Two other students had been forced to learn tap for the hostage show that spring. I was supposed to tap a duet with Matt, the Rock King, but in the end, it was only me, alone, dying of stage fright. I have the video. The leotard Robin made me, it's too tight. Way, way too tight. My camel toe is obscene.

My parents were so pleased with me. I'd been chosen. I was so good at tapping for the man.

"You've blossomed," they said, beaming.

I watched the spring burn off in my new job, with my new attitude. The new leaves stopped growing, hung limp like dicks in the afternoon heat. My eighteenth birthday was May 20, 1997, but I had long ago lost track of the date. There was no summer break at the Family. The imprisonment was year-round. But I sensed the gears slowing down. The time growing short. In the office, I saw a man's watch. There was a little number for the date: 18. I didn't know the month, but I figured it had to be May. Close enough.

I opened the door from the office to the outside. Nothing happened. The alarm didn't go off. Nobody was around. So I walked away.

I made it to the McDonald's around sunrise. Scrounged a quarter under the drive-in window. It was too early to call my dad. His office didn't open until 9:00. A small industrial business was down the street, sort of like a supply depot, with six large tanks behind it. I squeezed between them; there was a space in the middle where no one could see me. Even better, I could peek through an opening and see the time on an electronic sign outside a bank.

I snuck to the pay phone at 10:00. My father's secretary picked up.

"Oh, hi, Elizabeth, how are you?"

"I graduated, but my father's not here. There must have been a mix-up."

"Congratulations!"

"Can you get my father to pick me up?"

"He's in court, but he'll be back by noon."

"Okay. Tell him to come to the McDonald's. He can pick me up there."

I went back to my hiding place. Around 2:00, I heard tires squealing into the parking lot. I knew it was my father. He drives fast. I inherited that from him.

I found out later he had called the Family. Of course he had. A student must have picked up. There was a big board in the office with the names and photos of all students currently on the run. I must have been there. But when my dad asked if I had graduated, the kid had said, "That's right. Come pick her up."

The small love we show each other. The small acts of love. They mean so much.

"So is there paperwork or anything?" my dad asked as I hurried into the car.

"No," I said. "Mom took care of it."

"Oh," he said. "Okay."

And then we were gone, out past the trucks and gas tanks and onto the high road out of town. I stared out the window, not talking, listening intently for the pursuit. It was June 18, 1997, not May. I had been in 993 days. I couldn't believe I was free. I was incapable, in fact, of believing it was over. But as soon as we passed the Delaware County line, my body seemed to accept my freedom, and it did the only thing it could: it shut down. I collapsed and slept the whole way home, and I didn't dream a thing.

THE WOLF PACK

YOU BET WE'RE TROUBLE!

SURVIVOR 995

THE WOLF PACK

HERES How we Fought Back... And found love in the world.
A True story of survival, trauma and triumph.

9

One Hundred Cheeseburgers

I NEVER GOT ALONG with my mother. I think I've established that. I have a photo from my childhood. I'm about three, in an inflatable pool on the lawn, smiling at the camera. My mother is in a folding chair, staring away from me out of the frame, with an *I couldn't give less of a fuck* look on her face. That sums up our relationship pretty well.

I was close with my father. He was a personal injury attorney. I spent a lot of time in his office when my mother was having her bad days. He held my hand as he showed me his law books. He introduced me to his clients. He took me on his lap and explained, "These people have had bad things happen to them, but I'm helping them. I can't take away their pain, but I can make it better. That's what I do."

That's what my daddy does. He makes the hurt better.

I remember when he won his first big case. He took me and my younger sister for a car ride, and he whispered with a big smile, "Hey, let's go buy a house for your mother."

He took us to a big house. It was beautiful. *Yes, yes, we want this one*, we said. So we drove to an office, and my father pulled out a briefcase full of money, and he bought that house.

I realize now he had already picked out the house, and the money was probably for show, but back then, I felt like I was part of it. Like we had done it together. My father made me feel that way, before my relative started raping me. He made me feel like I was loved.

It wasn't like that after the Family. I returned to a house full of family photos, but none included me. It was the four of them now, my parents and younger siblings. I had been wiped from the family presentation. My sister was living in my old room, so my parents stuck me in a room under construction. They had been adding rooms to the house for years. We called it the Ianelli Family Compound.

My mother took me with her to the store. Once. Her friend smiled when she saw me. "Oh, Elizabeth," she said, "you're back. How was art school?"

So they had lied about me, too.

My father told me, "You're going to St. Bonaventure in a few weeks. Get ready."

I had not applied to St. Bonaventure. I had not applied to any colleges. I had not thought about colleges. I didn't even have a real high school degree. The one I received was from John Jay High School, the public school where my parents lived. I had never set foot in the place. But the Family got me into St. Bonnie, I guess. They were obsessed with their college acceptance rate. It was a big selling point. They wanted to seem like a good school without having to be an actual school. St. Bonnie was for them.

I was not ready for college. Understatement of the year. I was not ready to walk down the street, much less live in another city on my own. My father took me to a parking lot for one day and taught me to drive. I was too young for a permit when I went away, but I managed to get my license. Then I drove myself to college. My memory is a little fuzzy about this six- or seven-year period. Maybe it wasn't quite like that. Maybe my parents drove up, too? Maybe they helped me move in before saying goodbye? But that was what it felt like: my parents didn't want me back, so they dumped me off the edge of the earth.

I was so paranoid, I couldn't function. I had a roommate, but she beat it pretty quick, because I was nuts. Not angry: trauma-tized. I spent days in bed. I jumped at every sound, in a college dorm, where there was always sound. I didn't open my door ten times the whole semester, because I was terrified of what was out there. Every time I heard a noise in the hall, I thought it was the Family. They knew where I was, obviously. They were inside my head, reading my thoughts. Nobody escaped from them. Nobody.

If the Family wanted you, they got you. And they always wanted you.

I had nightmares about being black-bagged. That's when they throw a bag over your head, zip-tie it tight, and toss you into a van. It's a form of gooning, the word the TTI uses when kids are forcibly removed from their homes to a facility. Kids arrived at the Family drugged and tied all the time. I never saw a black bag, but Heather witnessed one. A kid was black-bagged by hired goons in the Family dining hall because he'd had sex with a white girl. She stayed; no one ever saw him again.

I peed in the sink in my room because the bathroom was down the hall. That was how paranoid I was. Do you know how hard it is for a girl to pee in a sink?

I drank water out of that sink.

Don't even ask about my grooming.

To leave my room, I climbed out the window. I attended one class. It was in a huge sunken room, with the professor down front, like a gladiator arena crammed full of spectators. It gave me a panic attack. After that, I only went out at night. I felt safer after dark. My father had given me a Mobil gas card. It took me a week of walking around to find a Mobil station and another two days to work up the courage to go inside.

The lights were bright. The air cold. That terrible buzzing. I bought a pack of crackers and cheese, a pack of cigarettes, a bottle of juice, and a carton of milk. My hand was shaking when I handed the clerk the card. This was it. I was about to be gooned. But he handed it back, and I walked out alive. I wasn't sure how the card worked, so I bought the same food and drinks every day, a safe purchase. That was all I ate for months, crackers and cheese. Hello starvation, old friend.

I roamed the campus at night, snatching any newspaper, magazine, or book left lying around and reading it in my room. I kept a notebook of things to research, like who the president was and what he was about. I listened to Top 40 radio and wrote down the names of bands and songs, then whether I liked them or not. I'd lost myself at the Family; I couldn't remember what I had listened to or trust what I liked. Eventually, the late-night clerk at the Mobil station started giving me unsold copies of newspapers they were going to throw away. Now I was really digging into this "real world" thing.

I took my notebook to the library. I asked the librarian questions like "Where can I find a book about putting gas in your car?"

"Oh, sweetie," she said, "there's no book for that."

After a few weeks of ridiculous questions, like "Is it okay to chew gum?" the librarian started taking me aside and explaining the world. It was late; the library wasn't crowded. She probably thought I'd been homeschooled.

The joke was on her: I'd been unschooled since the seventh grade.

At some point, I wrote a letter to Jon. I was unattached from the world; nothing seemed real; I needed proof of life. The letter was little more than *How are you? Here's my address.* I mailed it to his home, so I was paranoid his mother would get suspicious if I said more.

Months later, I got a phone call. I didn't know I had a phone. It was under my bed.

"Yes?" I said.

"Is this Elizabeth Ianelli?"

"Yes."

"This is the campus post office. You've had a letter sitting here forever. Are you going to pick it up?"

I got dressed and went out *in the middle of the day* to get my letter. I didn't know there was a campus post office, so I wandered. The letter was from Jon, of course, and it included his phone number.

The first question I asked him: "Was that real?"

"Yeah," he said. "It was."

"Is this real?"

"Yeah, I think so. You good?"

"I don't know. You?"

"Same."

I failed out of college. Bet you didn't see that coming. I moved home for a few weeks, then into my car. Eventually, I threw in with Jon at Vassar, where he was a student. Mostly, we stayed in his dorm room and talked. We asked each other questions like "What's the craziest thing you remember Tony doing? What's the craziest thing you remember Robin doing?"

"What was the worst Sanction?"

"Who was the worst staffer?"

We were trying to make sense of it. We had to nail it down because out here, in the so-called real world, it was hard to believe that had really happened to us, and we needed a witness just to make sure we weren't insane.

I tried to get past it. I tried to figure out how to function in the world: wash clothes, pay bills, buy normal food, talk to normal human beings. Jon shared his music. He explained politics. He taught me how to drive, because I had been faking that, too, white-knuckling it like everything else. Jon was the one who taught me how to put gas in my car.

"You having dreams?" he asked me.

"Yeah," I said. "I'm having nightmares." It helped, somehow, to know that he was, too.

My father sent me to Hamline University in Minnesota, where he had gone to law school. I barely survived. I was extremely suicidal. He sent me to his alma mater, Marist, in Poughkeepsie, down the road from Vassar. My father never asked me what was wrong. He never sat down with me and held my hand, like he used to when he showed me around his office, and said, "I see you're barely hanging on. I see you're hurt. I see your pain. What's wrong, Liz? How can I help?" He knew what was wrong: I was a piece of shit and a cancer on his good name. He had sent me to a fancy private school for losers . . .

Well, not fancy. Every parent who drops a kid off at the Family knows, even if they won't admit it to themselves, that those places are punishment. But that wasn't the point. My father had spent good money to give me the best chance in life, and I had done nothing but piss on his efforts.

And I'd done it crouching over a sink like an animal, no less.

But credit where credit is due: my father kept paying for college even as I kept dropping out. Many Family kids got less. Heather's grandfather had promised to pay for college for his grandchildren, but when Heather asked for hers, he laughed at her. "We spent your college fund on that school," he said. *And it didn't even help.*

Heather never went to college. She lived rough, with bad boyfriends, got hooked on opiates prescribed by a quack doctor. She's been Narcaned three times.

Katrina's parents refused to take her back, so the Family drove her to Binghamton and dropped her off at the homeless shelter. She was abused, sexually and physically, then addicted to heroin, then pregnant. Her parents took her baby and left her on the street.

My parents never took me back, not in their hearts. They never accepted or saw me. But they insisted college was my way forward, and they kept sticking me in colleges until, at Marist, it stuck. I told the registrar, "I can't do math." I hadn't had a real math class since the seventh grade.

"Try social work," she said.

I lived on campus for three days. My roommates were labeling the food, pledging sororities, and making paddles. It was terrifying, so I bailed. I lived in my car, a tan-and-cranberry Ford Explorer. I loved it in my car because it was only me, no walls. Because I couldn't be Landlocked. Because there was nothing to stop me if I needed to run.

Typical Family "graduate." We come out broken and fail to thrive.

Kevin, who they had called an alcoholic at eleven, became an alcoholic.

Heather, who had never taken a drug before the Family, became an opioid addict.

Neil ended up back at the Family, working in the office. He hated them, but he couldn't function on the outside. He worked there until he saw his baby sister being forcibly restrained and carried down the stairs like a slab of meat. The Family went after siblings. Siblings were easy money because the parents were already in the cult.

Neil's sister was shy and trusting. Very innocent. Totally harmless, almost surely on the spectrum. The desperate look she gave Neil as those girls carried her down the stairs, the lack of understanding and longing for release, any release, made him quit on the spot.

The Family broke her. She's remanded to the New York state psychiatric hospital for life. Neil won't talk about it. He loves her. He blames himself. It's too much.

Jon got me through. He kept me alive, because I was struggling to do ordinary things like eat and shop and sleep. I was good at social work, but he wrote most of the papers for my core classes, like history and English. Jon was always a writer. He let me crash with him at Vassar, when I needed a shower (terrifying) and a bed. In many ways, we were opposites. I wore my pain; he hid his inside. I lashed out; he spoke carefully. He had a way of clenching his jaw, a little sideways, as if grinding his teeth. I learned to recognize when that meant he was concentrating and when he was biting off his pain and frustration. Jon was wound tight.

We were angry. At our parents, mainly, but also at our failures. We were from upper-middle-class families; great things were expected of us. Things we couldn't do. Our three years of abuse had separated us from the outside world. We were aliens, looking at a new planet through glass. I watched how normal people talked. How they smiled. I didn't understand it. When was I supposed to smile? How was I supposed to feel? What did happy mean? I needed Jon to tell me, like he told me everything else. But he didn't know happy, either. He was lost, too, just not as obviously as I was.

I tried therapy. The therapist listened to me for an hour, then said, "Well, you have an interesting imagination."

There was no way back. I tried, Mom and Dad, I really did, but you left me here. Jon and I were drowning, slowly, and there was no way back to shore.

"You having dreams?"

"Yeah," Jon said, "I'm having dreams."

For more than twenty years, I have woken up almost every night screaming.

Eventually, we stopped trying to fit in and embraced who we were: outcasts. We embraced *who they made us*. I put on my leather jacket and released the anger I had barely been able to control. If someone startled me, I punched. If someone insulted me, I punched. I was dangerous. A ball of razor blades rolling downhill. Jon got into piercings and tattoos. He took every flyer from every pole in Poughkeepsie. I sat in his dorm room while he sorted through them, figuring out the night's best show.

We came together with our old Family gang, the Misfit Toys. It happened to a lot of Family survivors. We didn't have the momentum to escape the Family's gravity, so we fell back into its orbit. We pulled back into *each other's* orbits because nobody believed us. Nobody loved us. Nobody understood us except the people who'd been there.

Our groups were small, since we struggled with trust. They were geographic. This was before MySpace, Facebook, Instagram, and Twitter, so proximity mattered.

We called ourselves Wolf Packs, after nature's tightest families. Nature's misunderstood hunter-killers. Or maybe after German submarines. The German wolf packs of World War II were designed to protect the weakest members. They pushed damaged subs to the front so they'd never be left behind. That was what we did for each other. We were wounded and struggling in an enormous ocean of apathy and neglect. We were afraid; that was what nobody understood. Afraid of ourselves and afraid of our future, which seemed bleak.

Jay, God, he was a great kid, a metalhead with the heart of a hippie. But he came out of the Family with a self-loathing that curdled into self-destruction. A hundred nights we started out together before he disappeared into alcohol.

Marisa was on Long Island, working in marketing for Zima, a clear alcohol that was having a cultural moment. Once a month,

I drove down from Poughkeepsie and we had lunch. She always paid, but in the end, despite her smiles and celebrity stories, there was something haunted in her eyes.

Mike O'Donnell was our rock. He lived an hour away, in Middletown. He had a steady job as a case worker at Occupations, a center for adults with disabilities. They loved him there. Mike felt unlovable, that was what the Family had put into him, but it was impossible not to love him. He didn't drive (obviously), so Jon and I picked him up at his childhood home, where he lived with his parents. Jay was a chef, so he usually met up with us after midnight, and we hit the underground music scene. Rancid-style acid punk in basements or abandoned warehouses, no tickets or bouncers, just slam dancing and aggression until dawn. Mike played bass. He wasn't in a band, because there weren't many steady bands, there were just musicians in the scene, and everybody loved Mike. Jon sang. Jay drank. I danced.

One night, I was thrashing in a mosh pit when Jon grabbed me by my T-shirt and dragged me out, screaming, "You gotta be careful, Liz. You gotta be smart." Typical big-brother bullshit. He was only six days older than I was, but I was a girl.

Bite me, I thought. I loved the violence of the pit. I loved slamming and being slammed. "I can take care of myself," I screamed over the music.

But I loved him for it. I loved Mike and Jon for watching out for me, even though I didn't need it. Mike had jumped off the stage to rescue me that night, the blind-ass fool. I didn't notice the blood until we were halfway home.

New Year's Eve 1999, Y2K. I was in a club in Poughkeepsie, I don't know why, clubs weren't my scene. Suddenly, people started running and screaming. Shots were being fired outside. I walked out into the crossfire with my head back and my arms raised to the sky.

Something slammed me in the back. I went down. Hard. A cop had tackled me, got a commendation and everything. He probably thought I was on drugs, but I wasn't. *Everybody says this is the end*, I was thinking, *so let's see if it's my time.*

It was an experiment. Pure nihilism. I didn't care if I died. I was dead inside, anyway.

"You having the dream?" Jon asked. He meant being chased through a building with no exit, our nightly terror.

"Yeah," I said. "I'm having the dream."

I didn't do drugs. I didn't drink. I've been raped multiple times, inside relationships and out. I've been beaten countless times. Kicked. Knocked unconscious. I've watched Jay walk—no, run—no, sprint—into oblivion. The world is too dangerous to risk losing control.

The only thing getting me high was my anger. I wore it like a coat of nails. I was drawn to aggressive men. I liked boyfriends who punched me. I attacked them verbally, like I had learned at Table Topics, they punched me, and I punched back. It was the only kind of relationship I knew, the only intimacy I felt comfortable with. When a man punched me, it felt like what other people meant when they said love.

None of those relationships lasted long.

I got a series of horrible jobs, but none of those lasted, either. Because I was belligerent. My parents rented me an apartment because they thought it might help me finish college, but I never went there; I preferred my car. I got a tramp stamp of a phoenix rising that I thought was bad-ass, the new me, girl-strong, but turned out to be just ass. Never get a cheap tattoo in a filthy garage from a guy named Painter. Nothing from that period lasted long, except the tattoo.

"You having dreams?" Jon was struggling. I could see it. He was fighting himself. He has always fought to live up to his own ideals.

What could I do except be there for him? That's what survivors do for each other. That's all we can do. We can care. We can see. We can keep each other from being alone. *We hold on,* as Bishop Briggs sings in one of my favorite songs. Through the fights and lies, and fall and rise. *We hold on. Together.*

"Yeah, Jon," I said. "I'm having dreams. I'm running every night."

The only thing releasing me from torment was hunting the Family. I couldn't escape them, asleep or awake, but I could despise them.

"You're the angriest bitch I know."

Jon told me that all the time, especially when we left a show at 3:00 a.m., dead sober but electrified, and I insisted we head to Hancock.

"They put the wrong bitch in that blanket."

Jon said that, too. I think it was a compliment. I know he said it with pride.

We were hunter-killers. That's what Wolf Packs are for: hunting and killing. And nurturing. And tending wounds. And being a family of outcasts, yes, the unfairly hated; we were all those things. We had so much anger, we had to turn it somewhere, so we turned it on our enemy: the Family and its torturers.

We shaving-creamed their cars.

We egged their property.

We drove down Route 97 through Hancock at 3:00 a.m. on the Fourth of July shooting Roman candles and bottle rockets out the window.

What did you think we were going to do? We were still kids.

We called the Family office eight, ten, twenty times a day.

I called Mikey Argiros at home and vented every foul thing I could think of about every horrible thing the Family had done to us. He took it. I'm giving Mikey that. He took my abuse, too afraid to hang up.

We booked multiple rooms at the Delaware Inn, the Hancock hotel Mikey co-owned, then didn't show up.

We rented a van to kidnap a staffer's cat. Jon and I were the instigators, Mike the happy-go-lucky sidekick, as always. That's a cheap trick, kidnapping a cat, but these people didn't deserve cats, not after what Tony Argiros had made us do. We wanted to give that cat a real home. But the cat was so violent, we drove back to the trailer and opened the back door of the van, then hid in the bushes until it hopped out and sauntered home.

One Family staffer had sex with McDonald's cheeseburgers. There were two versions of the story. In one, he masturbated with the cheeseburger wrapped around his dick. In the other, he masturbated while eating the cheeseburger. It was a food and sex addiction. That was why he told us the stories. *He* told *us* the story. *Repeatedly.* In the classic version, he's driving, jerking off with one hand and eating the cheeseburger with the other. He loses control, but he can't decide which to put down, the burger or his dick, so he crashes into another car. That was how he met his wife.

Imagine what a fucked-up "school" you had to teach in, how divorced from reality and common sense you had to be, to think this was a good story to tell, *repeatedly*, to teenagers. And to have no one take you aside and say, *Hey, buddy, maybe you should keep that one in your pants and shut your mouth.*

And I know what you're thinking: Did he eat the cheeseburger in the first story? I don't know. He never said. But . . . hell, yes. He *devoured* it.

So what did Jon, Mike, and I do? We went to the Hancock McDonald's and ordered one hundred cheeseburgers. "Umm, like, that's going to take, like, half an hour."

"That's fine. We'll wait."

They brought us the burgers in a garbage bag. "Sorry, I hope this is, like, alright." They thought the burgers were for a party.

"Oh, no worries. That's perfect."

Driving to the man's house, because of course I knew where he lived, I heard crinkling. I looked in the rearview, and Mike was eating a cheeseburger.

"Mike! That's nasty. Those aren't for eating."

"Yo," Jon said, "pass me one, bro."

So we arrived at the house with, like, ninety-four cheeseburgers. We planned to throw them around the yard, but I tried the front door, and it was unlocked. So we went inside, throwing cheeseburgers everywhere. We took them apart so the ketchup and mustard stuck to the wall and slid slowly down, leaving a streak. Pickles stuck to everything, including the ceiling. Mike was so blind, he missed the walls. He was just throwing cheeseburgers. I laughed so hard I peed my pants.

It was juvenile stuff. Teenage pranks. But we were juveniles. We were in our twenties, but our development had stopped at fifteen, when we'd been jump-punched into the Family.

We never did anything destructive. Once the Family's chapel was defaced and its iconography destroyed. It was clearly personal and directed at the religious component of the Family. They tried to pin it on me, because I was the one calling Mikey and railing at him, but it wasn't us. A lot of Family kids were angry and hurting, struggling, wanting revenge, and more power to them. I'm not judgmental.

I have three rules. Don't do anything to hurt your children. Don't go to jail. Don't check out. Otherwise, whatever you have to do, more power to you.

I'm with you, survivor, in spirit. And if you need something more, I've always got a balaclava in my bag.

10

Emergency

I GOT MY DEGREE in social work from Marist, but my parents were wrong; that didn't change my life. What changed my life was a college job fair, because at that job fair, a woman pitched me on being an EMT.

Anger is an energy, and being an EMT gave my energy an outlet. As soon as I stepped into an ambulance, I stepped into my best self. The lightning bolt, they call it. True love. It hits like a hammer to the ribs, and you know. When a call came in, the adrenaline rush was the armor I pulled on to go to war against the world, and I loved it. It never bothered me to see sick or wounded people. It never bothered me to see dying people. It focused me. When I walked into an emergency, the world slowed down, I saw everything, and I took control. Slam the oxygen. Give or take an order. Nobody knows what's wrong, but give me half a minute, I'll figure it out and help keep this kid alive.

Being an EMT is how I know about tripoding, because I saw people struggling to breathe.

It's how I know about lividity, because we walked in on death all the time. And I didn't have to be the shoulder your wife or child cried on, I wasn't ready for that kind of emotional commitment, but I had to be nice. And that was new for me: jacked up on adrenaline, in a difficult and stressful situation, and nice.

Not always. Let's not get carried away. I was the craziest EMT in Dutchess County, and most EMTs are at least 42 percent nuts. We dealt with violent drug episodes. We dealt with aggressive drunks too tanked to know they were hurt. People attacked us in a state of panic. We took no shit. If my partner was driving the ambulance, and I said, "Waffle," he gave it a count of three and slammed the brakes. I was holding on; the unruly passenger flew forward and slammed into the plastic milk crate that held our paperwork, giving them a waffle face.

We had metal clipboards. I bent a few, I hit people so hard. But when someone is wild—I mean completely out of their mind on drugs or fear or panic—it's dangerous. You do what's necessary to calm them down.

I worked twenty-four-hour shifts. That way, I could shower and sleep in a staff room at a firehouse, because I didn't have a home. I preferred to be on the move, with only a handful of possessions.

I often worked ten nights in a row, eight hours on the overnight shift, because I was registered with three ambulance companies. Some months, I worked twenty-eight, twenty-nine days. I was an adrenaline junkie. The work never wore me down. It powered me up.

And I was proud. I was proud of myself, for the first time. I was helping people. I was saving lives.

I don't tell war stories. I mean, you want to hear about the guy who almost died of alcohol poisoning because he chugged a bottle of wine through his asshole? No, you probably don't. But one night, we took a call at a convenience store, and as soon as I heard it, I told my partner, "Get in the truck."

"Ah, it's an unknown medical," he said. "I wanna get a coffee."

"I'm driving," I said. "Get the fuck in the bus."

I took off at full speed, lights flashing.

"You want me to check the map?" We had paper maps then.
"No need."

We got to the address, and sure enough, it was Jon. He was passed out in his bathroom, leaning over the edge of the tub. Heroin overdoses make you feel hot and dry. Victims often pass out trying to reach cold water.

We hit him twice. We didn't have spray Narcan then; it was a double shot. He snapped up like they always did, wide awake and stone-cold sober. My partner threw him in the back of the bus, and I got in after him, screaming all the way to the hospital, "You stupid motherfucker. How could you, you stupid motherfucker?"

The ER attendants were like *What the fuck?*

My partner shrugged. "I think she knows him."

Jon was sheepish afterward. He didn't want to talk about it. He was struggling, and I knew it, so I didn't press. He had joined the army, been accepted into the Eighty-Second Airborne. This was around 2004, when the war on terror was kicking off. Jon craved the discipline and purpose. He needed to help someone. But he failed the psych exam. (Thanks, Family.) It was the biggest disappointment of his life; he told me that many times. It crushed him, that failure, but the Wolf Pack flanked him. We took him in. Marisa was drifting away. Jay was in and out of jail, mostly for stupid shit he did while drunk. Mike O'Donnell and I took Jon in.

The overdose was an accident. Jon liked party drugs, like ecstasy and molly. He never did them around me, because I didn't like it, but I knew they were his escape. He wasn't a heroin user. He was experimenting. Maybe he got it from Mike, I don't know. Mike relapsed pretty regularly. But it wasn't the overdose that scared me; it was his reaction. Jon didn't want to die, but there was a part of him, I could tell, that didn't mind how close he had come. That was why I didn't leave him for weeks. That was why I was always there, in person, on the phone, for my best friend.

Soon afterward, I met my husband. He was a cop. We met at a car wreck. I guess that should have been a sign.

We're still friends. I joke with him, "We had a great wedding, didn't we, Mike?"

"Yeah, Liz," he says. "We had a great wedding."

The rest of it? Well . . .

We had some good times. We had fun with each other. Mike was a veteran as well as a cop. His father had died unexpectedly while he was on a troop transport on his way to his first duty tour in Kuwait. My father became like a second father to Mike— the father he could never manage to be for me. And I was okay with that. I wanted that connection for Mike. And maybe for my dad, too, because I knew I wasn't what he wanted. Whatever I say later, because our life got messy, Mike was a good man. He has always been a good father and a stand-up guy.

We bought a little house, too small in my mother's opinion, but just right for us. A year later, in 2005, I got pregnant. The birth wasn't magical. Sorry. I wish it was roses and bluebirds, but I was a multiple-rape and trauma victim in a fragile emotional state. I felt vulnerable lying on the table with my nethers exposed. I felt echoes of abuse in the contractions. Then in walked a man I had never seen before. He was a substitute doctor, I guess that's common in obstetrics, but I didn't know this guy from Jesus, and before I knew what was happening, *he had his fingers in my vagina.*

I panicked. Not regular panic: soul-gripping, mind-destroying panic. I couldn't breathe. I felt like I was dying. By the time I was pushing, I was screaming, not in pain but in terror.

I don't remember my baby being born. I remember blood and shit, and someone holding me down. It felt like the blanket. I felt like a woman being wheeled against her will into a mental hospital in another B-movie. Nobody warned me. Nobody connected how my trauma would impact the act of giving birth. Nobody thought about me or my history at all.

I didn't bond with my baby. It was postpartum depression. It's accepted now as a pretty normal medical condition, but nobody had identified it then. Or if they had, they never told me. I thought I was broken. The Family told me all a woman was good for was having babies, and having a baby was the happiest event of your life. So why wasn't I happy? Why was I terrified instead?

My second night home, I was up with our baby, Patrick, at 3:00 in the morning. Mike was asleep. My mother wasn't there. I was alone. I called the hospital and said, "I don't want this baby. I'm not a mother. I can't do this."

"Don't worry," the very nice nurse said. "This is a normal feeling. It will pass."

I said, "No, you don't understand. I'm not normal. I don't know what I'm doing. I'm going to fail this child."

"Everybody feels that way sometimes," she said.

No, I thought. *They're happy. They know what to do. God put it in their biology. The Family told me so.*

I had been running since stepping out of the Family and taking off for the trees. I had been frantic to get away. But I couldn't, because what I was running from was inside me.

I couldn't even outrun their stupid ideas about motherhood.

Now I was bound. I couldn't run, because I had to be attentive every second, or this child would die. And I hated Mike for that. He tied me down in this house. He tied me down in this relationship. He bound me to this so-called happy, normal life.

I resented my baby. I hate to admit that, but it's true. My baby needed me, and I knew I was a fuckup. Even if I managed to keep him alive, I'd let him down.

It took me months to love my baby, and it never came naturally. I hope you understand this, Patrick. I'm talking about a baby. I'm not talking about you. I'm talking about an innocent, who had done nothing wrong. I was the one with the problem. I couldn't love my baby until I realized I was doing to him what my mother had done to me. She froze me out. She made me feel unwanted. I couldn't do that to my son. I had to love him, even though I had to work to love him.

I got pregnant again. My second son was born ten months after my first. I struggled to bond with him, too. I struggled with feeling worthy and able to care for him. But I did it. I put in the work to love my sons, which is what I want you to know, Patrick and Brenden. No matter what happened, I loved you, actively and aggressively, and always more than I loved myself.

I pulled the pin. I never knew that to have a real relationship, I had to open my heart. I had to be honest and vulnerable. I had to share myself and show someone who I really was.

I couldn't do it. I couldn't be open and vulnerable for my husband or submissive to anyone. So I pulled the pin on the grenade and blew myself up. I killed Mike's love for me with accusations and screaming. I recreated the Family in my family so that I could rebel against it. So Mike would never hold me or be close to me. So he would never ask anything of me. So I would never have to try to love and be loved in return.

It's what trauma does to us. It puts a self-destruct button in our heads. When we feel uncomfortable, when things get too bad *or too good*, we get scared, we pull the pin, and we're gone. Some into drink. Some into drugs. Some walk out. Some walk off the cliff into oblivion. I destroy myself with anger. I make myself a cactus so nobody will try to hug me, because hugging is a blanket, and a blanket feels like death.

I was no longer an EMT. Being an EMT is physical labor. At any moment, you might need to lift and twist with a few hundred pounds. You can't do that after a certain point in pregnancy, so I had to quit my job. I already assume you hate me because of my struggles with motherhood, so let me admit one more thing: at that time, I liked being an EMT more than I liked being a mom. I'm too old for the job now, and I still mourn the loss. Sometimes, I park across from emergency rooms and watch the ambulances come in. I don't watch the patients; I watch the EMTs. I can tell what they are doing and why, just from a few movements. I can tell whether they are good at the job. I can tell if they love it like I loved it. I don't do that when I'm sad. I do it when I'm happy. It's a celebration. I still fall asleep, when I can sleep, to the rumble of a diesel ambulance engine on my phone.

I tried being a call dispatcher. Worked it for a year. It wasn't the same. So while pregnant with my second son, I decided to pursue a master's degree in social work. Weekends and nights, I drove to the Fordham campus in Tarrytown to take classes.

And I loved them. I couldn't love my husband. I struggled to be present for my family in body and soul. But I fell passionately in love with social work. Because social work was powerful. It gave me the same adrenaline rush as being an EMT, but for the opposite reason. Being an EMT meant moving fast, improvising, not following protocol but doing what's right in the moment, because that's how you save a life. Social work was working steadily and methodically. It let me be my childhood hero Nancy Drew, because good social work was following clues, asking questions, building a solution.

Jon came by regularly during both my pregnancies. He worked at Planet Wings, a few blocks away, so when he was delivering chicken wings in my neighborhood, he'd stop by. He loved kids, both my boys and his nieces. I'd like to think my steps into adulthood, as stumbling as they were, inspired him, because his life was changing around then, too.

Jon was a rabble-rouser. He was a stand-taker. He believed in the righteous cause. He liked to rage against the machine almost as much as he loved the band. "Rally round the family with a pocket full of shells," he'd shout, a Rage Against the Machine lyric, whenever we headed out on a mission to Hancock.

He became increasingly active with trauma survivor networks. Through those contacts, he connected with the Community Alliance for the Ethical Treatment of Youth (CAFETY). The founder, Kathy Whitehead, had survived the notorious Mission Mountain School, and the group advocated for victims of the TTI. In 2007, Jon joined their board. That was how he found out about Maia Szalavitz's *Help at Any Cost*.

"We have to read it," he told me.

We were so broke, because I was in school and not working at the time, that we decided to go halfsies on one copy. I went to his apartment, and we read the book out loud to each other. I wasn't hiding from my family. Jon had always been my refuge. I had spent a couple nights a week with him since he answered my letter a year after we escaped the Family. Some people think we should have been together, as a couple. It was never like that, and I give my husband credit for understanding. I would have dated Mike O'Donnell. I should have told him that. He thought no girl would want him because he was blind, but he was handsome and sweet and a hopeless romantic.

Jon and I had a different relationship. It was more than friendship. It was a sophisticated, elegant love that connected us at the heart without either of us wanting more. We came through the fog together: failing at college, destructive relationships, family rejection, lost jobs. He was the one person in the world who truly knew me, and he loved me anyway. He was the only person I ever opened my heart to and was completely honest with. And he loved me anyway. Do you understand that? He saw me, and he accepted me, in all my messiness. He was there for me, no matter when and no matter what.

And I was that one person to him, too.

The first night we read *Help at Any Cost* together, it smashed through my heart like a message of hope. It changed my world. We weren't alone. What happened at the Family was happening all over the country, in a hundred schools and wilderness camps, to thousands of children. Someone was documenting it. Someone on the outside saw us. I felt lighter, a great weight lifted. I felt relief. Things were going to change. With Maia sharing the burden, I could be free. We could all be free.

Then I began to feel hot. It was a physical heat. It started on my skin, then built inside me, overheating me, until my organs melted and leaked out on the floor. These "schools" were everywhere. This was happening all over the country. It had been happening for decades. It was happening right now. I will never forget that moment when I saw my pain tearing through an endless crowd of children. That was the moment when this pain became a cause. When I stopped lashing out wildly and embraced the power in a rolling ball of razor blades.

"We have to support the Miller Bill," Jon said.

The Miller Bill required free phone access for children in residential care facilities and schools so they could call 911. That's it. One phone with one number. No other regulations. No credentialing. It was, anyone should agree, the bare minimum.

In early 2008, CAFETY started seeking survivors willing to testify before the US House of Representatives on behalf of the bill. Jon and Kathy Whitehead decided to testify. I wanted to testify. I wanted to walk into that chamber and tear their hearts apart with the truth. I wasn't going to be gentle, and I wasn't going to be kind. Too many lives were at stake. I could picture it: forcing those dirty old men to confront what they had condoned.

But I couldn't do it. I had been recruited out of my Fordham master's program to Veterans Affairs. It was a contact through my husband, Mike, who was a veteran as well as a cop. This was the height of the war on terror; the VA needed good social workers for wounded warriors, and I needed a purpose. My hiring was pending a government review, which I was already stressed about since I hadn't actually graduated from high school. I couldn't risk my job with public testimony.

That was my excuse, anyway. The truth is, I wasn't ready. I wasn't strong enough yet to speak publicly about what had happened to me. The truth is, I let down the kids in Troubled Teen Programs. I let down my friend Jay, who died by suicide in 2007. I let my Wolf Pack down. I let Jon down. I let survivors down, because I was weak when I could have been strong.

Maybe. I don't know. I have learned since then that you have to love yourself. You have to do what you can and not beat yourself up that you didn't do more.

I'm trying. I'm trying to give myself that grace.

"I'll help with your testimony," I told Jon. "I'll be there with you in DC. But I can't speak with you."

A few days before the trip, I asked Jon what he was going to wear. "My usual," he said. Jon's usual was a punk T-shirt and faded jeans.

"Oh, no," I said. "We're getting you a suit."

We drove an hour to the Goodwill in Danbury, Connecticut: the classy Goodwill. Jon tried suits off the $5 rack.

No. Too pimp.

No. Too grandpa.

Too meh.

Didn't quite fit, but not bad.

"Good enough," Jon said. "How about this tie?"

Brown suit, purple tie. Are you kidding? Hell, no. But I couldn't talk him out of it. Jon loved his ugly tie.

A few days later, we were on the Poughkeepsie platform, waiting for the train to New York City. We were catching a train to DC from there, but I was anxious. This was big. This was our chance to speak. To be heard. This was public. This was forever. This was a long, long train ride. A night in a hotel. A place I'd never been.

By the time the train pulled up, I was freaking out. I wanted to be there. I wanted to support Jon. But my anxiety, my fear . . .

"I can't do it, Jon. I'm sorry."

He looked at me. He dropped his bag. He knew my struggles. He knew them better than anyone.

He gave me a hug. "It's okay, Liz. I got this."

I shoved all the cash in my wallet into his hand, a couple hundred dollars. As the train pulled away, he walked back through each car all the way to the end, smiling, his thumb up, letting me know he was okay.

Jon nailed his testimony. It was beautiful. It was broadcast on C-SPAN, and the video went all over, through all our rudimentary social networks. Survivors remember it. They still talk about it. The first time I saw one of us being respected. The first time one of us was seen.

We celebrated like kings the night Jon got back to Poughkeepsie. Mike O'Donnell was roaring. Jay was gone, but Marisa was there. We felt good. We felt we had turned the corner. There was no way the world could ignore us now.

When the hearings warranted no mention outside Troubled Teen circles, we were devastated. But then again, when had the world ever listened to us?

When the bill failed, we were disappointed but not surprised. Who was stronger: abused children or child abusers?

"Well," Jon said, with his tight, determined smile, "I guess we have to do this ourselves."

11

The Truth

MAIA SZALAVITZ'S BOOK starts with a burglary: Richard Bradbury and a friend drop through the skylight at Straight, Inc.,
Nancy Reagan's favorite Troubled Teen Program, in the middle
of a cold Florida night in 1987. As a teen, Richard Bradbury
had been forced to endure years in the abusive program after
having been "evaluated" for five minutes at the facility by two
fellow teens. Afterward, he worked there before realizing what
he was witnessing was physical, psychological, and sexual abuse.
For years, he had picketed the facility, usually alone, hoping to
reform it. He had requested records. He had contacted news
organizations. Nothing happened. That night, he was looking for
files that could expose the program. He didn't get any files; in
fact, he barely escaped the police. A year later, in 1988, he was
arrested for disrupting a Straight charity benefit and sentenced to
1,250 hours of community service.

By then, he was in his early thirties, with no college education because of Straight, working as a maintenance man for six
dollars an hour. He was broke, and nearly broken. But Richard
Bradbury realized something clever. He had to serve his 1,250
at a charity, but nothing said it couldn't be *his* charity. The sole

mission of the nonprofit he founded, Community Improvement, Inc., was to shut down Straight, and its approach was Richard Bradbury's second genius idea: he contacted Straight "alumni," seeking their testimony and support. Straight had facilities in seven states; Community Improvement soon had chapters run by angry survivors in all seven. It took another five years, until 1993, but the combined strength of their testimony about the abuse within Straight's walls finally shut down the program.

Richard Bradbury was the OG. He was the Man. He created the plan. Straight was one of the most powerful Troubled Teen Programs of all time. Mikey Argiros "owned" Hancock, New York. He owned the nice hotel, the flophouse motel, and the movie theater. He paid to update the downtown park. He had the police and the locals, he always said, in the palm of his hand. Straight "owned" Tampa, Florida. They had state legislators and regulators running interference for them. They had senators and presidents (Reagan and Bush I) publicly supporting them. But one bad-ass survivor, using nothing but the truth and ten years of constant work, shut them down.

Jon's Truth Campaign was straight from Richard Bradbury's blueprint. The main difference was social media. Instead of writing hundreds of letters, Jon started a Facebook page. At first, it was anonymous, but it was clear: we're survivors. We were there. Tell us what happened to you at the Family.

No response. Kids were scared. No one on the outside had ever believed us. Nothing good had ever come from our honesty. The Family had put it deep inside us, and the world had confirmed it: speak and it's a lie. Speak and die.

So Jon stepped forward. He posted his story under his real name. I don't think anyone except Jon could have pulled off the Truth Campaign. He was well known in our communities because of his congressional testimony. And he was respected by those who had been at the Family with us. When Jon put his name on the campaign, people knew it wasn't a trap. It wasn't bullshit. I was never a leader of any resistance. That's the bullshit. Jon was our leader. Always.

Look, Jon said, *I've done it. I've gone public. I've told the truth. If you join us, you will not be doubted, not here, and you will not be alone.*

Jon and the others—at its height, ten or twelve survivors were helping run the Campaign—promised full control. The Campaign posted exactly what survivors sent, no changes. Some terms Jon didn't know, like Anchoring, the new word for Land-locking, but the Campaign posted them anyway, knowing kids from that era would understand. The Campaign didn't have to know you, or even know exactly what you were talking about. It trusted, and that was the secret sauce. Jon trusted survivors. The only rule was you had to include your real name or initials. Sorry, Batmans.

The campaign got a lot of Batmans, anyway.

A lot of Jokers who just wanted to see the world burn.

The testimonials mattered. They changed lives. I didn't know my friend Heather then. She was confined at the Family from 2001 to 2003. We became friends later, online, in our survivor network. She told me she read every testimonial posted by the Truth Campaign. She was deep in her opiate addiction and utterly alone. They were her way back from the edge.

Her mother, Jacqueline, is a good one. She realizes she made mistakes. She had a strict father and alcoholic husband. When her husband abandoned the family without warning, she went to work full-time, leaving Heather, who was eleven, and her younger brother alone until late at night. Heather started skipping school. She often sat alone on the hill outside the school, refusing to come inside. She was depressed—who wouldn't be if their world exploded like that?—but Jacqueline didn't have the confidence to talk with her. She was scared. She didn't think she could help her daughter, because every man in her life had told her she was nothing and no good.

So she turned to the Family, and the Family destroyed them. They used Heather's forced "confession" to brainwash Jacqueline into thinking her daughter was a drug addict. They refused to let Heather call home. They told Jacqueline that Heather had been misbehaving, so she couldn't go on the school choir trip to Canada. Jacqueline wasn't wealthy. She scraped to send Heather to the Family. Now she had to take off work, rent a cabin, and stay with her daughter in New York, because Heather was the worst of the worst. Even at a school for troubled teens, Heather stood out.

It was bullshit. Heather couldn't go on the trip because she was Canadian, and on the advice of the Family, and with their consent and planning, she had entered the country without a visa. If they took her back to Canada for the trip, they couldn't have gotten her back across the border. So the Family lied and blamed her for being left behind. They lied about everything. It was how they survived.

What actually stood out was the Family's abuse, because Heather had it bad. The school religious leader and another staffer made her dig her own grave. They made her lie in it while they berated her. She would burn in hell, she would be tormented, she would decompose and be eaten by worms. *Feel the flesh rot off your bones*, they preached at her. *Feel your eyes turn to jelly. Your brain to mush. This will happen to you, Heather. You will rot. You will be consumed by maggots. You will be tortured, at the burning end of hell, for eternity.*

They did this each day for weeks. Why? Because Heather was an atheist.

"I sat in his office and told Mike Argiros," Jacqueline says now, "that our family were atheists. He looked me in the eye and said they were not a Christian organization. They accepted all beliefs and would never impose their ideas on anyone. He lied, Liz. He lied to my face."

After Heather came out of her grave, it was Terry's turn. Terry's controversial, because a lot of Family survivors, including Jon, think he was okay. There's a Family survivor with Terry's face tattooed on his body. To me, that's a sign of the abuse; that reaction is as screwed up as mine. But I'll let you be the judge.

Terry was the opposite of Mikey; he was a *fanatic*. You know how many Jewish temples have an old guy who's an expert on scripture? You have a Torah question, this guy's got answers. That was Terry. You have a Big Book question, Terry's got you. He lived that AA shit like it was God's own word, because he thought it was. He was a big man at the Family because of that. The other staffers looked up to him.

Terry's dead now. Face-planted in his mashed potatoes. Massive heart attack at Thanksgiving dinner, with his whole family gathered around.

Terry put Heather on Exile Sanction. No one could talk to her. No one could look at her or acknowledge her existence, and you know the kids followed those rules. We always did. Heather was confined to a non-temperature-controlled metal walkway that connected two buildings. She slept in the boiler room. She read out loud from the Big Book an hour a week while kids looked the other way and pretended she wasn't there. She needed human contact. Reading from the Big Book was the only speaking Terry allowed.

Terry told her she could beg for forgiveness and acceptance back into the community once she accepted God—their God— into her heart. Heather wouldn't do it. So Terry kept her in Exile *for eleven months*. Robin Ducey and all the rest of the staffers: they watched Terry do this to a teenage girl, and they approved. I can almost hear the creaking of Robin's demented smirk.

To me, Heather's Sanction was worse than the blanket. Worse than Neil's month in the closet. It was eleven months of torture. And when she tried to explain it to her mother in that cabin in New York, when she told her own mother what was happening to her, Jacqueline didn't believe her.

Instead, she believed Mikey Argiros when he told her, "With these kids, if their lips are moving, they're lying."

So she sent her daughter back to Exile. And that's the worst betrayal of all: when you reach out to your father and mother with the truth, and they turn away.

Even after Heather came home, Jacqueline pushed her away. Everything was manipulation, she insisted. Even when Heather slipped into addiction, and Jacqueline feared every day she would get the worst call a parent can receive, she stuck with the idea the Family had given her: the only way to help her daughter was to be cruel. The Family had saved Heather's life. The Family knew best. It was like the mafia. Never go against the Family. You don't want to think about what will happen if you do. Dead daughters are the least of it.

Then the Truth Campaign came along, and Heather found the proof. Not the truth. She knew that. *The proof.*

So she popped a handful of oxy for courage, went to her mother's house, and said, "Look at this, Mom. Look at this. These are other kids from the Family. I don't know these kids. I have never talked to them. But they have the same stories. They went through the same things I did."

Her mother read the Truth Campaign. She sat with it for a day, then read it again. And she believed. After years of denial, the Family's control broke, and she believed everything Heather had told her.

"They hurt my daughter," she says. "They cost us eight years. They destroyed my family. For money. That's all it was to them, Liz. It was money."

How many other Family kids had a similar experience because of the Truth Campaign? How many finally found acceptance and belief after years in exile from the people they loved? How can we thank Jon enough?

My father yells at me when I mention what happened, especially with my relative who raped me. "Well, what do you want me to do about it?" he says. "If I had known, I would have punched him out. I would have protected you. But what can I do about it now?"

You can listen. You can see me for who I am. You can understand how I got this way. I don't want you to fix me; I want you to respect me and help me, right here, and right now.

I learned the power of that approach at the VA, because miracle of miracles, I was approved for government service, even without a real high school degree. In 2008, just as the Truth Campaign was launching, I joined the Operation Enduring Freedom (OEF) / Operation Iraqi Freedom (OIF) / Operation New Dawn (OND) intensive case management team in the Returning Combat Program at Castle Point Duty Station 620.

Intensive case management was the EMT of the VA. We took the hardest cases; you pretty much had to lose a major limb to be on our rolls. We took every call, like a dispatch desk, because we never knew the trauma or despair on the other end. We went to our patients instead of them coming in. We met them where they lived so we would know them, and we met them where they were physically, emotionally, and psychologically. I won't share details, because I'm not allowed to, and I value their privacy. My veterans lost legs and arms. They lost families. They lost their homes. They had drinking problems, drug problems, depression, or all three. They took those losses for us.

We were a team of four, with office support, and we handled everything: our patients' paperwork, errands, medical emergencies and long-term treatments, prescriptions, and care. We found them housing. We sat with their loved ones and tried to explain. Twice, I talked armed veterans off their roofs. This was during the height of the war. Our veterans had Fallujah-level trauma, an actual medical term for the highest level of PTSD, as measured through our tests, observations, and questionnaires. Several had fought in the battle that gave the trauma level its name.

I sat with one veteran many times. He had been pinned down in a watchtower during a major assault, and he couldn't stop reliving it. *I heard my friends dying*, he said. *I heard them screaming. But the enemy fire was so heavy that if I raised my head, it would have been blown off.*

I closed my eyes, trying to see it, trying to feel a trauma so severe that it took hours to coax him down from the tower after the enemy left . . . and I flashed on the Family. The violence. The intensity of that violence. The deafening sound of assaults that played forever in my head. The helplessness of your battle buddies being destroyed and knowing you could do nothing to stop it.

Why am I here? he asked. *Why did I survive when I did nothing? Did I survive because I did nothing? Did I let my friends die for me?*

Survivor's guilt. It's a cancer.

I went in a kid, he said, *and I came out a killer.*

Drop a dart on the map of my life: I'm there. Oh, my God, I'm there, too.

Obvious, right? But it's hard to see yourself. To feel compassion for yourself. I had to see him, and know his feelings were justified, before I could see that my behavior made sense. My anger. My paranoia. My inability to connect or feel understood. My constant circling back to my trauma. My pin-pulling. My wretched relationships. It was complex PTSD. I hadn't been in combat, but I had been through the same type of war.

"You can drown in two inches of water or twenty feet." That was an important saying at the VA. It meant trauma is trauma. Don't measure or compare it. Respect it and see it from the perspective of the person who feels the trauma.

I wasn't in combat, but I was brutalized. I didn't watch my friends die, but people I knew were dying because of the Family. Jay was gone. Meghan, a girl from my dorm, was gone. The suicides had started, though I didn't realize yet how bad they would become. I just realized, because of this soldier, that there was a name for my behavior. There was a reason.

My parents said everything was my fault. I was ruining my life. I needed to stop being weak. I knew they were wrong, both to treat me that way and to see the situation that way, but it's poison. Every time they stab you with the knife, the filth comes off inside you. You believe it, despite yourself. You're consumed with anger and then shame and then self-hatred.

But once I named it, I understood the symptoms. I understood the reasons. And when there's a name and a reason, there's a solution. It's a long way off. It's a hard walk from here. But there is a path.

Those long talks—not therapy sessions but real talks, between equals—changed us both. My vet grew to trust me as he never had anyone else. Many soldiers did. They knew I believed in them. I never told them about myself, but I kept it real, and I was always honest. Always. Honesty is essential. I made sure they knew I didn't blame them for the wrecked cars, the wrecked bars, the wrecked homes. I never considered them problems or bad people. They were victims. They needed others to understand that, and believe that, before they could get well.

I was a good social worker: emotionally, energetically, I was there for my soldiers. I have their letters to prove it. I keep them in a scrapbook. It's with my other mementos behind my desk. I can reach over and open it right now, and I often do. Those letters are proof of life. They are proof my life matters.

"You understand me," my veteran said. "You understand me like nobody else."

Because I'm there, too, I'm with you, I thought but never said. I would never compare my two inches to their twenty feet. I just treated them the way I wanted to be treated.

It helped me. It helped me in my daily life, because I was still haunting the Family and its minions. I sent social media messages, canceled their oil deliveries, followed their posts. Sometimes, after my family was asleep, I left my house and drove the two hours to Hancock. I kept my car packed with the things I needed for these trips: extra clothes and shoes, extra food and water, duct tape, knives, bulletproof vest, complete medical bag, toilet paper, latex gloves, and a large Maglite flashlight, heavy enough to crack a skull.

That sounds like a serial killer kit, but it was purely defensive. I was in my late twenties, with a government job and a family, and I was still paranoid that the Family would snatch me. I packed as if I was running, with everything I would need to protect myself from (human) predators for a few nights in the woods.

I drove past their houses, past the McDonald's, past the entrance to the Family behind that collapsing farmhouse. I never went down the one-lane drive because I was terrified of that place, but I drove up and down Route 97 looking for runaways. I want to say I wasn't dangerous, because I never did anything, but I have to admit, I had the potential for violence. I was a submarine, sliding quietly beneath the surface, bristling with missiles. I never attacked. I never found any kids on Route 97 to rescue. Every morning, when my husband and sons woke up, I was home, waiting with a smile. I took out most of my aggression, and it was considerable, on my husband, Mike.

My work helped me help Jon, too, because things turned ugly after the Truth Campaign started a website. The tech members of the team (all survivors) created a site that looked like the Family's site, with similar colors and a nearly identical crest. One survivor was a genius at optimizing it. He knew how to work the algorithms. He created a tagline that, in a Google search, made our site look like the official Family site—the "truth" part was cut off because it exceeded the maximum visible spaces. He tweaked the site constantly to make sure anyone searching for "Family School" saw it at the top of the results. When parents clicked on the link, they didn't get the propaganda and lies; they got the truth: the allegations of abuse and first-person testimonials to prove it.

The Family optimized their page. Our guy optimized better. They complained to our site administrators. We tweaked our interface. They sued us for copyright infringement. We changed the crest. They never said we lied, because they couldn't. We were telling the truth. But they came after Jon.

They threatened to ruin him. Not the Campaign, but him. They threatened to put him in prison. They tried to run him into the ground financially. They sent notices to their followers denouncing him as a liar, a malcontent, a loser who was angry his life hadn't turned out the way he wanted. They portrayed everyone who posted a testimonial that way: as sour-grapes losers solely to blame for their own problems. They attacked, as always, in deeply personal terms, and Jon was our leader, our public face, so he took the blows. It wasn't a fair fight. They had three hundred students at about $30,000 apiece, so maybe $9 million a year. Jon was barely making nine dollars an hour at Planet Wings.

Tony was gone. He was in Florida, balls-deep in Alzheimer's.

Robin was gone. She died in 2006. Ass cancer. She spent her last year being fed through a tube. The Family inmates had to go to chapel every day to pray for her.

"That backfired," they laughed, "because we all prayed for her to die."

I hope her hair lifted her up on a cloud of rapture, I really do. If anyone needs to meet her maker, it's her.

But Mikey was still there. He had been there all along. He had to have known. He cleaned the place up after his father moved away: new classrooms and dorms, a gym, full-time teachers. They started a respected soccer program; one Family survivor became a professional soccer player. The school has produced doctors, lawyers, and other professionals. Kids are resilient. Plenty succeeded, despite the abuse, not because of it. We even have a porn star. I mean, I guess she's a star. She sends me raunchy promos for her videos, so I guess she's doing alright.

None of that excuses the abuse. A porn actress's success doesn't make the rest of us losers, like the Family tried to paint us. That's not how abuse-induced PTSD works. It doesn't strike the weakest. We don't know how it works, honestly, but it's not a moral failure. It's the result of catastrophic circumstances that are not our fault and are beyond our control.

I was there for Jon. That was my role in the Campaign: I sat watch on my people, guarding their quarter. Jon was on a mission; I was a mother holding down a good job. We didn't go to underground punk shows anymore. When we needed a break from the grind, we hung with Mike O'Donnell at the skate park in Middletown. Mike (like Jon) was an incredible skateboarder. He had skated his lanes so long, he didn't need to see them. Music, skateboarding, Occupations: Mike could feel his grooves.

He had his classic look by then: dark sunglasses, even indoors and at night. What did that matter to a blind guy? Fedora or slicked-back hair. Black leather jacket with a full-back painting, Mexican folk-art style, of a woman praying the rosary. "Lowbrow," it said up top.

"They love my look at Occupations," he said with a smile. "They love my hair." He meant the adults with disabilities, not the bosses. Mike was always with the underdogs. He was my role model in that. He had been my hero since the day he survived a grand mal seizure on the dining room floor. Or maybe from the day we "killed" that kid in the kitchen. Jon and I were always happy with MOD.

It's time for a meeting, Jon would text me. That meant he wanted to talk about the Family. We never talked about the Family in our regular life. We never said the F word or wrote it in a text. Speak the devil and he appears, right? We were paranoid as hell, still, after more than ten years.

We met in Waryas Park, by the river in Poughkeepsie. I smoked cigarettes; Jon drank beer; we watched the prostitutes and the crackheads—it was that kind of park. Jon's life was messy. He had gotten married in 2009, but it fell apart in less than a year. He kept getting into fender benders and minor legal scrapes. My father was an attorney, so he helped him out; he always liked Jon. My father could see the good in everyone but me.

After his marriage, Jon started dating girls in their early twenties with problems. I called them his lost puppies. He was trying to help them. He felt guilty; that was his cross. He had given tours to parents that convinced them to send their kids to the Family. He was their Golden Pen, writing their newsletters full of lies, whitewashing their abuse. He never forgave himself. But it wasn't his fault. They made him do it. They made us all do it. They made us what we were.

I hated those girlfriends. They brought him down. They clung to him like rocks, like drowners in deep water. I threw several out on their asses when they wouldn't let him go.

Jon was happy, though, with the Campaign. Every time we met at Waryas Park, he was full of ideas. Find parents. Write to therapists and school counselors. Change laws. Hunt for a sympathetic reporter. Above all: respond to every move the Family made—every move—by posting the truth, and nothing but the truth. The truth, Jon always said, was all we needed.

The blowback was intense. The Family called Jon a loser, a malcontent, a sad lost nobody who blamed them for his own failures. They tried to destroy him in order to destroy his message. And people believed them. Some of his own friends and family believed them. I won't tell you it didn't hurt him, because it did. Once the Family sent him a message so savage, Jon curled into a ball. He curled in on his pain. Jon was strong but wounded. He could be depressed for days. He hated cruelty, which is why the Truth Campaign was never cruel. He never understood or accepted the need for savagery, even when he saw it in others. He believed that only right made right.

I assured him that he was doing right and we were behind him. I helped him flesh out his plans. I gave him someone to confide in. That was my role, to remind him that it was real: the trauma and the cause. He came to Waryas Park wound tight, but he was smiling by the end, because that's what friendship does. It reminds you that you are loved. It helps you see the good in yourself.

"They put the wrong bitch in that blanket," he always said with a laugh when I got him back on track. I could always make Jon laugh.

That was how we lived: as a pack. Together. For each other. If Jon called anytime, night or day, I picked up. I came to his apartment. I met him at the park. I bailed him out or drove him home. I threw out his lost puppies when they wouldn't leave him alone.

And when I brawled with my husband, when I struggled with motherhood, when I had a shit day and was hanging on by my fingernails, I called him, too. He talked for as long as I needed. He let me come over. There was nothing we wouldn't do for each other. Nothing. There was no moment Jon wasn't with me, even when he was across town. That's what it takes to be a friend to a person in need. That's what it takes to survive what we—and you—have survived. I see you, survivor. I see you like Jon saw me, and I needed that. Always. I couldn't live without it.

Eventually, the Family asked for a truce, because the Truth Campaign was working. Neil was back inside, working on their computers, but really, he was our mole. The Family's social media and outreach claimed all was good, but through Neil, we knew their enrollment was dropping. They fought Jon like those girls in the boot closet, like that chaperone fought me in Croatia, but no matter how hard they punched, he held firm. He might bend for a few days, but he was never going to break. So they asked for a meeting at a neutral location.

"I have to go," Jon told me. "I have to hear them out."

"You don't," I said.

"Yes, Liz. I do."

Jon believed anything could be talked out. He believed, even after everything, that every person was inherently good. He thought that once they realized what they had done to us, Mikey and the others would change. That they were mistaken, not evil. He was Mr. Honorable. Always.

So he met with Mikey and another administrator at a diner, and they went back to Hancock touting a breakthrough. We read about it in their socials. A framework to resolve some minor problems, they said, had been established.

I sat with Jon in our place, a triangle of grass on a busy corner outside Dunkin' Donuts. The Planet Wings where Jon worked was down the block. I had handled a lot of car wrecks on that corner as an EMT. Drunk drivers, mostly. It was our place.

"Is it over?" I asked him.

It wasn't over for me. I wanted to ride these fuckers through the wall. But I knew Jon was tired. It's not easy being out front, taking every blow.

He watched the traffic. I could see his jaw working. They put it in us, accidentally, when they beat us so badly. The will to power as a way to get through.

"Hell, no," he said. "They have kids in there, Liz. It's not over until it's done."

12

Eat, Prey, Kill

I TOOK ADVANTAGE OF my job at the VA. Not the physical resources . . . okay, fine. I printed a few flyers. I used their paper, ink, and paper clips. I'm joking, a bit, but the government takes that seriously. They count their paper clips. They would have dinged me for theft of a few hours of their time. It's no joke at the VA.

What I really used, though, was my knowledge. There's more information in the world than you can imagine. The US government preserves everything. But you have to know how to find it. As a federal employee, you learn to work the system: what, where, and how to request. It's all about forms and files. If you don't become a master of forms and files, you won't be a good federal employee. And I was an outstanding federal employee.

Most importantly, I learned how much information was available to me as a citizen. The Freedom of Information Act (FOIA) gives every citizen access to government records. I'd say all you have to do is file a request, but you really need to file the right request the right way at the right time. And you have to do it over and over because nobody wants to give you what you're entitled to. But if you keep going hard enough and smart enough, you can't be denied.

Submitting FOIA requests (on my own time) was how I found out Tom Hogan granted the Family an absolute charter to become a school after the Division of Alcoholism and Alcohol Abuse (DAAA) said they weren't qualified to treat substance abuse issues in 1990. How I found the notes where Hogan went to bat for the Family when the DAAA wouldn't back off. How I discovered the Family was forbidden from offering drug or alcohol treatment, even though parents were led to believe that was the foundation of the program.

It was how I found out that Fox News had been sniffing around the abuse story in 1993 but never found what they needed.

In 1998, a judge in New Jersey asked for an investigation after a juvenile he'd sentenced to the Family said he'd been restrained with duct tape. Tom Hogan was one of the three people who investigated. The Family admitted using restraints, but "school staff estimated that 4–6 physical restraints were used per year." *Per year.* That's a Burger King–level Whopper.

The father wrote a letter to the judge saying he believed his son had exaggerated the use of isolation, blankets, and duct tape (there is an acceptable level, I guess, for duct-taping children) and that "I also gave written permission for him to be restrained."

"I believe that basically the Family School is a respectable and effective school for very difficult teenagers," he wrote. "I think my son recoiled strongly against their methods because he was unwilling to accept their help. . . . Any reports of them being a torture chamber are greatly exaggerated." Dear Dad, you, sir, are an asshole.

The Family agreed to stop using duct tape to restrain students, along with a few other minor tweaks. Then they went right on doing what they had always done. What a joke.

The whole New York state apparatus was a joke. The charter school division was, in effect, working with the school to quash investigations. The judicial system was apathetic. I FOIAed the Hancock police department logs to see how many runaways had been booked and what was in the reports. Out of at least a thousand runaways, I found seven reports. Seven! None said anything negative about the Family.

For years, I tried to get my hands on my personal records. I asked. I sent official requests. I FOIAed. I lawyered up. I walked into the Family office and straight-up demanded them from Mikey, sending him cowering into a corner. Nothing ever came of it. Later, when the lawsuits from survivors started, the school claimed to have lost or destroyed most of their old records, including mine. It's been an open wound for decades that there are no personal files for survivors to hold and see. It's like we didn't even matter enough, as human beings, for them to document our existence.

Honestly, I don't think the Family destroyed the required records. I think they never kept them, as this incident from 1997—corroborated by Neil and a few others—makes clear.

Layne, a recent arrival, was wild. She was a foster kid, came from a wilderness program, and nobody had ever loved her or given a shit. Most kids at the Family, as I've said, were depressed, acting out, or on the spectrum. Layne was the exception. She was an extremely troubled kid.

I was in the main building, minding my own business, when Layne came running in with a field hockey stick—no idea where she got that—and smashed me in the head. I was looking the other way; I never saw it coming. Never protected myself. And she swung hard. I went straight down.

A staffer jumped in. He grabbed Layne and they fought, physically, until she grabbed him by the balls, squeezed, and didn't let go. Neil was there. He said it was the most unholy, and satisfying, scream he had ever heard.

As more staff jumped in and the fight escalated, Neil and another kid dragged my body down the stairs and out of harm's way. Ten minutes later, by Neil's estimate, after Layne was subdued and the staffer's testicles tended to, the staff noticed me lying unconscious in the yard. They started debating what to do.

They finally decided to strap me to a spinal board—the hard, flat board EMTs use to pick up patients when a rolling bed isn't practical—and load me into Audra Runge's beat-up Ford Tempo. They tried to shove me through the door, but the board wouldn't fit, so they opened the hatchback and slid me in from the back. The board twisted and almost flipped me off. At one point, Neil says, I was sideways, hanging head-down in the passenger-seat foot compartment. When they tried to close the hatch, the board was too long. It hit the glass. They jammed me farther in, got the hatchback closed, and tore away from the property.

An ambulance met us on the road. I woke up briefly as I was being transferred. The EMT was an older woman; I remember that and not much else.

I woke up in a hospital, with a nurse bending over me. I grabbed her by the wrist and looked her in the eyes. "Help me," I said.

She stared down at me, then slowly pulled my fingers back, one at a time, until I was forced to let go. She turned and looked across the room. Audra Runge was standing there, watching, a few feet away.

The nurse put something in my IV. The next thing I knew, I was back in my bunk at the Family. I didn't know my diagnosis. I didn't know my treatment. Neil told me I was gone for two days. The staff never mentioned me or explained to the other kids what was happening. I was simply gone. Two days later, I was back.

No medicine. No time off or special treatment. They never called my parents. Nothing.

Here's the kicker: I have been searching for fifteen years, and I cannot find any record of my ambulance ride or hospital stay. I don't know what hospital I was in, but there are only four possibilities. This shouldn't be hard. But the Family clearly didn't use my real name, and I can't figure out the name they used.

The system ghosted me. If a child is knocked unconscious at a state-chartered school and hospitalized with a head injury, a report has to be filed. No report was filed. The police, I assume, were never involved. My parents were never informed. Nobody at the hospital asked any questions or supported me in any way.

It was all gaslighting. Everyone was working to bury us, to destroy the evidence, to make others doubt us and make us doubt ourselves. I doubted this memory, in fact, until it was confirmed by Neil and other witnesses.

"Well, Elizabeth," my first therapist smirked. "You have an interesting imagination."

We've all had people in positions of power, with access, with the ability to help, laugh at us. Where's the proof? It's buried. Where's the proof of that? We are the proof! The kids who went through it. The thousands who tell similar stories about the TTI. Fuck that nurse. Fuck that EMT. Fuck the hospital administrators who buried a child with a massive head injury. Fuck whatever lie made that nurse turn away from me in disgust. We are here!

The Truth Campaign had testimony from forty-eight survivors. Not anonymous testimony. They came forward with their names. They told personal stories of violent restraint. Beatings. Jewish kids forced to eat pork. Gay kids demeaned and debased. The blanket. Many kids were bound in the blanket. Sat in a corner for days. Stood for sixteen hours without a break. Dug their own graves.

"[Phil] picked me up by the scruff of my neck, threw me across the Family 3 dining room, right through a door leading outside. He followed me out, smacked me again, then kicked me down the back stairs. I got up and ran, but this man, this staff member charged with taking care of minor children, followed me into my dorm, into my room, picked me up again and threw me on the bed, then ripped my coat in half."

That's from a survivor who is ambivalent about the Family. Who thinks it might have helped him. That's the stuff of Stockholm syndrome right there.

PTSD. Anxiety. Nightmares. It's in the testimonials, over and over. Survivors can't sleep. They were hospitalized for anxiety and depression. One girl was under cardiac care because her nightmares were so severe they gave her heart attacks.

We collected this information for years: from students, from sympathetic staffers. Nine parents gave us their testimonies, and that wasn't any easier for them than for the survivors, because they were publicly airing their greatest shame. I had dozens of pages from old state investigations and correspondence. I dumpster-dived for files. That's how vital this campaign was to me. I drove dozens of times to Hancock on garbage night to see what the Family was throwing out. I created fake personas to access their Facebook pages. Catfished for information. Social engineered.

By March 2010, the Truth Campaign had more than two hundred pages of testimonials, letters, and reports. We took our findings to the New York Office of Mental Health and the Center for Quality Care of Youth with Disabilities (CQC). We gave them copies of everything. Seven volunteers testified in person about the abuse they had suffered. In June 2010, the CQC conducted a two-day unannounced inspection. I have it listed in my files as "NYS EPIC FAIL."

The inspection found seven pages of violations, including overcrowding and unsafe conditions in dorms, unqualified staff, lack of record keeping, noncredentialed clinical services, solitary confinement exceeding acceptable guidelines, forbidding poorly performing students from taking the state Regents Exam (to keep the school's "success rate" high), false and misleading marketing, erroneous medical records, Sanctions that "would not be allowed and could be considered harmful in licensed mental hygiene programs," and "inconsistent descriptions of the use of [isolation] rooms . . . from administrators, staff members and students." The rooms were small, bare cubes with nothing inside but a security camera. The school claimed the use of the rooms was voluntary, even though they locked from the outside.

Still, the report essentially exonerated the Family since the inspectors did not personally observe students being physically abused or neglected. Shocker! They didn't beat students right in front of you?

"Many of the students interviewed," the report said, "reported positive experiences with the school and were appreciative of the staff's efforts."

Of course they did! Are you unaware of the concept of coercion? *You interviewed them at the school, within sight of the staff.*

Mikey Argiros was riding so high, he had the tiny balls to respond that when the report said the Family's past practices "arguably constituted abuse and neglect," it was a "serious distortion of our record." The commission stood by that finding but praised Mikey for "your strong statement that physical and mental abuse is 'anathema' to your calling."

Yeah, if Mikey said it, it must be true. Just pretend those isolation cells (the only things you can't hide at a moment's notice) are for volunteers, interviews on site aren't compromised, and our forty-eight firsthand reports of violence and emotional abuse are lies, sour grapes, or old news. Give them a slap on the wrist and empower them to keep right on going. Same as it ever was.

We were learning the lesson Richard Bradbury and everyone else who took on the TTI eventually learned: the regulatory bodies and media will come in only at the very end, after everything is proven and the facility is dying. You have to do all the work, and even then, honestly, you're probably on your own.

That was why we built the Truth Campaign: it was an engine that didn't need the outside world. We could run it all day, every day, on our own.

It was other survivors who told me Marisa was in trouble. She drifted away during the height of the Truth Campaign, but I didn't think much about it. Maybe I was distracted by my dumpster-diving and file gathering. Maybe I was too focused on my revenge. I didn't know she had lost her job. I didn't realize she had fallen into addiction. I didn't know the bomb in her head had gone off, and she had pulled the pin. That's trauma. It's always in there, working its poison like a worm.

When I found out what was going on, I called Marisa immediately. I tried to talk her into coming upstate and staying with me for a while. She declined. But we talked every day for a few weeks, and I thought she was getting better. Then she called, and I heard it in her voice. I was an emergency dispatcher for a year and a half—I know the sound of suicide.

"I'm calling to say goodbye," she said.

I was in a CVS parking lot in Westchester. I remember the view across the intersection. I remember the parking spot I was sitting in when I heard those words. I threw the car in drive and sped toward Long Island.

"Where are you?"

"It doesn't matter."

"Marisa, where are you?"

I had my work phone for the VA. I kept Marisa on my personal phone and called 911 from the other. When that phone number comes through, it says government employee. That's supposed to carry weight. I have a social worker license. That's supposed to carry weight, too.

I told the dispatcher, "I have a mental health situation 937. I have a suicidal subject on the line—requesting ping." An MHS 937 is an involuntary commitment to a mental health facility for seventy-two hours. As a licensed social worker, I could arrange that.

They wouldn't ping her phone.

"Please," I said. "I know suicide." It has a sound. I've heard it many times, and I heard it from Marisa. "I was an EMT. I am a clinical social worker. My friend is planning to commit suicide."

I was tearing down the highway toward Long Island, listening to Marisa, listening for background noise to identify where she was, because that's what dispatchers are trained to do, but all I heard was traffic.

"Please. She's on Long Island."

"Which district?"

"I don't know. That's why you need to ping her phone."

"I'm going to transfer you."

I talked to dispatchers in several districts. I talked to at least six police officers. Marisa was distraught; they could hear her on the speaker. I was doing 90, trying to get to her, desperate to save my friend's life, and I couldn't find her.

I just couldn't find her.

"Liz," she said, "I love you. Thank you. You've done all you could."

She hung up. I called and called, but she didn't pick up.

I didn't know what had happened. I didn't know where she was. I hoped for the best: she'd changed her mind. But the next day, I found out she had hung herself in her childhood bedroom. Her family hadn't lived there for years. Marisa killed herself, alone, in a stranger's house.

She wasn't the first close Family friend I'd lost to suicide. She was the third. But she was the first I lost that way: when it was my fault.

When I could have done something more.

So I worked my end alone, in the darkness, like a submarine slicing through the water, angry, silent, bristling with bombs. I sat overwatch on my shit list, the staffers who'd abused us, never letting them out of my sight. I followed them on social media. I called their phones. I canceled their internet service. I sat in my car late at night, watching their houses, not doing anything, just watching. Just a ghost in their machine.

The asshole who'd put Heather in the grave got a job selling cheese door to door. Yeah, that's the quality of these people. He lost that job over an anonymous report of his past abuses.

A known pedophile got a job at a church in Ohio, working with children. No way I was letting that stand.

Tom and Mary opened a pizza restaurant in the dirty South. I ordered fifty pizzas to the local children's home, payment on delivery. Let that be a down payment on everything they owed the children of the world.

"They put the wrong bitch in that blanket," Jon said, shaking his head.

"They should have killed me," I said, "because they only made me stronger."

I started calling the Family's office phone, jamming their lines. I spammed their fax machines and social media accounts. Two hackers from the Anonymous collective were running Operation Liberation, a campaign against the TTI. I reached out to them. I don't know who they were, and if I did, I wouldn't tell you, but I know this: they were women. A lot of shitkickers on the web who you think are fat guys in basements are women. Probably in basements. I know these two survived a program, probably WWASP, because they knew the lingo, they knew the perversions. We recognize, even if we went to different "schools."

They taught me about disruption. They taught me the power of being in the way. Every time the Family put out a public invitation for prospective parents to call and ask questions, I led a campaign to jam their lines. I wasn't going to let another parent of a child like Marisa fall victim to their propaganda.

I called the hall phone, where we had made our Sunday calls home. If a student answered, I tried to talk to them. "Are you a student? Press one button if yes."

Most hung up. They knew the consequences. But once, there was a long pause. Then: beep.

"Don't speak. Just listen. I went to that shithole. My friends went to that shithole. We know what they are doing to you. We are shutting them down. We are getting you out. We will not leave you behind. We are standing overwatch on your ass."

Silence. Then: "Who are you?"

"Remember this number." I gave him my number. "Memorize it. Spread it around. If anyone needs anything, call that number. And if you get in trouble for this, tell them Liz Ianelli made you do it. You drop my name, you're home free, because I am their worst enemy."

I never got a call. I doubt he shared my number. I wouldn't have. Too dangerous. But he knew. I hope he knew we were out here, fighting for him.

It was about then, at the height of my personal revenge campaign, that my life hit another bump. Or fell off a cliff.

At the VA, I had noticed a problem between two groups I cared deeply about, cops and veterans. Cops were encountering veterans in crisis, but nobody had trained them to recognize and handle PTSD. So incidents that might have been defused were spiraling into confrontations, arrests, felony charges, and, in some districts, deaths. This wasn't good for my veterans, and it wasn't good for cops. Nobody wanted it to escalate.

So I developed guidelines. With another VA employee, I created a framework for de-escalation. We took our First Responder Initiative to police and fire departments. I worked with EMTs. We wrote a book—well, a chapter in a book. One of my professors at Fordham invited me to speak to her class, and I ended up teaching an Introduction to Social Work course for a few semesters.

I wrote and designed a pamphlet for vets. It listed behaviors and feelings and, if you were experiencing them, where and why to get help. The government took five months to approve it (typical), so I made the first batch on my home printer. The pamphlet folded into the size of a driver's license, so police officers could slip it to drivers unnoticed when handing back their license. That was how I'd want it done for me. Don't make a scene, especially in front of my spouse, my kids, or my friends. Don't talk to me about it. Just see me, give me the information, and let me make my own decisions.

Officers gave away so many pamphlets, and the VA got so many calls from veterans who received them, that my partner and I were given a congressional citation. We started meeting with police captains and prosecutors around the Northeast. We flew to overnight conventions. We were making a difference. We were helping a wounded, vulnerable population.

Until it came out that my trusted colleague was improperly engaging with her vets. The VA said I should have known because some of the incidents had taken place while we were on the road at conventions. They shut down my program. They threatened to take away my congressional citation.

I had no idea what she'd been doing. None. I worked the late shift on Wednesday. I didn't know she had been going to my house while I was working, hanging out with my kids, cooking them dinner, and telling them not to tell me about it.

I didn't know, but Mike knew. *He let another woman come into our home every week and pretend to be an aunt to my kids* without telling me. I mean, I know things were bad for him. I never cooked. I wasn't nurturing. I was a cactus. I own it. But Mike pulled the pin on our marriage, because that felt like an unforgivable betrayal. He accidentally helped pull the pin on my career, because I got demoted. I know people loved to see me fall. I'm not easy to get along with. I'm feral. I have an anxiety disorder. I'm an outsider. I don't play well with others. But I was clinging to that job like the oxygen mask in an airplane going down. It was my lifeline, even though my life was doomed. I was a great intensive case management social worker. I loved it. It helped me not hate myself. And I helped a lot of veterans who needed someone like me.

I filed for divorce. It got ugly. I'm sorry, Mike, for how ugly it got.

I took a lateral move to become a caseworker at the Vet Center in White Plains, north of New York City. The head of the office was a wounded Vietnam vet. When a grenade landed in his helicopter, he jumped up and tried to throw it out. His fellow soldiers were saved, but his face and upper body were badly burned in the explosion. He was an incredible man. He had an instinct for vets in trouble. He saw them between the lines of newspaper articles and police blotters, but he didn't like to go out because of his injuries. So he sent me, and I knew how to bring them in.

I remarried. An older man with money. I didn't love him; it was a classic Liz survival plan. I moved into his house near White Plains. He treated my boys well.

Geographically, I was farther from Jon, but emotionally, we were close. We got together once a week, when it had been a couple of times a week before, but we talked and texted every day. We didn't have to talk, though: that was the magic of our friendship. We didn't need to be there to be there, you know? We never left each other's side.

I pulled back from the Truth Campaign. They didn't need me. Jon and the others had it locked down tight, and the Family was reeling. They tried to hold a fundraiser in New York City, but Jon and the Truth Campaign were there. (You know who else was there? Tom Hogan, the head of the state's charter school division.) They changed their name to Allynwood, a common tactic in an industry used to muscling through bad publicity, but the Truth Campaign was there as soon as the new name was registered. Allynwood was dead on arrival.

After that, the fight went out of them. They knew Jon wouldn't quit. Whatever they tried, he'd find them. Wherever they went, he'd be there. He wasn't just throwing information on the web and praying. We weren't just researching. Jon pursued the Family to the gates of hell. That's what it takes. Relentless pursuit.

It was horrific at the end. As their enrollment fell, the Family cut a deal with a facility for juvenile sexual deviants. Some of the kids were rapists, remanded by the courts. The Family put them with the regular kids without telling anyone, including the parents paying full freight. I feel sick about it, because it slipped by us. Violent sexual predators need treatment. They should not be left with other children overnight, especially not in a group, and especially not unsupervised.

The Family has never answered for that, and the extra money did nothing to stop their slide. Neil, our mole who had gone back inside, fed us the numbers. Under eighty. Under fifty. We started counting down every kid. Forty-one. Thirty-eight. Thirty-four. Under thirty.

And then, on July 31, 2014, the Allynwood Academy, aka the Family Foundation School, announced it was closing. Eight kids stayed for a few months, because some parents were delusional, but most of the staff was dismissed, and all the other kids were sent home. They were free. After twenty-one years, America's children were safe, at least from them.

Jon and I met at our place, the triangle of grass outside the Dunkin' Donuts, the next morning. We had been texting and talking all night, because we believed, we knew it was coming, but when that torture chamber actually closed its doors, an evil was taken out of the world, a hell portal was closed, and we realized how much its gravity had been crushing us, how heavy this campaign had been.

I have never been happier than when I saw Jon step out of his car that morning, smiling an easy smile, his usual tension gone. We hugged. So unusual for us. I despise hugging. We laughed. We got our large coffees (never doughnuts) and sat, as always, with our backs against the only tree. The tree was two inches thick, so really, we were sitting back to back, supporting each other.

So I didn't see it, I felt it, when Jon started to cry. They were tears of relief. Tears of joy, because the effort had been so much for so long. You don't know how hard it is to kill, even with a wolf pack, until you've pulled down prey. Until you've felt them fight against the end. But those tears of joy soon turned to tears of frustration, then tears of despair.

"We fucked it all up," he said.

"What?"

"We didn't do anything."

"We killed them."

"No. We didn't. They still get to live their lives."

"Jon," I said, "you're a hero."

He didn't say anything for a while until he whispered, "I wish."

He had closed the school. He had destroyed their tool. He had saved the last kids to ever be tortured in that secluded hellspot, with its collapsing farmhouse, scattered trailers, scythe-toothed tractor, and dark, dank pond.

But our abusers walked away. Nobody was punished. Nobody was charged or publicly accused by anyone but us. They were never called to testify. They were never investigated. They were allowed, unchallenged, to float the narrative that bad kids had brought good people down. Twenty years and thousands of damaged lives later, including more than seventy dead, they were allowed to leave with their reputations, their money, and their excuses intact.

Jon saved the children of the future, but we were left behind. We never got relief from our pain. We never got an apology from our abusers. Society never backed us or cared. Our parents never understood. They didn't praise us or say they were proud. Nobody ever said, *Good job, you did it, you made the world a better place.* They only blamed us for throwing away our chance at normal, for wallowing in our abuse, for wasting our best years taking down the only people who had ever tried to help us.

"Get over it." That was all my parents ever said to me. *Let go, loser. Move on.*

So all Jon and I had to lean on that morning, every morning, was each other and that scrawny tree.

It wasn't enough. It hurts like hell. It's like lava in my chest. Because it wasn't enough. Despite everything he accomplished, despite everything we meant to each other, Jon Martin-Crawford, my rock, my best friend, took his own life on October 24, 2015.

13

If I Ever Leave
This World Alive

SURVIVORS REMEMBER JON'S congressional testimony and his suicide and think the two were linked. They weren't. They were more than seven years apart.

I'm doing the same thing: I'm putting the end of the Truth Campaign and Jon's suicide together when they were fifteen months apart.

Jon's life was more beautiful than that. He was more than his pain and the campaign. He was thirty-five, a brother, a son. He loved his nieces. His sister was nine months pregnant when he died, and he should be here, doting on that girl. He wanted children of his own, but his wife divorced him after he attempted suicide. He was dating lost puppies in their early twenties and failing to save them. He had two master's degrees. Did you know that? Jon was a scholar.

He was a riot. We once ate nothing but Taco Bell for three days. Imagine that: Taco Bell for nine straight meals. Then we drove to Hancock and took massive taco shits on Tony Argiros's grave.

And if he was here today, he'd be laughing, saying, "Hell, yes, tell that story, Liz. Don't make me out to be a saint."

He had recently gotten his dream job, teaching reading and writing to inmates at a maximum-security prison. I know why he took the position. He needed to help others. He loved the inmates because he loved underdogs. They gave his life purpose. He loved to write; he took any opportunity he could get to do it. But that place was loud, like the Family. It was chaotic, like the Family. It was violent, like the Family. It was putting himself back in the cage.

He should have been the one writing this book, not me. That's the reason I'm doing this: Jon can't, so I have to do it for him. I am writing the book he should have written. I am telling the story he should have told.

I suspect you don't like me much. I'm erratic; I'm antisocial; I'm foulmouthed and angry. I'm not America's sweetheart. I'm not Satan's little slut, either. I'm a good person at heart, but you wouldn't want me for a daughter. My own parents don't want me for a daughter. I embarrass them. I screwed up their retirement plans. I wrecked the family. Everyone's life, they say, is worse because of me.

So be it. I didn't ask for their help. I never wanted their money.

So be it. I am what I am. America's cautionary tale.

But you would have loved Jon. You would have wanted Jon as a son. He was charming. He was kind. He hated hypocrisy and mistreatment. He cared about people, not just the good people but everyone. He had potential; he just struggled to reach it. They put broken glass inside him at the Family. They put it in all of us. Every time Jon reached for something, it cut him up inside, where no one could see it. Every time he made a move, it bled him until he weakened and fell.

My parents think the Truth Campaign was harmful. That holding on to our pain is killing us and the only path forward is to forget. But the truth is the exact opposite. The Family killed Jon Martin-Crawford. The Truth Campaign just *failed to save him* from the damage they had done.

When he left us, it wasn't the worst day of my life. It was the end of my life. I was in my car, on the way to the Vet Center, when I got the call from the chief of police. He knew me. We had worked together. I'd been a Blue wife. He knew how much I loved Jon. He said, "Liz, are you driving? Pull over."

I pulled off to the side of the road, and he told me Jon was gone.

I didn't believe it. I couldn't believe it. I had to see it for myself.

"Don't try to drive," he said. He could hear how hard I was crying. "I'll send an officer."

I hung up, turned the car around, and was at Jon's apartment in forty minutes (it was normally an hour's drive). Everything was there: the crime-scene tape, the EMTs' discarded gloves, the bright green dog leash. He had hung himself in the early morning, around 2:00 a.m., when everyone was asleep and no one could help him, not even me.

I called his mom. "Where is he?"

She told me the name of the funeral home. I arrived before he did. They wouldn't let me wait inside, so I sat on the steps, shaking so badly I could barely smoke. They told me I couldn't do that, I had to leave the property, so I jumped in my car and took off, the tears coming so hard I could barely see.

I pulled into the parking lot of my father's office a few minutes later, going so fast my tires screamed at the corner. I was yelling as soon as I hit the door. Yelling for my parents. Yelling at my parents. I backhanded the files off my father's desk. I knocked over a chair. I was yelling that Jon was dead, my best friend was dead, and *you did this, you did this to us, you sent us there.*

"Enough," my father screamed so loudly I actually stopped.

"What is the matter with you?" my mother snapped. She's my father's secretary and mouthpiece and always has been.

"My best friend just hung himself."

"Well," my mother said, "I'm sorry, but we don't have time for this."

I looked at my father. He was hard, like when he pulled my confession out of his pocket. He was a cactus. I learned it from him.

"What's in the past is past," he said. "We're not going backward. You need to go to work."

That was it. I wasn't getting more. No love. No sympathy. They didn't have one molecule of kindness or understanding to offer. So I flipped over a filing cabinet and stormed out.

By the time I made it back to the funeral home, Jon's father had arrived. He lived down South. He had flown up. Jon never forgave his father for sending him to the Family, and I wanted to tell his father that, to hurt him like I was hurting, but the man was so destroyed, and his anguish so genuine, that we collapsed into each other's arms and cried.

When the body was ready, he let me go first. "Have a minute," he said. He knew how close I was with Jon.

The casket was on a riser in the middle of an empty room. It was dead quiet. An overhead light reflected off the wood. The rest of the room was in shadow. I approached slowly because I didn't want to see him. I didn't want to make this real.

Jon's face was pale. I put my hand on his cheek, and it was cold. I looked closer and saw his head was resting on cloth bags of ice. His neck was wrapped in a frozen towel. I started throwing the bags out, heaving them over my shoulder, not caring where they went. I tried to climb into the coffin. I had to warm Jon. I didn't have anything but my own body heat.

The coffin was too high. I couldn't get in. So I pulled a chair over from the corner. I took off my shoes, climbed into the coffin, and lay down next to Jon, my body pressed to his. I cried my makeup onto his cheek.

"Oh, my God."

It was a woman. "Oh, my God, you can't be in there."

I held Jon closer. "Try me."

"Look, I'm sorry, I understand, but you can't be in there." It was a man.

"I'm not ready," I said.

There were several men now. "You can come back."

"You can't make me leave."

"We can."

"You better call the marines, then, because the only way I'm getting out of this coffin is if you take me out."

They were big boys. They pulled me out. They walked me to my car, my knees so weak my legs didn't work. They stood there, on guard, while I hunched over the steering wheel, bawling.

The word was out. Our networks were activated. I was getting messages one after the other: "Are you okay?" "R U OK?"

Matt called. "I'm at the airport. I'll be at LaGuardia in three hours. Pick me up."

Matt, the Rock King. He was small. Quiet. Angry. After he turned eighteen, he worked at the Family. He hated them, like Neil, but he didn't have anywhere else to go. Jon and I drove out one day and told him, "You're better than this. You're coming with us." He came with us. He lived in Georgia now.

"Where are you staying?" I asked him.

"With you."

He was taking possession. That sounds bad, but it's what we do for each other. When a survivor needs help, we stay with them. We make sure they are never alone. It wasn't just Matt. Every survivor was worried about me. Without Jon, they didn't think I'd make it. They thought I was next.

Matt saved my life.

The funeral was at Vassar, in the cathedral. Family kids flew in from all over the country, sixty or seventy, maybe more. We waited on the lawn because we have a thing about churches and enclosed spaces; nobody wanted to be inside. I was sitting on a bench when I saw Jon's dad coming up the walk carrying a brown box. It was so small. So ordinary.

I went wild with grief.

Nobody told me Jon was being cremated. That I would never see him again. The box wasn't even all his ashes. It was half his ashes. His parents had decided to split them.

I saw Jon's mom in the back of the cathedral. "Don't be sad, Liz," she said. "The Family gave us three more years with Jon. Without them, he would have been dead before now."

My brain exploded. How could you, here, after everything . . . ?

Family kids took possession of me, pulling me back.

I sat in the fifth pew with Matt, staring at Jon's box on the altar. It was tiny, the size of a cigar box, and plain. It didn't even have his name on it. It was cold. Empty. He was alone. There wasn't a single flower.

His sister, nine months pregnant, read a passage from the Bible.

I gave the eulogy. His family didn't know him. I knew him. I was the only one. There wasn't a dry eye, including mine. I don't know how I made it through.

After the service, I ran into Jon's girlfriend, the last sick little puppy he couldn't save. She handed me a piece of paper.

"What's this?"

"His suicide note." He had tried thirteen days before and failed, but she hadn't told me. Nobody had told me.

I went to the bathroom to pull myself together. Two Family girls were in a stall, laughing and snorting coke. "What the fuck is this?" I said, throwing open the door.

"You want some?"

Let me get this right, so you understand: I closed the stall door, locked it behind me, and then beat them with each other.

I took their heads and slammed them together, repeatedly, until they couldn't stand. One girl hit the toilet tank. The other hit the floor.

"Don't come out," I told them. "Don't even dream of fucking coming out."

Matt caught me outside. He took me to my car and drove me home. There's one picture of me that day. A group photo with Family kids. Everyone is smiling except me. I have the look. The look survivors remember from the Family. It wasn't defiance then, and it wasn't now. It was pain.

Fuck you, I was thinking. *This isn't a reunion. It's our funeral.*

Matt stayed with me for a few days until he thought I was okay. I thought I was okay, too. But within hours of dropping him at the airport, I was on my back in the big field beside my husband's house, staring at the black night sky. The tall grass reminded me of the fields at the Family, grabbing at us as we tried to run away. The stars were cold and far away.

I lifted a Glock 9 and pressed it to my temple.

I was a bad mom. I was in a loveless marriage. My parents hated me. My brother and sister resented me. My boys wouldn't miss me; they'd be better off without me. I was a rock, dragging everyone down. There was nothing for me here. Nothing but pain.

I wanted to be with Jon. He was the only one who had ever cared.

My phone rang. Bang.

It startled me so badly, I almost pulled the trigger.

Bang. It rang again.

I didn't recognize the number, but I answered it. It was a filmmaker, Mikaela Shwer. She was making a documentary on the TTI. She wanted to interview Jon, but she missed him. By four days. Maia Szalavitz had suggested she interview me instead.

I thought, *Why not? The footage will be my suicide note. I'll kill myself after.*

But I didn't. The fever passed, and I never put a gun to my head again.

Instead, I spiraled into darkness. I started drinking. One night, I told my husband I was going out. He said, "When are you coming back?"

"I'm not."

"Okay."

I never did. I left with nothing, not even my boys, who were living with my first husband, Mike.

I bounced into another relationship, the kind from the bad days, when I was just out of the Family. I suspect a part of me wanted someone to kill me, since I let Jon die. But I also wanted to live, so we fought like wolves. Even our silences felt violent.

I drove to Monticello, New York, to a crack-ridden trailer park. I slammed on a door. I heard someone moving, but nobody opened the door, so I went around back and started to climb in the window.

"What are you doing?" It was Linda, the prostitute-turned-staffer. I knew where she lived. I knew where they all lived.

"I'm coming in, Linda, one way or another. I need to talk to you."

She opened the front door and stood on her cinder-block stairs, smoking under a bare bulb and a haze of mosquitoes. I asked her why. Why did she do it? What was in it for them?

She had no idea. No answers.

Nobody had any answers.

So I beat myself. Ever since leaving the Family, whenever it felt like my life was spiraling out of control, I would go into my garage, or a closet if I didn't have a garage, and beat myself with a hammer. Always in the same place, my left ribs, under my arm, until I felt something inside me give way. I have great shame about it. I'm a social worker and therapist. I'm a helper. How can I give advice to trauma victims when I beat myself with a hammer? Who would want advice from someone like me?

I beat myself, my new therapist, Dorothy, recently pointed out, in the spot where Robin had kicked me through the blanket. Twenty years and I never realized that.

They killed my friend. They killed my *friends*. I felt a murderous rage over that. I felt it all the time. But I couldn't hurt them, so I hurt myself. I beat myself until it hurt to breathe.

I called Mikey Argiros and cursed his family, his fucking name.

I drove to Middletown. Mike O'Donnell knew I didn't want to talk, so he snuck me into his childhood bedroom in his parents' house.

"It's okay, baby girl," he told me as we lay together on his bed, fully clothed. He always called me baby girl. "It's okay."

Mike and I drove to the Family compound. Mike was always there for me, no matter what I needed. No matter what I asked. The compound was shuttered. It was haunted but empty. They were gone. So we went to Mikey Argiros's house. His tween son let us in. He was home alone, so we sat with him in the living room, not talking. He said he had to go to basketball practice, but his dad would be home soon.

We said we'd wait.

We were alone in Mikey's house. My God, what do you do in your enemy's home when you feel like he murdered your best friend? We wandered around, checking things out. It was ordinary. Boring. I like to take trinkets. I broke into Jon's apartment after he died and took a few of his things. I have his favorite hat. His favorite shirt. I didn't take anything from Mikey's house. It was so banal there. The banality of evil.

I was in his master bathroom, checking out his toothbrush, when inspiration hit me. "Hey Mike, can you leave him an upper decker?"

"Hell, yes."

That's something I love about guys: they can shit on command.

Do you remember that, Mikey? The upper decker? That was a gift from the legendary MOD.

I voluntarily separated from the Vet Center. I guess that's another way to say quit. But those men and women were precious. They needed someone better than me. Somebody unbroken. Mike took me in and took me to the skate park in Middletown. I hung with the skaters, like I used to with the BMX boys, because they were the only ones who would have me. I didn't say a word. I couldn't. I ended most nights in the bottle, or with Mike, talking about Jon.

Bubby saved my life.

Bubby, my third son. I got pregnant with him in the late spring, when the leaves were greening, and that slowed everything down, because I couldn't hurt a child. I couldn't abuse him by abusing myself.

We decided on a marriage of convenience. My boyfriend wanted his son to have his last name; I needed his health insurance. We lived together, but my real emotional connection was with Mike. I drove to Middletown almost every day to take him to Dunkin' Donuts. He was my refuge. The last member of my pack. He always ordered the same drink: a medium hazelnut-blueberry coffee. It was disgusting. The smell was disgusting, but I'm smiling about it now. The smell of Mike.

We drifted apart after the anniversary of Jon's death. We went inside ourselves to wrestle our pain. Maybe Mike was using again; I don't know. He had slipped a few times over the years. We texted, but his responses were slower. My visits got less frequent. After Thanksgiving, when I hadn't heard from him for a few days, I texted to see if he was okay.

I'm okay baby girl, he wrote.

Did he want me to come over?

No. I just need to get out of New York. Jon had said the same thing in his last message. But I didn't connect it. We didn't connect.

A few hours later, around midnight, I heard that Mike was dead. It's raw. It's still raw, like Jon. It hurts so bad right now, I can't contain it. Don't kill yourself. Please. It doesn't take away the pain. It only transfers it to the people who love you.

The funeral was closed to the public. Family only. I asked if I could come. His family said no. They never told anyone what had happened, so I don't know for sure. I don't know. The announcement said only that Michael O'Donnell died unexpectedly at forty-one years old.

But I have footage from one of Mikaela Shwer's interviews, the only one of Mike and me together. We're in a park. Mike's wearing his sunglasses and fedora. He looks great. He sounds great. My Mike. So cool. But his words.

"I don't deserve. I'll say that, I don't deserve."

"I don't know what happiness is."

"This was wrong. It was bad. It hurt a lot of people. It hurt a lot of families. . . . Being there really changed my outlook on how cruel people can be."

Mike's friends gathered in a park across the street from the funeral home on the night they said goodbye. It was the dead end of November, dark and cold. They played Mike's favorite music and danced: the misfits, the skaters, the punks-gone-middle-aged. Then they huddled in the cold, their hands in their pockets, and stared at the lights across the road. I wasn't there, because I was nine months pregnant, but I hope they played "If I Ever Leave This World Alive" by Flogging Molly.

After Jon died, Mike played me that song. We played it over and over, a hundred thousand times. On the one occasion I gave in and let him drive, on a long, straight road at two in the morning, Mike put on that song and kicked my car to eighty-five.

It's a man telling a woman that, despite being gone, he's always with her. And the woman replies that it should, because he said it would, be okay. Be alright. Be okay.

SURVIVORLAND

14

I Believe in You

WHEN I TOLD a therapist about the Family in 2000, he laughed and said I had an "interesting imagination." So I walked out. He wasn't a therapist, not with that attitude, but he ruined my trust in the profession, at least as it pertained to my situation as a TTI survivor, even though I went on to be trained in therapy, traumatology, and social work. Honestly, subconsciously, maybe I got those degrees because he was such a shit. I didn't want other survivors to go through that.

I didn't go back to counseling until 2011. This was during my divorce and the scandal at the VA, and my anxiety and depression were slipping into suicidal ideation. I never made a plan. I'm not a planner, guys. I just thought, at least once a day, how nice it would be to check out and leave this pain, this mess of a life, behind.

I needed help. If you have suicidal ideation, you need help. But I was terrified of therapists. That's the thing about being a therapist: you know how much damage a bad one can do. Plus, I didn't trust their discretion, and I didn't want to lose my job over an ugly truth I revealed about my life. I had never gotten over the feeling of being a fraud because my high school diploma wasn't real, even if my college degrees were, and because I'm bent by self-doubt. I knew the abuse I'd suffered at the Family wasn't my fault, but I thought if people found out about it, they'd blame me. They'd see me as the problem. That's how it works. The self-hatred they grind you with, when they grind you down, it never goes away.

So I found a psychiatric nurse practitioner. A psych NP is trained to evaluate and treat mental illness, but like a doctor, not a therapist. If you're struggling with trust, get a psych NP. I chose Kay because she was in her sixties and retired from the VA, so I figured she'd understand what I was going through on the job—and what not to put in my chart. I described my problems; she asked questions, then prescribed drugs. It was the first time I'd been medicated since Four Winds at fifteen. It was a lifesaver.

I didn't tell Kay about the Family. Or the rapes. I didn't even tell her about my suicidal ideation because I knew the word "suicide" triggered protocols. (A mistake: please be honest in therapy.) Instead, I told her how hurt I'd been by Mike's secret Wednesdays, my collapsing marriage and VA career, my work partner's betrayal. I told her I feared my parents were right: I didn't deserve good things, and I was too awful for any to last.

This is Survivorland. This feeling. Many of us who have lived through abuse live here, in this mix of anxiety, distrust, fear, betrayal, and pain. Survivorland is the island where our abuse has stranded us. The island where we keep ourselves, out of fear and embarrassment, and where society exiles us because it can't see or accept what's wrong. An island we desperately want to escape, and yet . . . to even consider leaving is to sharpen them again: the anxiety, distrust, betrayal, and pain. The feeling that no one will come. No one will help. No one, in my case, except Jon.

Kay said, *You're not alone, Liz.* She was the first person to tell me that. *You're not alone. Other people struggle. Other marriages collapse. Other people feel desperate and unworthy. Don't beat yourself up.*

I didn't think about the Family. I mean, I thought about them all the time, but I never connected the problems in my personal life with what I'd endured there. I know, crazy, right? So many insights in this book I never quite understood at the time or took to heart. I knew I had complex PTSD; I knew it was a result of the Family's abuse; but the poison they'd put in my parents' ears, about what a vile and hopeless shit I was, they'd poured in my ears, too. And inside, in some small but vital part of me, I believed their lies. They were evil. They were wrong. But they wouldn't have abused me without a reason, right? My parents wouldn't have sent me away if I wasn't unlovable, right? It was my fault my husband betrayed my trust, because I suck. It was my fault my colleague ruined everything we'd built. I was broken, an unlovable wreck since the day my abusive relative "dumped" me at twelve years old. What did I expect? Of course my life was a clusterfuck.

But Survivorland is not just a feeling; it's also a place, a loose network of people coping with the fallout of their abuse, mostly online. Jon was a hero in that Survivorland, in that place we go *to survive*. People knew him and valued his opinion. I followed him into that Survivorland, but as a lurker. I read Reddit threads and message boards for hours, but I never posted. I never felt I had anything to say.

You're not alone, Kay told me. But she didn't know the Family. We met every month, but I never mentioned the rapes. And that's fine. Go at your own pace.

Survivorland, to me, was the proof that Kay was right: I wasn't alone in my trauma. In those Reddit threads, I saw hundreds who had survived abuse, mostly in the TTI, and in them, I saw myself.

So slowly, tentatively, I started to reach out. If I saw a smart post or someone struggling, I tracked them down offline, and I called them. This was not done; even in 2015, nobody called on the phone. But it was the way I worked with Jon: never write it down, never leave a trail. It was paranoia. It was part of my personal Survivorland. Most survivors ignored my calls. Survivorland is not, at its core, an open place. We're skittish, like all wounded animals. But at its best, Survivorland can be a bond of trust: if you are here, then you have been where I am; you understand me; you speak the language; you know the despair and isolation; you are on this island, too.

Then Jon died. Jon was a complicated and beautiful person, with complicated problems, but I knew to my bones that his problems had grown out of the years of brutality we'd endured in that dark and sucking hellhole, where we'd been both tortured and torturers, deep in the New York woods.

And if the Family had killed Jon . . . if they had killed Jay and Mike and Marisa and . . . holy shit, they were killing us all.

I compiled a list of the lost lives—the suicides, the overdoses, the accidents. It took me months, since even the Truth Campaign had never connected the dots, and it sank me to my knees. The list was over eighty dead kids long.

I had an online identity, Survivor993, for the number of days I'd been imprisoned at the Family. I started posting on Facebook, on Instagram, in our Reddits, as Survivor993. This was a terrible time. Family survivors were hitting their thirties and forties, and we were dropping. You can hold a fractured life together for only so long before you get tired, before you feel hopeless, before something—a mere pebble, a stray word or encounter or mistake—shatters the delicate tower you've built on the shifting shit of your trauma. I know, because I've been exhausted. I've been lost. I've been to the edge.

I posted my phone number online. Nobody does that, but I couldn't stand aside and watch my people go down. A million desperate survivors were out there, trying to get through the day. Not just survivors of the Family or the TTI, but of all abuse: sexual, physical, verbal, emotional, psychological, spiritual. We hang on. We hang on. We're waiting for someone to see us and reach out.

That's why I called when I spotted survivors in trouble. But sometimes, that's not enough. So I gave survivors what I wanted when I was at my lowest: a phone number. A private support to reach for when the water was too deep.

And they seized it. Before long, I was getting three or four calls a day. A man in his forties. A woman in her twenties. "I went to the Family," they said. Usually, that was it, no name. The Family was our code. That was all I needed to know.

One evening, it was a woman with a soft Southern accent. "I went to the Family," she said, and I heard the crack in her voice, and I knew, I recognized that pain.

"I'm sorry," she whispered. "I can't do this anymore."

I heard wind in the background. She was outside. The sound of cars ... thumping over something hollow. Driving over a bridge!

"Don't jump," I said.

She started crying.

"Are you there?"

"I don't know. I don't know why I called."

"Yes, you do. Because you don't want to jump."

This wasn't my first call from a suicidal survivor. I received a couple a week. With most, I put them in touch with local services. But there was no time this time to find out where she was, call around, ping her phone. It was just the two of us. Like Marisa.

"Get in your car," I said.

"I'm sorry," she said. "I don't know you. I don't know why I called you."

"Yes," I said, "you do."

Because you don't want to go. Because somehow, through Survivorland, you knew you weren't alone.

It took ten minutes to get her into her car. Another twenty and she was still there, on the shoulder of the bridge. I could hear cars honking as they passed.

"Look," I said, "someone is going to call the police. When they come, they will put you in a cell under suicide watch. You do not want to be in a cell under suicide watch."

"No," she whispered. Our police interventions, even when well intended, are often the worst solutions.

"Then take your ass to the ER," I said. It's called a warm hand-off; the only acceptable way to leave a suicidal person is with professionals. "Drive now."

I heard her engine start.

"You're not alone."

"Thank you," she said.

She hung up, which I didn't want her to do. Which scared me. But I knew. In the same way I knew Marisa was dead, I knew this woman survived.

The experts told me, when writing this book, to concentrate on my story. One raped and tortured teenage girl is a tragedy, the saying goes, but sixty-three thousand are a statistic. Too many victims dull the knife edge of the pain.

I didn't feel that way. The deeper I got into Survivorland, the more I felt the pain. My experience didn't matter because I didn't matter, but knowing there were thousands of victims struggling because of the TTI, and hundreds taking their own lives, and the abusers were still out there, unpunished, taking in fresh victims, *and more programs were starting each year than were being shut down* . . . it was unacceptable. It created a desperation to do something I couldn't deny.

But where could we turn? We had been screaming since 1972, when the Seed was exposed. We'd been banging on your door since *Bradbury v. Straight* in the 1990s. Jon died for this. And nobody listened. Nobody believed. Survivorland was a little island in the middle of an indifferent ocean, lost in the fog. Very few on the outside even knew it was here.

I posted a ridiculous number of schemes to rectify the problem: Get a billboard. Paper New York City with flyers. Bombard news organizations. Hire an independent reporter. Post and link, post and link.

Let's put stakes along Route 97 between the old Family site and the Hancock bridge, I posted, *one for each Family kid who died, with their name big enough for passing cars to read.* This wasn't just publicity; it was commemoration. I didn't want to forget my friends, and I sure as hell didn't want Hancock to keep pretending they'd never existed.

Survivorland hated that idea. I mean, they *hated* it. Of all my harebrained ideas over the years, this was the most despised. Survivors were like: *We'll get in trouble, it's not public land, that's stupid, what's the point, shut up.*

I was pissed off. I was pissed off a lot, as you probably know. *Fine,* I posted. *But if you happen to drive by, you'll see me in my jeans, sitting with my head high and my eyes low, in the back of my truck, with the list of my friends in my back pocket to keep me company.*

One person DMed back: *Hi. I went to the Family too. If you need someone to sit with you I'll go.*

I didn't recognize the handle. She had never posted before. Her profile contained no biographical information. But you know me: I tracked her down.

She was terrified. She had been lurking in Survivorland for three or four years; the last thing she wanted was a phone call. But we ended up talking for hours, entirely about the Family. In the last half hour, we broke through. I told her a cook had raped me twice, once for power and once for revenge. It was the first time I had spoken the act aloud to another person.

"I was raped there, too," she said.

She described what had happened: the grooming, the basement dorm, the staircase from his living quarters that was supposed to be locked, the empty top floor of the big red barn, the shame. This happened years after I left the place, but I could see it, every horrible detail. Worse, I could feel it.

And I was livid. I was so on fire, I couldn't even lie down in my bed that night.

I didn't know, while at the Family, that anyone was being raped. A girl got pregnant by a staffer, another girl ran off to a sex cabin with a staffer, but I just thought, *Do what you gotta do, girl.*

Well, not exactly. We killed those girls at the pole. We railed at them as sluts with dead-fish vaginas. They got *punished*, and we enjoyed it. Because it didn't seem like rape. I didn't understand, then, that abuse was coercion.

By 2017, I knew numerous kids who had been raped at the Family. This girl was the seventh child-rape victim I knew of for that particular staffer. But the other six—in fact, every Family rape victim I knew of at the time, other than me—were boys.

The cook was a predator. His rapes were crimes of opportunity. The staffer who abused this girl was a pedophile. And I knew from my social work that raping girls and boys made him a nonbiased predator of either sex, the most dangerous kind.

I got out of bed, since I was burning so hot I couldn't touch the sheets. I stood in my backyard, smoking American Spirit Golds and staring into the darkness. I had tracked this guy for a decade.

Seven known victims, plus how many I didn't know? How many in the last ten years? How many in the next ten? It was madness to let him walk the earth. It was criminal. He needed to be put down. But what could I do?

I went inside and googled FBI offices. The office in New-burgh, New York, had an opening at one o'clock the next afternoon. I took it. Eight hours later, running on exactly no hours of sleep, I stormed into the FBI compound, ready to burn the ocean if I had to. And by stormed, I mean I slammed the buzzer on the security fence, then gathered myself and walked calmly through another security fence and two security doors. You do not storm an FBI office. You do not even walk fast. My storm was only on the inside.

The lobby was small and bare, with a short sofa and large metal detector. The door to the bullpen was bolted. Cindy, my soon-to-be favorite receptionist, sat behind glass. She told me to walk through the metal detector. She took my cell phone.

"Front room," she said.

Two meeting rooms were off the lobby, with no access to other parts of the building. Number One was for serious inter-rogations. It had equipment. Number Two was for appointments and intake interviews. It had a table and four chairs. The door locked automatically. I heard the ominous click.

Two male agents entered. It did not go well. They were not ready for the fire I was laying down. A little brush-off, a mis-placed joke, and I was at their throats. I couldn't have climbed down from my anger even if I had wanted to, and I didn't want to. It's that Spiderman thing, right? My biggest strength, my greatest curse. That's my anger.

"Okay, then," they said, and I heard the ominous click as the door bolted behind them.

A few minutes later, a woman walked in. Special Agent Diana Savage. Thirty-three years on the force, the most experienced female FBI agent in the state of New York. Murder investigator. Former vice. Newburgh, a postindustrial city across the river from Poughkeepsie, had the highest per capita murder rate in America until Agent Savage and her teammates scoured the streets. They got a commendation for that. Now she was the crimes against children coordinator for the Hudson Valley.

"I'm Agent Real Name I'm Not Allowed to Use in This Book," she said, like we were casual acquaintances meeting over coffee.

She sat down. She was small but not slight. Serious but not harsh. She didn't have anything with her, because she didn't need anything. She could handle herself; that was obvious. A younger woman, clearly her partner, pulled out a yellow legal pad and put it on the table.

"How can we help you, Elizabeth?" Savage said.

I launched into the details of the rape I had heard about the night before. I was scared. No, I was terrified: of that office, of federal agents, of telling our truth, so I was rushing, trying to talk my way past my fear. That was what had put the male agents off: the rush of my fear.

Agent Savage slowed me down. She asked questions. She made me explain this girl, this man, this place in the forest where children were locked in trailers and basements. Soon, I was explaining the Family. The reasons kids were sent there. The beatings. The verbal abuse. The Sanctions. The sexual assaults. I didn't tell her about my rapes or what Father Stephen and Robin had done when I reported them. I told her about other kids who'd been raped. The trauma we suffered. Our car-wreck lives. I was not subtle. I laid it out in graphic detail. I shocked them. I had this idea that the FBI was going to hear our horror story, storm out of the room, and arrest everyone.

"What's the list?" the younger agent asked.

I stopped. I hadn't realized I had mentioned the list. I had stacks of papers, the proof I had gathered over the years, but I had been talking so feverishly I hadn't used them. I pulled out my list of dead Family kids and threw it on the table. I carried it everywhere. They were my motivation. My purpose. The lost souls I kept in my pocket to keep me company so I was never alone. Neither agent said anything as they studied the list, but I saw the shock on their faces.

It was 2017, less than two years since I'd started keeping the list, and there were almost a hundred names.

The rape victim—who I will not name in this book, at her request—wasn't happy when I told her I had gone to the FBI. That's fair. I hadn't asked for her permission. I'd just reacted. It's what I do. If I thought about half the shit I throw at the wall, my life would be easier, but nothing would get done.

She was paranoid. She thought this was going to blow back on her somehow, and she would get in trouble. Who can blame her? The only person arrested in the Straight saga was Richard Bradbury, the victim and advocate. The only person arrested at the Family was . . . no one, although I had been threatened with arrest a dozen times. The aunt of two girls traumatized by the Family gave the Truth Campaign a large donation. We used the money to mail a letter detailing our allegations to every address in Delaware County. We put extra copies on windshields in Hancock. The sheriff did nothing with the allegations but tried to arrest us for littering. It was a near miss. We had to spend the last of our money on a lawyer to get us out of the charges.

But my visit to the FBI . . . was the exact opposite of that. Savage and her partner listened to me for an hour. They took notes. They asked questions. They nodded at the appropriate times, like they were hearing me.

At the end of the session, Agent Savage reached across the table and took my hands in both of hers. I tried to pull away, but she was strong.

"Liz," she said, "I believe you."

I had to leave the room because I could barely hold it together. I walked fast to my car, two gates away, because you don't run at the FBI. I got in the driver's seat and broke down in tears. Out of joy. Out of relief.

Then I picked up my phone and called the first number on my Survivorland contact list. "They believe us," I said. "The FBI believes us."

I hung up and called the next number. I didn't have phone numbers for most of Survivorland, but I made twelve or fifteen calls from the FBI parking lot that afternoon.

"The FBI believes us." Hang up.

"They believe us. The FBI. Yes. The FBI."

Twenty-five years since being sentenced to the Family. Two decades of badgering cops and shouting at the world. Savage and her partner were the first law enforcement officials to take us seriously.

"Someone believes us," I said.

"Someone believes in us."

"Someone sees us. Yeah, really, yes, and it's the FBI."

She believed me. *Agent Savage* believed me. When she took my hands, it was a shock. I hated it. It was the first time I had been gently touched in six years.

And then, "Liz," she said, "I believe you."

It was May 20, 2017, my thirty-seventh birthday. Yeah, that's right. I celebrated my birthday at the FBI. Those four words are the best gift I have ever received.

15

Operation Roscoe

'M A CACTUS. I have spines. You brush against me, even a little, and I'm under your skin.

It costs me to be that way. You have to break off a little piece of yourself to hold a person to your cause. It hurts my reputation, and that hurts my pride. But it's the only way I know to get what I need. You brush up against me, you show any interest in the TTI epidemic, and I'm never letting go.

I thought my FBI contact would be the younger agent. The two of them had a hard-cop/soft-cop routine, and she was the soft one. Savage was kind but intense. She scared me a little. Plus, she was in her fifties; her partner was more my age.

It didn't work out that way. I called the FBI office almost every day, looking for the younger agent. I had a lot of "good" ideas to share, and I was in a hurry. She was nice about it, accommodating, but it was Savage who ultimately took the lead. It wasn't charity. Savage was a professional. She researched my story: studied the Truth Campaign, checked the obituaries, read news articles. The suicides got to her, she told me later. That was when she became emotionally invested, when she saw how many Family kids were dying.

She believed us. It comes down to that. When you actually listen to a TTI survivor, and you believe them, it's hard to turn away.

She not only believed in me; she recognized me. What male officers had for years dismissed as hysteria—a sexist word, since "hystera" is Greek for uterus—Savage correctly identified as desperation. My overzealous advocacy, so often laughed at and belittled, proved to her I was telling the truth.

Oh, Robin Ducey, you gave me the wrong tools, girl. You made me into your nightmare.

"What do you need?" I asked. Anything. I would do anything.

"Corroboration," Savage told me. Victims needed to come to the FBI, in person, for interviews.

"I'll have to bring them in," I said. I knew survivors. They would never trust the FBI enough to come alone.

"That's fine."

"And I'll only bring them in to talk to you."

I didn't want survivors harassed, dismissed, or laughed at. I had to trust before I could convince a vulnerable victim to trust, and I only trusted Savage.

"Agreed," Savage said.

So Survivor993 dove back into Survivorland. My first call was to the survivor who'd tipped me off to her rape, but I didn't stop there. I knew a dozen Family sexual abuse survivors who had communicated with me directly or whose stories were circulating in Survivorland. I didn't bombard them with messages. I didn't even contact them directly. Survivors are skittish, like deer. I couldn't come on like the wolf. Instead, I put it out there, softly, that I had a contact in the law enforcement community, and they were looking for victims who had been sexually abused at the Family.

I worked my close contacts, too. The thing about Survivorland: it's not one place. We struggle to trust three or four people;

how could we trust a couple hundred, or even fifty, even online? How could we be open if we were in the open? Even in Survivorland, we kept our wolf-pack structure. I had maybe twenty people I counted on and trusted. I reached out to them. They reached out to their twenty trusted contacts—mostly people I still don't know by name. They vouched for me. That was required. You aren't trusted on the island without being jumped in by a friend.

Survivorland was a spider's web. Not the web of a black widow or a brown recluse but one of those beautiful orb webs with a thousand delicate strands connecting pivot points. I wasn't the center. Nobody is the center of Survivorland. But I was a pivot point, a place where strands came together. I like to think of myself as a point of strength. Like a concrete pillar. I might not be pretty, I might not be covered in gold or even paint, I might be mostly buried underground, but I'm helping hold up something important. I put a lot of new strands in my web with this effort. We built something pretty life-sustaining out of our work for the FBI.

It wasn't easy. We are afraid of you. Most survivors recoiled out of fear. But others begged me to hear their horror stories: beatings, concussions, lifelong physical injuries. They had PTSD. Nightmares. Broken relationships. They had been accused of being addicts so often and for so long that they became addicts. Alcoholics. Prescription drug abusers. Far, far more addicts came out of that place than went in, I guarantee you that. The Family wasn't addiction treatment; it was an addiction factory. Survivors were getting older, and they were breaking down. They were homeless. They were in abusive relationships. They were too hurt to leave their rooms or hold a steady job. The only thing many had left was a dream of justice. Of revenge. They wanted the people who hurt them as children to pay.

I had to tell them, *I care. I hear you. Survivorland will be here for you, whatever you need, for as long as you need. But the FBI is only investigating sexual molestation and rape.*

It was devastating. It meant traumatized victims hearing that their pain didn't count. And then taking that pain to Survivor-land and claiming Survivor993 was a stuck-up bitch keeping the FBI to herself.

It wasn't like that. Savage and her partner wanted, on a personal level, to see the sociopaths and rapists brought to justice. But they were not our emotional support blankets. They were not our therapists. I loved Savage. She took my calls, even when my calls were dumb. But she wasn't coming to my birthday party, you know? Not that I ever had a birthday party. I haven't celebrated my birthday since Jon died, because our birthdays were six days apart, and we celebrated together. But you get the point, right? I trusted her, but we weren't friends. This was about making a criminal case.

I never would have succeeded if I hadn't had my social work training. If I hadn't worked with wounded soldiers. If I didn't know to be honest, patient, and real. I never would have understood I had to go to their apartments (or cars, for those living on the street) and do their errands, donate groceries, arrange babysitters.

I went to a crack house in Allentown, Pennsylvania. It smelled like piss, sex, and porn. I pulled a kid off the floor and drove him to Port Jervis, across the New York line, where Savage interviewed him. I helped half-a-dozen other survivors sober up and detox. I waited for hours while one barricaded herself in her house, afraid to leave, even though she had invited me and knew I was coming. It's the evil of the TTI: they screw you up so bad that you aren't in any condition to come after them later. It's the time bomb they put in our heads. It's for their protection as much as for our destruction.

In the end, I found about a dozen verifiable victims of sexual crimes. I was able to convince several to talk to Savage, including the girl whose rape had set me off. I picked them up and drove them to the FBI because, as I'd predicted, they wouldn't go alone. I wasn't allowed in the interview room, so I waited on the uncomfortable sofa in the lobby. Sometimes, it took an hour. Sometimes, it took three. Didn't matter. I would stare into space for an entire year, bored out of my head, if it meant victims were being heard and Savage was getting what she needed.

Her corroboration. Her proof. A clear pattern of abuse. She got it.

But nothing happened.

After the Family closed, a friend and I put on bright yellow workmen's vests to steal their sign. We were standing on a ladder in the bed of a pickup truck wrenching that rusty thing apart when a state trooper drove straight by us on Route 97. I ducked so fast, and so stupidly, I almost knocked the ladder off the truck. The trooper didn't stop. He didn't notice us any more than he'd noticed all the runaways over the years. Now, out of frustration, the rape victim and I took that sign to a gun range and blew it apart with automatic rifles.

Finally, after about a hundred calls, Savage sat me down at a local diner and straightened me out. Sex crimes, she said, were hard. Some male agents were uncomfortable with the emotional commitment necessary to connect with victims. Female agents were too often victims themselves. Proving cases was difficult with a he-said, they-said crime. Victims backed out when they realized how public their rapes would become. They weren't credible on the stand because the rapes affected their mental health. They needed an outcry witness: someone they'd told about the rape at the time or who had recognized a change in their behavior, like how I'd become angry and sullen after my abusive relative raped me. (Nobody noticed. Or rather, they noticed and exiled me for it.) With teens, in a coercive and secretive environment like the Family, meeting these criteria was difficult.

And then there was the historical nature of the abuse: the school was closed, the cases old. All these cases, including mine, fell beyond the statute of limitations. The government was not allowed to prosecute them, even though Savage wanted to.

"But most of these people are alive," I argued. "They will rape again."

"I know," Savage said, "but we have to work within the rules."

It was crushing. Forget the Family for a second: we're talking about a place with four known (to me) rapists on staff, including a serial rapist of children. How could there be a get-out-of-jail-free card for a man like that?

"It's alright, Liz," Savage said, taking my hands. God, I wish you could hear her voice. She had a slight Southern accent that made it sound like *Liiiz*. "We'll get 'em, Liiiz. You just have to be patient. God's work takes time. And I believe in you."

I took matters into my own hands. I have always been a self-starter, as you know. Always thought of myself as Nancy Drew, ever since reading those books at six or seven years old. Always believed I could solve the case and bust the asshats if I worked hard enough, even before hooking up with the FBI. And there was that one Family staffer atop my takedown list: the Pedophile.

I had sat overwatch on his ass for years. Called his phone. Followed his socials. He moved, trying to escape his past. It was an ordinary lower-middle-class home in an ordinary blue-collar town. An anonymous box on a street of similar boxes. But I found him.

I rang the doorbell, and there it was: his sad-ass face, staring around the edge of the doorframe.

"Hey, motherfucker," I said. "You remember me?"

I saw the fear in his eyes, but he stuttered out some denial.

"Don't worry," I said. "That's fine. I sure the fuck remember you." I looked around. "I'd say nice place you got here, but . . . you know. You better watch your back."

Eventually, I evolved my tactics. I softened my approach. I had a long, friendly correspondence with Father Stephen, the ex-priest who hadn't reported my rape to the authorities, before a Family kid who knew me from social media warned him I was probably trying to set him up. And I was! I wanted to break someone off from the mafia. I wanted someone on the inside to tell the truth.

Nobody warned the Pedophile, probably because he didn't have any friends among Family survivors. For years, even as I drifted toward *I just want to talk to you, I want to understand*, he never responded. And I worked him hard, like a punching bag. There's a power in letting them know, *Hey, motherfucker, I'm still here. I'm still thinking about you.* He was probably sweating more over my softness than over my anger.

Then one day, after I'd left a voice mail at his brand-new job advising him to check under his bed, he responded. I was in the middle of getting a tattoo from my regular guy, a Family kid; we stick together. It was the word *warrior* on my left wrist.

"Holy shit," I said. I showed the tattoo artist my phone. "It's him."

"Answer it!"

I picked up. He was breathing heavily already. He wanted to meet.

I said, "I'll come to your office. Where do you work?" I knew where he worked. I knew everything about this guy. This was the first good job he'd had in years.

"No, no," he said.

"How about somewhere on your way home, then."

"Sure."

"The Roscoe Diner."

I could practically hear him sweating. "Fine," he said. "What time?"

"Five thirty." He'd have to come directly from work.

"Fine. I'll be there."

I checked my phone. I had two and a half hours. The Roscoe Diner was an hour and a half away.

"I'm out of here," I told my tattoo guy.

"Hell, yeah," he said, patching up the *warr* in bloody ink on my wrist. "Take him down, Ianelli."

I called the FBI, but Savage wasn't in. I got the two male agents from my first interview instead.

"Don't do it," they said. "It will just be your word against his."

"I'll record everything." I knew the laws. New York was a single-consent state. As long as both parties are in New York state, one can record the other without their knowledge.

"It's not safe."

Please. I knew this guy. He was as dangerous as a fart, and twice as rank.

"I'll bring my gun."

"What! No. Liz, do not bring a gun."

"I'm joking. Jesus. Settle down."

And that was when the other agent chimed in: "Does your husband know what you're planning?"

Yeah, he went there. He said that. There was no way I was backing down now.

I had lunch with Savage every few months. She filled me in on the investigation, asked me questions, but most of the time we just talked. She gave me advice and the kind of pep talks I had given Jon in Waryas Park, and I knew it was real, she had faith in me, even before she took my hands at the end of every meal, like a benediction, and said, "Liiiz, I believe in you."

I observed her, more than she knew. Agent Savage, with all her rule following and explanations of the finer points of law, taught me how to pay attention. She always chose the same type of restaurant: open, public, casual, and busy. She always arrived early, before me. She always sat at a back table on the far side, with a clear view of the door. She knew her order, so she didn't have to look at the menu. Everything was set up in advance so she could be alert the whole time.

So I arrived half an hour early to the Roscoe Diner. I talked to the waitress. I told her I had an important meeting, like an interview. No, not a job interview, for information. I said it, you know, like a cop on television. Like I was trying to keep it quiet.

"I need your help," I said.

I could see her excitement. "What's going on?"

"I can't tell you that, but here's what I need you to do."

I asked her to turn down the music when my mark arrived. I asked her to come immediately and take our drink order. He would order decaf coffee, but I wanted her to bring him regular. "Keep filling it up, but be slow about any food."

"Okay," she said. She was in deep, I could tell. Her eyes were bugging. But I gave her twenty bucks to make sure.

"Another twenty at the end," I said, "if we get it right."

I chose a small booth in the back, with a clear view of the door. He would have to walk a long aisle in full view. I moved the table closer to his side. He wouldn't realize it was uncomfortably tight until he sat down. I put my phone on the table. When he arrived, I would make a show of turning it off so he'd know I wasn't recording him. But I had an old iPod. I was going to record him with that.

He arrived as expected, huffing uncomfortably down the aisle. He squeezed into the booth and tried to push the table away for extra room, but I put my arm out, subtly, to prevent it. The waitress was there immediately, staring at him so wildly I thought she might give it away. He ordered decaf; she brought regular.

I was hoping he'd order a cheeseburger, for old time's sake, but no such luck.

"Can you turn down the music, please?"

"Oh, yeah," the waitress said. "Sure. Yeah. Sorry."

Five minutes into our conversation, the Pedophile was sweating. Ten minutes in, he was jittery. I poured on the butter. *I know you're not a bad guy. I know you're a Christian. God is always watching. Why would you sin? I don't want to hurt you. I just want to know why it happened. I want to understand.*

It was a weird time, he stuttered. *It was a bad place. Things should never have happened, but it was the place. The attitude. They made it seem . . .*

"You had sex with the students."

"No."

He was trembling from the caffeine and the guilt. He was sweating through his shirt. I have no sympathy. I know he was molested as a kid, but I don't care; repeating the cycle is not an excuse. There are staffers from the Family who couldn't care less what they did. They haven't lost a second's sleep. But sitting close to this guy, for the first time since my imprisonment, I saw that he was eating his sins, and they were eating him up. I could smell it. I mean, it was body odor. The guy reeked. But it was also decay: the rot in his soul.

I was convinced he had come to confess. And why not? Legally speaking, unless there were rapes I didn't know about, the statute of limitations made him close to untouchable. Why not save himself from hell, in this world and the next? All I had to do was find the right words.

This isn't your fault.

I know how that place was. What they made you do.

We were brainwashed. Me and you both.

I understand. Tell me what they did to you. What they made you do.

Don't you want to be free?

He kept tiptoeing to the edge. But it wasn't a drop. It was a wall he couldn't bring himself to climb. I suspect he built that wall in his mind to hide from himself what he had done to us. He wouldn't speak the acts, only that he was wrong, he was sorry. He was very, very sorry.

I didn't get it. He didn't confess. It wouldn't have been admissible in a criminal case anyway, Savage told me later.

But I wanted it for myself. For his survivors. And I didn't get it. I failed.

The next morning, I called his place of work. I asked for the man in charge. The operator wouldn't put me through. "Well," I told her, "I am a concerned citizen, and I heard you have a suspected pedophile working with the public."

I was put straight through to the director. That afternoon, the Pedophile was fired. He won't be working a quality job anytime soon. If I have anything to say about it, he won't ever work again.

Is that too harsh? Does it make you uncomfortable?

Well, tough titties. I'm a cactus. I keep pulling off my fingernails to leave in this motherfucker, and I'm going to see it through. You hear me, Pedophile? I'm never going to let you go.

16

Jersey Girl

I WAS BUSY, AND not just with my FBI work. I was meeting Kay, my psych NP, every two weeks. I still hadn't come clean about the Family, but I was figuring out how to find the holes in her schedule where she could give me forty minutes, even an hour, of conversational therapy.

Kay introduced me to art therapy, a brilliant tool for dealing with trauma. After a few months, I developed a style. I found passages that evoked moments or feelings from my life—a few words or a page, written by me or cut out of a poster or magazine—and glued them to a canvas. Then I painted over them, usually in tones of ocher and blue, until the words were completely hidden. The patterns were abstract, but I tried to make them beautiful. The meaning was in the creation of beauty.

Eventually, my name found its way to a therapy group in New Jersey. It was invitation only, for survivors of cults. I was the first survivor of the TTI. In fact, I introduced the leaders, the Goldbergs, to the TTI, and they helped me understand I had been in a cult. Maia Szalavitz defines the TTI that way, but it was the Goldbergs who showed me how much the Family was based on psychological manipulation and the destruction of identity.

I opened a traumatology practice—therapy related to trauma, for which I had a master's degree and a license—out of the house I shared with my toddler, Bubby, and husband of convenience. My husband hated that, but I had a separate outside entrance and a stubborn disposition, so I didn't care. I worked only with survivors of the TTI. I rarely charged them, because they struggled with money and didn't have insurance. My husband despised that, too. But these survivors needed help, and ordinary therapists were shitting the bed when it came to treating us. Therapists struggled with the basics, listening and believing, because our stories were so brutal and our symptoms so severe. For decades, they had retraumatized us with their disbelief. There weren't many Agent Savages willing to embrace us in the therapy industry but a lot of underinformed, overconfident jerks. Fifty years of abuse, and therapists still have their heads up their asses about the TTI.

I had been through it. There was no horror my clients could tell me that I wouldn't believe, because I'd seen it. I knew the industry lingo, and I knew its methods. I knew what survivors wanted to say, even when they backed away from the abuse or couldn't put it into words, and I knew how vulnerable they felt reliving it. I never blamed them. I never rushed them. That's important for survivors: never rush, and never pry.

"Remember me?"

"Of course." I was receiving a dozen calls a day from survivors, since I still had my number posted online, but this one was special. It had been a year, but how could I forget her voice?

"My name's M—."

"Hey, M—. I'm Liz."

"You saved my life that day on the bridge."

"Bullshit. You saved your own life, girl."

"I'm starting a podcast."

"What's a podcast?"

"It's about us, you know, survivors, and the Troubled Teen Industry."

"Okay."

"I want you to be my trauma expert."

Hell, no, I thought.

But then again, most of my work with survivors broke down into four categories. The first was assuring them that what they had experienced was real. *Yes, it happened, no matter what your dad says. It was abuse. It wasn't your fault. It had a profound effect on your life.*

The second was explaining those effects: *This is complex PTSD; this is anxiety; this isn't being a lazy shithead like your mother keeps telling you; it's depression.*

The third was how to work the system, where to get medicine, and what services were available.

The fourth was dealing with a panic attack, because good God, we have a lot of panic attacks.

All this was personal, but it was general, too. It could be communicated in a podcast, and the format would emphasize my core message to survivors: *You're not alone. We've been there. And we're here for you, too.*

So M—'s podcast became part of my outreach, and M— became one of my best friends in Survivorland. She was a beautiful strand in the spider's web, but she wasn't the only one.

Jodi Hobbs's Survivors of Institutional Abuse (SIA) defined institutional abuse and listed programs engaged in it. It was a clearinghouse for information—we thought cops might use it, but they never did—as well as community and confirmation. *Yes, we see you, survivor. Yes, you were abused. Yes, you are one of us.* I helped her define the cult aspects of the TTI and served on her board.

SIA cast a wide net: if you were hurting children, no matter how small your program or focused your methodology, we tried to find and list you. Natalie was our eyes. She was a free spirit: always traveling, no real home. Natalie checked out in person many of the rumors we heard online.

I went to programs, too. I rented a van once or twice a month, when my husband was off and could watch Bubby, and parked it outside TTI programs in the Northeast. I stood on the roof of the van with a bullhorn and yelled, "If anyone wants to leave, come now. I am a survivor. I will help you."

I worked out a good rental relationship, and for a while, we had a small fleet of vans. Survivors stood outside programs with bullhorns: "If you are eighteen, they cannot legally hold you. If you are eighteen, you are free. Come outside. We will help you."

The programs locked their gates tight when they saw us coming. No child was ever rescued.

So we switched tactics. I started placing moles in jobs inside TTI programs, like Neil had been at the Family. Only men did that. No female survivor, that I know of, ever voluntarily went back inside. We hoped to win the trust of the teens and create a mass breakout, but again, we failed.

I had an alter ego, Margaret. Margaret was a "concerned parent" with a "troubled teen" who asked questions and recorded the answers. The TTI programs were bad. They repeated the classic lies about being gentle and using aggression only in extreme cases; about the rigorous proof behind their work; about their misleading or nonexistent credentials and fantastic track records with whatever affliction "my teen" happened to have.

The companies that gooned kids were appalling. They required no paperwork or documentation. All they wanted to know was "Are you the legal guardian?"

If yes: "How much are you willing to spend?"

Margaret's answer, "I'm desperate, money is no object," meant nothing was off the table. Big guys to hold him down? *We'll bring six.* He knows karate? *Our guys know MMA.* Handcuffs?

Encouraged. Knockout drugs? *We'll supply them.* Black bag over the head? *It always calms them down.*

"I don't know what to do with him."

"Don't worry, Mom, we know a place. We'll take him straight there."

I found abandoned houses on Google Earth and sent companies there for "interventions." It worked a few times, but they got wise. Gooners have Google Earth, too.

All this time, I was also taking in survivors. It started with Katrina, the girl the Family had dumped at the Binghamton homeless shelter. She was off heroin, someone in Survivorland told me, but in an abusive relationship. Could I check on her? I didn't know Katrina, but Kay talked to me about abusive relationships all the time: how to spot them, what they were. Agent Savage talked about them, too. Saying he was going to punch you, then punching a chest of drawers, they said, was domestic abuse. Throwing things in your direction, even if he didn't intend to hit you, was domestic abuse. Breaking things in anger was domestic abuse. Even harsh criticisms, said softly, could be domestic abuse.

Domestic abuse, I realized, was rampant in survivor circles. We were conditioned for relationships like that because our programs were run by abusive men, and we not only fell into those familiar relationships, we stayed.

You are not alone, Kay told me. They were her four words, the way Savage's four words were *I believe in you.* Four words can change your life.

I tried to talk Katrina into leaving her boyfriend. I explained why the way he treated her was domestic abuse. It wasn't happening. She was dependent on him, financially and emotionally. So I went to her house and, essentially, forced her to pack a bag. I can be very persuasive when I have to be. She didn't have anywhere to go, since her adoptive parents still didn't want her, so she came to live with me. Before long, she was in her own place and moving on with her life.

I took in several more female survivors over the next months, mostly because of homelessness or an abusive relationship. My husband hated it, but by that point, we weren't speaking. Our relationship was so bad he started working the night shift so we wouldn't see each other. I watched Bubby in the morning so he could sleep; he watched Bubby in the afternoon so I could see my traumatology clients and work in Survivorland. After Bubby went to sleep, I logged on and spent much of the night in Survivorland, too. There was endless messaging and brainstorming because there was an endless need. They say social media is addictive, and it is. It's even more addictive when you believe in your mission and believe you're doing good.

I was still getting a dozen calls a day, including from a strange man who wouldn't quit. Young(ish) woman on the internet, right? It's a hazard. Especially when you post your number.

This guy had a husky voice and a thick New York accent. He left voice mails telling me he'd tried to reach me online; I needed to call him. He had an offer. I could almost hear it: *It's an offer you can't refuse.*

If this guy isn't mobbed up, I thought, *I'll eat my jeans.* Yeah, I wear them ripped to bits, but that's still a lot of denim to bite through.

Finally, I'd had enough. I called back: "What the fuck do you want?"

"Your cooperation. I'm calling on behalf of a lawyer."

"Fuck your lawyer." I hung up.

He called back. For days.

"I told you to fuck the fuck off."

"Don't hang up."

"Why not?"

"I'm a private investigator . . ."

Click. No way.

He called back.

"I've got cop friends, motherfucker. This is harassment."

"Hear me out, Elizabeth. This is a good thing."

"What kind of good thing?"

"My client is a lawyer. He needs information."

"On what?"

"Abuse. Institutional abuse."

Hmmm.

"How did you find me?"

"He's been looking for someone like you."

Ominous or interesting, I wasn't sure.

"What does he think I can do for him?"

"I should let him explain."

I did not want to talk to a lawyer. I had no trust. None. But it felt like it might be a way forward, and moving forward was always a risk.

"Fine," I said. "He can call me at this number."

Two minutes later, the phone rang.

"Elizabeth Ianelli?"

"Yes."

"Survivor993?"

Holy shit, this guy had a stronger accent than the private dick. I could almost taste the hair gel. "What's it to you?"

"My name is Ralph DeSimone. I'm a personal injury lawyer."

Yes, there was a 10 percent chance this DeSimone character was a leg-breaker and a 50 percent chance he was an ambulance-chaser. But my father was a personal injury lawyer. That was . . . complicated. He'd smashed our relationship on the rocks of his disgust for me. But as a kid, I'd idolized him. I'd believed it when he told me it wasn't about the money; it was about helping the powerless gain control over the powerful forces crushing them.

"What do you want, Ralph?"

"To understand."

After a minute, it was clear what had happened: he had taken on what he thought was a basic institutional malfeasance case, and it had quickly gone dark. Restraints. Beatings. Daily verbal abuse. And rape. This Ralph guy couldn't get his head around it. Could all this be true? To me, it was obvious right away that it was not only true, it was a Troubled Teen Program. The abusive behaviors are so similar across the industry that we recognize the stench.

I had to do it. Had to. Every molecule in my body rebelled against putting myself out there for this guy, but if I didn't stand up for survivors, who would?

"What's the program?" I said.

"It's small. You wouldn't know it."

"You'd be surprised."

"I'd rather not say."

"Tell me."

"It was called the Family."

Fuuuuuuuuuuuuuuuuuuuuuuuuuuuuuuuuuuuuuuuuuuuuuuck!

Okay, Liz, breathe. Breathe, baby girl, breathe.

Fuuuuuuuuuuuuuuuuuuuuuuu . . .

"Whatever you need, Ralph, I'm there."

"Let's meet tomorrow. I'll send a car."

"No way."

I did not want to get in a strange car. I don't take public transportation because you have no control. Who knows where that bus is actually going? So I cannot stress strongly enough how much I did not want to get into a black Town Car in the deep darkness of 6:00 a.m. and head to . . . freaking New Jersey.

This was an assassination. They were definitely shooting me in the head and dumping my body in the Meadowlands. It was the perfect trap. Use my commitment to survivors against me.

And sure, I'm not important enough to be the victim of a hit, even a TTI hit, but people have died for less. Jay died, after all, because some dime-dicked adults thought it was fun to rail at a kid over his cleft palate.

And that was why I had to do this. I had to take the bullet for Jay, for Jon, for Marisa and Mike and all the others.

Plus, I researched Ralph DeSimone. I started three seconds after I hung up the phone. I used the internet, my law enforcement contacts; I took the deep dive. He was a former Brooklyn prosecutor. He had his own firm. They had an office on Fifth Avenue, the ritziest street in Manhattan. He looked legit. If he murdered me, he'd do it right. He'd make it classy. What more can a girl like me ask?

The car was swank. Free water in tiny bottles! The hotel the car pulled up to was *swank*. Valet with gloves! The conference room Ralph had reserved was *swankity-swank*. The refreshments were . . . terrible, but I'm not complaining. I ate two trays of dry pastries.

Ralph was a good-looking man. Tall, bronze, slick hair, immaculately put together. He was a star, I could tell. I sat with him and his people for most of the day. I explained everything: the isolation, the abusive philosophy, the so-called school, the AA-adoring, dry-drunk staff, the weird religion, the incomprehensible vocabulary. I told them about the horribly oversexualized environment we'd lived in as teens.

Girls stripped to their panties while adult men talked about their vaginas.

Boys stripped naked so staff members could smell their penises and inspect them for "irritation" to make sure they hadn't been masturbating. This happened every week; sometimes every morning. Kevin Argiros told me Paul Geer had done this to him, in front of a dorm full of older teenagers, when he was eleven years old.

A boy got a girl pregnant. He was sent home. She had the baby and was sent back to the Family.

A staffer got a girl pregnant. He was fired. She was sent back.

A staffer ran away with a girl. They were found in a cabin a hundred miles away. Yes, they'd been having sex. He was fired but not arrested, even though she was underage. *She was sent back and punished.* I don't know if her parents knew she was missing. Maybe they did. But regardless: *she was sent back to a place where a staff member had statutory-raped her and punished for it.*

A whole system supported the Family's abuse: the town, the cops, the state charter school division, the DAAA that had ceded control, the parents. Think about everything that has happened in this book. Think of how many people had to *willfully become blind and deaf* for it to occur.

Even now, people are skeptical. New Yorkers say, "It's not that bad up there." They have a second house in Delaware County. They drop in for the weekend to enjoy the views, the funny locals, the investment opportunities. They drive Route 97, past the entrance to the Family, and think it's lovely. Which it is! It's rocky, mountainous, tree-covered terrain.

"It's rough, sure," they say, "but it's not, like . . . middle of nowhere."

Oh, yeah? Have you tried running through the woods at night, with no trail, for eight miles? It's a little different than tootling along in your Subaru or pedaling your fancy road bike.

That's not the disconnect, though. It's not money or circumstance or looking at poverty porn instead of living it. The disconnect is experience. If you haven't been forced to stare abuse in the face, it's hard to believe how ugly the world can be—and how easy it is for seemingly ordinary people to become monsters when the door is closed.

Ralph had been a prosecutor in Brooklyn. He was a personal injury lawyer. He knew the world. Like Agent Savage, he'd seen what human beings are capable of. That afternoon, I saw not only his belief but his anger. Ralph DeSimone had a quiet hatred for the people who had abused his client and a burning desire to bring them down.

So I shared the papers I had collected. I shared "The Ianelli Tapes," the recordings I'd made of the goon squads and at the Roscoe Diner. The FBI wouldn't take them, but maybe they did Ralph some good.

He's handled a bunch of Troubled Teen cases now. I don't know how many, and I don't care. I was never involved with clients, testimony, anything like that. I was there for background, to help his people understand the Family, because that's a deep, dark lake, and there are a lot of buried bones.

I didn't have to know the specifics, because when I walked out of that hotel that evening, I knew this: the Family abused us because they thought "bad" teenagers abandoned by their parents were weak and easy victims. With Savage and DeSimone, the calculus had changed, and we had some bad-ass, pipe-hitting motherfuckers on our side now.

17

I See You, Survivor

O N NOVEMBER 30, 2017, a few days after Thanksgiving, a young man died in the Bronx. He was discovered in a bathroom at a school, beside the syringe he'd used to shoot up shortly after classes let out for the day. The school was for disabled students between the ages of thirteen and twenty-five. The man was a beloved teacher. His name was Matt Azimi. He lived near me, in the town of Carmel. He was a survivor of the Family.

I went to his visitation. It was my first since Jon, so I was raw, but Family kids show up for each other. Matt had two young children. They clung to his coffin and cried. His wife was visibly pregnant, like Jon's sister at his funeral, and visibly shattered. His parents, her parents, numb with grief. Everyone was crying. And then there was the Family girl from my era, drunk off her ass. A Family boy was so hammered he parked his car half in the front yard of the house next to the funeral home. I came out for fresh air, because it's heavy when a thirty-six-year-old father dies without warning, and the Family kids were aggressively making out on the hood of her car.

Why do we have to be like this? Why is this our lives?

"I'm out of here," I said to a survivor who had served his time at the same time as me. I couldn't take it. Not that day.

I met that survivor and another Family kid at a diner. We hadn't seen each other in years. They acted like it was a reunion, the way Family kids had at Jon's funeral. But Matt was dead. Another Family kid was dead. A wife, two kids, and one more who would never know him, not even for a day, left to carry the pain Matt couldn't put down. How hard would it hurt them? How long would the generational trauma echo?

The female survivor was working for a shady operation that felt a couple turns from becoming the Family. The man was an addiction counselor, and that worried me. He had given the Truth Campaign testimonial about being punched, thrown down the stairs, and beaten in his room by a staffer, Phil. I was there on another day, when the kid was brought back after running away, and Phil ran across the room and punched him so hard it knocked the kid back out the door. Phil turned to us with satisfaction; the kid jumped up and started running. Phil saw us staring and took off after him, but Phil was a juicer. Steroids make you strong, but they wreck your lungs. The kid got away.

Now, he told me, he and Phil were friends. "I needed that punch," he said. "That punch straightened me out."

What are you talking about? I wanted to scream at him. *Getting away from that place straightened you out!*

Worse, though, far worse: the two of them were proud of me. They loved the Truth Campaign. They followed me online. They knew about my traumatology practice for TTI survivors. They asked about my connections in the FBI. They were proud of me for having my life together. A leader of the resistance, maybe, finally?

My ass.

My life was not together. My life was hell. I was still with my third husband only because I didn't have the money to leave him. Looking back, I probably took in so many strays as a sub-conscious protective measure because I was afraid of him. I was afraid for my son. I struggled with being a therapist while my life was a wreck. It makes me a better listener, I know, because I understand and empathize, but I felt like a fraud. How could I counsel those in need when I was back to breaking my ribs with a hammer to ease my pain? When my fear was so crippling, I sometimes wore a bulletproof vest? I bought it when I worked at the VA because we intervened with armed men and women in crisis. We never lost a vet on my watch. I'm proud of that. Now that vest was the literal armor that protected me.

So, no, sorry, I wasn't doing great.

I had a hard night after Matt's visitation. I didn't sleep. I stared at the ceiling, yards above my head in a nice big house, and thought about how Matt seemed to have pulled it together, to have weathered the storm, to have made the pieces fit, but it wasn't true. He was still damaged, and he was still lost. I'd heard former Family staff were coming to the funeral, so I couldn't attend. I knew myself. There would be a confrontation. That wasn't fair to Matt's wife, his poor children, the people who loved him. I was hurting badly: for Matt, for everyone on the list, and for everyone I feared would be there soon.

So I sat down in my office an hour before the funeral and recorded a video on my laptop. Just me, in a collarless black band T-shirt, one take with no edits, speaking from the heart.

I said my 993 days at the Family had changed me. When I came out, I couldn't understand myself, or my feelings, or why I couldn't make anything work.

"I had to make a lot of mistakes," I admitted, "for every one success."

I wasn't okay. That was what I wanted listeners to know. I had anxiety. I had OCD and PTSD, with nightmares so bad I thrashed and screamed. I had trouble trusting. I made bad relationship choices. I struggled as a mother because I didn't know how to express emotions. I had seriously contemplated suicide, both inside the Family and after.

"I want you to know that I see you. That if you're struggling from depression or having a bad day or you're stuck in addiction or you're missing a friend . . . you are not alone. There are many of us who feel the same way."

I feel the same way.

"I see you. I know what you're going through. I'm no different than any other survivor trying to make sense of what happened to them."

What we're doing isn't working, I said. *Too many of us are dying. The Family didn't save us, and they won't help us now. It's up to us. We are fighting for our lives.*

"Our best revenge is living a good life," I told them, and we couldn't do it alone. We had struggled separately. It was time to come together now.

"We are not the lying, manipulating pieces of shit they told us we were. We are strong, and we struggle, but that doesn't mean we won't come out the other side."

I see you. I see your strength. We are survivors. We survive.

The video was a message to Matt—and to Jon and Mike and Marisa and Jay, because everything I do is for them. It was a message to everyone who felt alone in their grief. Mostly, it was a message to myself, because I needed Survivorland. It wasn't a cry for help; it was an offer of community.

I posted the video to Facebook a few minutes after Matt Azimi's funeral was scheduled to start, under #ISeeYouSurvivor. Then I collapsed into sleep.

I woke up fourteen hours later to "OMG."

"I saw you, girl."

"Congrats on the campaign."

What?

"Check Facebook."

My video had gone viral. #ISeeYouSurvivor was ripping through our networks. It would become a rallying cry, used more than one hundred million times, reaching around the world and into thousands of survivor communities. But my pride that morning was in those closest to me. In my video, I asked others to post videos, to not be quiet, to let us know how they were doing, and my people responded.

Katrina told of being dropped off at a homeless shelter by the Family. She cried talking about her heroin addiction and the death of friends, including Matt.

"I see you," she said. "I'm here. If you're struggling, reach out. I don't care if it's four o'clock in the morning . . . I had people who were up at four o'clock in the morning to support me. You have the same thing. I'm here. I see you."

That's a victory.

Heather committed to not drinking before 5:00 p.m. Victory.

M—'s podcast helped me find my voice in Survivorland. She posted an #ISeeYouSurvivor video more than twenty minutes long. Victory.

A woman from the Nevins Road house, the 1980s precursor to the Family, showed up at my door. She didn't know how to film a video. She wanted me to film her. She wanted to apologize to the younger survivors for not stopping them. If only she had done something, she said. If only . . .

I knew the feeling. But to say it, to unburden, after so many years, was a victory.

An older gent from England who had been abused in orphanages in the 1950s posted a message of support. Victory.

The *New York Times* reporter contacted me. Again. Not a victory. I don't like talking to outsiders.

He had written an article about Matt Azimi. I had read it. Immediately. Obviously. I took exception to a few lines, like a positive description of the Family that only mentioned in passing "a system of punishments that could be severe."

A friend described Matt as saying of his addiction issues, "This is my problem. I have this problem. I'll never get over this problem."

There is a positive way to view addiction as a lifelong struggle. *You're an addict, Matt, and we love you.* That's the actual AA philosophy. Matt's words felt like the self-destructive negativity of the Family. *You're an addict, Matt, and that makes you a piece of shit, a loser, and that means everyone hates you.* They made us feel doomed to failure, and we took those words into our souls. They turned our troubles into comfort and our addictions into excuses. Of course Matt reached for heroin again; the Family told him he was a piece of shit, and that's what pieces of shit do. The article didn't see that. Nobody has ever understood how the Family used addiction-speak as a weapon, not a tool.

But Matt's wife had participated in the article, and it was well written and respectful, so I agreed to talk to the reporter.

Mike Wilson and I had actually talked before the article. He was looking for context for Matt's overdose, so he contacted the Truth Campaign, since Matt had once posted there. I saw the message and called him.

"What did you think when you heard Matt had died?" he asked me.

"Honestly, it didn't surprise me," I said. "He's ninety-three."

"Ninety-three what?"

"He's the ninety-third Family kid to die."

Long silence. "Can I come see you right now? I'll get on the next train."

I hate it when they come in person. Why do they always want to come in person? "Sure," I said.

The snow was deep; that's what I remember about Mike's visit. He was wearing fancy loafers, the worst shoes for snow. He was a city guy, and that's a different animal than us up here. But I trusted him. He wasn't a hungry hipster out for a scoop; he was an old-school working-class grinder who came out of Alabama and just wanted to keep plugging away at his dream job, the crime beat for the *New York Times*. In other words, he wanted the truth.

He got it.

And he didn't blink. He took it in like a sponge, as much as I could pour into him, then went away sloshing. None of that information made it into the article about Matt's death, but Mike Wilson didn't quit. We talked multiple times after the article came out. I gave him other names, and I heard through our networks he was poking around. He came upstate many times. He pursued information for months. He even went to the Family compound, which had been bought by a sports camp. He never saw it at its worst. He was twenty years too late.

But he was here now. He was taking our stories more seriously than any reporter ever had before. He heard us, like Savage. Like Ralph.

He was, I hoped, another link in the chain.

18

A Place of My Own

SHORTLY AFTER THE first interview, my husband and I moved to a townhouse a few miles from my parents. Except for three semesters in college, the only time I have lived more than an hour from my parents was my three years at the Family. My husband had a new job in the area, but it didn't last. Before I realized what was happening, he was on disability, and we were splitting. I had craved it for years. I had dreamed about it. And then, suddenly, in a blink, it was here. I was on my own.

I panicked. I had no money. No job. What was I going to do?

My parents came through. Bob and Peg, for once, showed up for their daughter. They lent me money so I could buy my husband out of the townhouse. They were doing it for Bubby, they told me, or at least that was what I heard.

Twenty-two apartments and houses. I had lived in twenty-two apartments and houses, not to mention my car, since leaving the Family twenty-three years before. Now I had my own place—a place of my own!—for me and my sons.

This was progress. I was losing my bad-husband baggage, and for the first time, I wasn't desperate for another. I didn't need a man to make me feel safe. I wasn't antsy to run out the back door as soon as I walked in the front. I had feared living alone because I feared myself. That's a fear the Family put inside me. But I was ready.

I bought sixteen locks. I bought a dozen security cameras and motion detectors. I configured my home computer into a neural network for security. I changed my phone number, took my old one off the internet, and then scrubbed my personal information. Agent Savage taught me how to bleach my online footprint; she was big on internet privacy. I painted my bedroom black, bought a pair of night-vision goggles, and downloaded an app so I could cut the lights from my bed. Nobody was trapping me in my bedroom. I was creating a trap, a DIY safe room. For a year, I slept on the floor on the far side of my bed. I have often slept on the floor since leaving the Family.

I stopped taking in TTI survivors. My husband had always hated that; he said it was a risk. He had a point, some of those survivors were too troubled to help, but Bubby was never in danger; I made sure of that. I created a safe space for him, in my life and now in my new home. He had his own bedroom on the second floor, with toys. I created a space for my older boys on the bottom floor, separated from my office by a handmade privacy curtain. I was never comfortable with the sliding glass door to the patio. I had an urge to seal it. But I knew the boys needed light and access, so I put a bar across the door and a wooden pole in the corner for self-defense.

Then I shut down my traumatology practice. People make fun of those puffy red float-on-a-ropes lifeguards throw when they swim to drowning people, but there's a reason for them. Someone did a study, and lifeguards were dying because they were grabbing drowners, and the drowners were pulling them down. Distance meant safety; thus the float-on-a-rope.

I had been drowning, and it wasn't just my relationship with my husband. Survivorland is an ocean. It looks calm on the surface, but it's deep, and it's dark. I had been trying to be a lifeguard for too many people. I had been getting too close. And the predators were circling. After the success of the #ISeeYouSurvivor campaign, a group of survivors came after me online. They were the popular crowd. They thought they owned Survivorland, but nobody owns the ocean. I got into an online argument with one of them before realizing it was making me miserable, and it wasn't doing any good.

We couldn't fight each other. It was a dead end. We had to keep our focus on the real enemy, our abusers, but too many survivors never left the Table. They tore other survivors down. They had learned the Game too well.

So I settled my patients with dependable therapists and lay low, for myself and for Bubby. My dive into Survivorland had been a deep dive into my past. It had stirred up a lot of hurt and a lot of sadness. I knew I needed to do something with that grief, so after the stakes-by-the-road plan blew up and I simmered down, a friend and I decided to plant a memorial tree. I wanted to plant it on the old Family grounds, but the sports camp wouldn't let us. Neither would the church down the road, where Tony Argiros was buried. That turned out to be for the best. The tree was for visiting, and it was too painful for survivors to return to the scene of the crimes.

My friend secured a location several miles away on the grounds of a one-room church. After way too much research, we decided to plant a green vase zelkova, a beautiful tree capable of growing to more than fifty feet with a lush green crown. What we really liked, though, was her legendary hardiness. She could survive the toughest conditions, of cold and rocks, heat and drought, and thrive.

I told Survivorland we were going to Delaware County on Saturday to plant her. Immediately, a survivor wrote back, "I'll be there."

Then another. And another. The woman whose rape had sent me to the FBI came. Kevin Argiros came. I had found Kevin, the wheelbarrow kid, in a long-term institutional care facility. His family had put him there after he contracted a brain-eating parasite. The parasite had saved his life, Kevin told me. He was an alcoholic. He went through withdrawal while in a two-month coma, and he hadn't had a drink since.

"How long ago was that?"

"Three years."

"In here?" The place smelled like piss. The average age was about 103.

"Yeah." He shrugged. "I guess this is my home now."

"I'm getting you out," I said.

He was nervous about the tree planting since his family ran the Family. He thought we might blame him. But he was one of us, a survivor of their abuse. I think it was Neil, my old kitchen buddy, who hugged him first.

Neil had taken possession of me after Mike died, and it changed our relationship. He was married. He had a steady job. But whenever I needed him, Neil picked up the phone. In desperate times, he drove hours to sit with me, sometimes in the middle of the night. And I did the same for him. I came when he was hurting. Between survivors, taking possession is a sacred promise and a pact. As a survivor, you need a "3 a.m. call." You need one person you can count on in an emergency. I never thought that person would be Neil, but it was.

It was a brutal dig, mostly because it was 150 degrees (my estimate) with high humidity, and we didn't have good tools, but when the hole was complete, we held a ceremony. The night before, a friend and I had written the name of each dead Family survivor on a scrap of paper. We burned them one by one, along with two blanks for those coming behind. Then I burned my master list of the dead, the one I had shown Savage and carried for years. Those kids were in my heart. I didn't need them in my pocket anymore.

We took the ashes and placed them in the bottom of the hole.

We planted our tree.

We built a small wall around her with stones we'd boosted from the old Family property. I had put out a call: *If you want to honor a loved one, send a stone.* I received hundreds of responses. Many sent rocks. Others sent money, with a request to say a few words, or a prayer, while placing a stone. A mother sent a professionally engraved stone in memory of her son. A couple sent hand-painted stones that looked like they had come from a flowerbed or a local creek. We placed those stones on the top row. Neither Jon's nor Mike's families responded. I haven't heard from either since they died. No judgment. It's hard to lose someone you love. I painted and placed two stones for them.

Mikaela Shwer, the TTI documentarian whose call had saved my life, had interviewed me a few times over the years. She came from California to film the planting of the tree.

Afterward, she took Neil and me to the Hancock McDonald's. She told us, "Order anything you want."

As kids, we had hidden in their bathroom. We had eaten out of their dumpster. Neil and I *housed* their food that day. We ate fries, Big Macs, McNuggets, hot apple pies. We drank the Coke machine dry. We ate everything. Almost.

We did not eat a cheeseburger.

The next day, Suzanne lay down in her bed in Colorado and never woke up. She was an anesthesiologist. She took herself out with an IV full of drugs she lifted from the hospital where she worked.

Her best friend, Lauren, lived in Connecticut. They had been at the Family with me, in my dorm. Lauren wasn't in my Wolf Pack, but she was close.

She came to my house after she heard the news. She cried on my porch. She felt guilty for not stopping Suzanne. She felt guilty for not joining her. She would have joined her, she admitted, if Suzanne had asked. Lauren had the Family diseases: anxiety and depression, complex PTSD, horrible relationships. She loved her son. That woman is dedicated to her son. Her son kept her here, just as mine have kept me.

I think of Lauren and Suzanne every time I visit the tree. That's what makes her special: the memories. The people she represents. Mike Wilson, the reporter, roamed upstate New York on his own, talking with parents, former staffers, and survivors. The one place I asked to personally take him was the tree.

When a photographer from the *New York Times* called in the summer of 2018, almost a year after my first interview with Mike, I asked to be photographed at the tree. I didn't want my photo in the newspaper. I didn't want anyone, especially survivors, to think I thought for a second this was about me. Then I realized I could wear Jon's favorite hat, which I had taken from his apartment after he died. I could let Jon know I remembered him. I loved him. I was doing this for all of us, the living and the dead.

That was when I told Kay, my psych NP, about the Family. Kay was precious to me; we'd been together seven years. I only told her because I had to. I didn't want her to read it somewhere else.

I'll never forget it: she was taking notes, and the pen dropped out of her hand. She hunched motionless over her notepad, then looked up slowly and stared at me. She didn't say anything. She let me say what I needed to say, *and then she never asked me about the Family again*. The door was open. She was inside now. We talked about the Family a lot after that. But she never pressed; she let me say what I needed to say, in my own time.

A few weeks later, Mike Wilson's article ran in the *New York Times* under the headline "'It's Like, Who's Next?' A Troubled School's Alarming Death Rate."

The article was evenhanded, meaning it gave ample space to defenders of the Family. There was this sentence, for instance: "Former students sought to find someone to blame, their first target being the school, only to come to terms with a more likely truth, that their dead classmates had been overcome by the sources of despair and addiction that took seed in their youth and brought them to the school in the first place."

Yeah, Mike, we were diseased when we got there. It was our fault those good people couldn't save us. Same bullshit we'd been hearing our whole life.

But the article, on the whole, was with us. It saw us. It described the school as controversial. It mentioned abuse like Table Topics and the blanket. It talked about how many of us ran away and tried to commit suicide at the Family. It featured my suicide attempt: how I tried to drink bleach after being "groped" and then "reprimanded" for reporting it, only to discover the bottle was vinegar.

Yes, the article placed our deaths in the context of "'high-risk kids . . . in an opioid epidemic and a suicide epidemic,'" as one parent who lost her son to suicide said, but it didn't sugar-coat the fact that our friends' early deaths—102 by the time the article was published—were fucked up and that something had clearly gone wrong at the Family.

And it featured a photograph of Jon. It quoted from his congregational testimony: "The nightmares and psychological scars of being dragged from your home to a place in the middle of nowhere; restrained in blankets and Duct tape; assaulted, verbally and physically—those scars and that trauma never go away. For my friends who have since died from suicide because of the nightmares or those who still suffer the nightmares, our time and our voice will not be in vain."

We were heard. Forget the "context" and double-speak about troubled kids; we were seen. The article was one of the most read of the day. It was picked up in Norway and in other countries around the world.

"Last year," it concluded, "Ms. Ianelli and others from the school planted a tree near the property in Hancock. They placed a plaque before it and named it the Lost Souls Tree. Up close, markings can be read on rocks, remembering dead friends, but in the winter, the tree is bare and slight, easily missed when passing by."

Never missed, Mike. Never missed. For a long time, I went to the tree every month to commune with my friends. I got a tattoo on my forearm, a compass point with her longitude and latitude, marking on my body our tree's specific spot on Earth.

When people ask me what the numbers mean, I tell them, "It's home."

19

The Nexus

L ARRY NASSAR CHANGED everything. In case you've been living under a rock, or found this book buried in the rubble
a thousand years from now (hello, future!), Larry Nassar was
a doctor for the US national gymnastics team. He was credibly
accused of sexually abusing more than 265 victims under the
guise of medical exams, although in his plea deal, he admitted to
only seven. Since at least the early 1990s, victims had been telling
people in power about the abuse, but their reports were covered
up or ignored.

Credible allegations were brought to the FBI in 2015, but the
FBI refused to open an investigation. The male agent who interviewed the victim, *who was world-famous Olympic gold medal-
ist McKayla Maroney*, didn't write a formal report, as required.
According to Maroney, his response to her hourlong testimony
was "Oh, is that all?"

He filed a report seventeen months later, after the *Indianapolis Star* published accusations against Nassar by Rachael Denhollander and another gymnast. That report, lawyers for the victims
claim, was factually inaccurate. The agent was ultimately fired
and his boss forced to resign, but not before it became national

news that the FBI's failures had allowed Nassar to abuse at least sixty-three, and possibly more than a hundred, additional victims.

As Denhollander said before Nassar's sentencing, "I do want to thank you, Judge Aquilina, for giving all of us the chance to reclaim our voices. Our voices were taken from us for so long, and I'm grateful beyond what I can express that you have given us the chance to restore them."

Denhollander was fifteen when Nassar began sexually assaulting her; she was thirty when the story in the *Indianapolis Star* finally broke and thirty-three when she made that statement. If it takes that long for the world to listen to its Olympic heroes, you can understand our frustrations as struggling, nonfamous survivors. As of this writing, the FBI is being sued by Nassar's victims for more than a billion dollars.

"Nassar is the reason the Family case has gotten this far," Agent Savage told me. "Child sexual abuse is a priority right now."

Savage was straight with me. She had been working with a female assistant district attorney. They had tried every direction. They were invested; they wanted this badly. But they didn't have a nexus.

"What's a nexus?"

The victim had to be under twenty-eight, putting the crime within the statute of limitations for child sexual assault. The pedophile had to have traveled across state or international lines to commit the act; otherwise, it fell within the state's jurisdiction, and the state of New York had no interest in our cases. For Savage's office to build a case, the pedophile had to have committed the crime in or traveled through the Hudson Valley area of responsibility (AOR) with the intent to commit the crime. The Family's compound fell outside Savage's AOR by eight miles.

"We have two agents coming down from Albany," Savage told me. This was what Nassar gave us: a second chance, when before, the case would have been shelved. Albany was the main office for upstate New York; these agents had jurisdiction my agent didn't.

"We've given them everything we have, but I need you to get all the information in one place. Explain everything, Liiiz. Make it simple." She stressed that several times: *Make it simple.* "Don't make these boys have to figure it out on their own."

I spent hundreds of hours putting together a book for the Albany agents. It was the book the Truth Campaign had given the education department in 2011, updated with everything I had discovered in the seven years since. Even though I removed most of the nonsexual abuse, it filled a six-inch four-ring binder. I gave one copy to Savage and one to the men from Albany: Agent Smith, a standard-issue white man like the guy in *The Matrix*, and Johnny Cash, who dressed in black and slouched in the corner.

Smith took the book, flipped through it, and then set it aside. They listened to me talk for an hour but didn't say much—and in Johnny Cash's case, not a word.

I was antsy after the meeting. Had it gone well? Had I screwed it up?

Savage took my hands. She wanted this almost as much as I did. But she never got angry or frustrated. Never raised her voice. I never saw her lose control of herself or a situation.

"Be patient, Liiiz. These things take time. You're doing everything right."

She was a devout Christian. She spoke often about her faith, because after three years of meetings, our conversations had gone far past the case. She hadn't had an easy life. She'd been married twice but raised her children mostly as a single mom. We talked about relationships and why they didn't work. She understood the way men broke women down.

Even after everything she'd seen—and FBI agents see horrible things, done by horrible people—she believed in the goodness of the universe. She believed in a universal goodness that directed all things.

"Karma's a bitch," she told me. "God provides. Liiiz, these people will get what they deserve."

I wish I had her faith. I wish I could tell you that, free from my last marriage, things were going well, because I want to be a positive example for you, survivor. I want you to see that the universe rewards bravery, and it bends toward fairness and good things.

But my life was hard. I couldn't hold a job because of frequent anxiety attacks, and I struggled to pay my mortgage. My parents rarely came by, but when they did, it was usually to bring food for my pantry. I didn't ask for it, and I didn't want it. They had to do it for my kids, they told me. Not wanted to, *had* to. They were good to Patrick and Brenden in ways I couldn't be. They took them skiing and to Martha's Vineyard, places I wasn't invited and could never provide.

They resented me, though, for those things. They called me a loser, unstable, an embarrassment. They told me to get my life together. "Quit looking back," my father said as my mother nodded in the background. "Move forward. Get a job. Be an adult."

Every gift I took from them cost me because they took a piece of my pride. It was their fee. But I paid it for my boys.

I had no hobbies. I didn't watch television. I didn't drink, take drugs, play sports, or crochet. I had three friends. I worked as a trauma therapist when I could. I was a mom to Bubby the half of his life he was with me.

On the nights Bubby wasn't with me, I often drove to Hancock. I still kept my trunk packed with the things I needed for these trips: extra clothes and shoes, extra food and water, duct tape, knives, bulletproof vest, medical bag, toilet paper, latex gloves, and a large Maglite flashlight, heavy enough to crack a skull. I drove through Delaware County for hours, looking for ghosts. I often ended up outside the emergency room in Pough-keepsie or Newburgh, watching the sun rise, the ambulances coming in, and the EMTs working.

The rest of the time, I was in Survivorland.

It was dark there, beneath the surface. A few years before, Jodi from SIA and I had agreed to appear on *The Doctors*, an interview show distributed by CBS, to discuss Troubled Teen Programs. Survivors were furious. The show starred Jay McGraw, son of "Dr. Phil" McGraw, and survivors despised Dr. Phil. If there was one person we could turn to dust . . . well, it would be our chief tormentor. (Hello, Robin.) But other than them, it was Dr. Phil, a man who had sent dozens of kids to Troubled Teen Programs on his show. The man who did more than any other person to legitimize these programs for suburban parents.

"We need to be there," I argued. "Survivors have to be part of the conversation."

Survivorland didn't agree. Their hate was so relentless, I stood on the roof of my hotel in Los Angeles, looking at the ground eight floors below, trying to work up the courage to throw myself off. I huddled in the green room before the taping, reading through my socials and crying. They didn't get the crier on *The Doctors*, though. They got the bad-ass bitch. But putting on my armor when it's time for battle doesn't mean I'm not hurting like hell.

The backlash from the *New York Times* article was worse. Someone left a bottle of bleach on my doorstep. Someone sent a hollow-point bullet, carved on the tip for extra damage. Someone mailed me thirty-six cents, an old mob message. Thirty-six cents used to be the price of a bullet. The message: *Try this.*

It wasn't survivors or the Family. You think I didn't call Savage to check? It was random haters. You stick your neck out for a cause—for anything, really—and a thousand people will try to chop it off. That's the world we live in. The messages I got online . . . it's crazy how hateful people can be. All I did was admit to attempting suicide after being raped. My mother found it embarrassing. Strangers begged me to try again.

The items sent to my townhouse were disturbing because I don't know how they found me. I was careful. I wasn't listed any-where. The response from Survivorland was heartbreaking. The popular kids who'd attacked me over #ISeeYouSurvivor attacked me again, but this time others joined in. I was a stuck-up bitch. I thought I was all that. I was in it for the fame.

I was getting a lot of tattoos at the time. I got *Survivor993* on my forearm. I got the Mexican woman from Mike's jacket on my other forearm. The tree tattoo. *Lady Luck*, one of my nicknames, on my knuckles. This was another thing my parents hated about me, my low-class skin. I found my tattoo artist, a Family kid I had known for decades and who I thought was a friend, trashing me online in Survivorland.

I've never told him that. I still go to him for tattoos. I'm out-spoken, but it hurts too much, sometimes, to speak your pain.

I turned my anger on the system, or what I thought of as the system. I argued with Savage. I badgered Ralph. I got in a fight with Brenden's principal. I'm sorry, Brenden; I know that made your life harder. I had knock-down, drag-outs almost every time I saw my dad.

I found out about Bob Runge's funeral a couple hours before it started. A few Family kids were going, so I drove to Hancock, top speed, to meet them. His wife, also a Family staffer, smiled when she saw us. "How nice of you to come."

His daughter, Audra the Viking, pointed to me and said, "Do not let her in here." She had worked at the Family, too. She was the one who'd taken me to the hospital after I'd been knocked unconscious.

I walked past her to the casket, open at the front of the church. I looked down into the face of the man who punched me at my admission, who dropped the knife for Table Topics, who made Carl eat his own vomit. I held this man, and others who'd run the Family like a POW torture camp during the time we were there, responsible for the death of my friends.

I bent close . . . and spit in his face.

Okay, I didn't spit. I thought about it, I tried to stop, but a drop of saliva dripped from my lip. People were staring as I straightened up, wiping my mouth. So I turned, and I strutted—fast—out of the church.

I could hear Audra yelling, but everyone else was in shock. I made it to the last pew before one of the Family kids with me said, "Holy shit, let's get out of here."

We bolted to our cars and tore out of the parking lot. I don't know if they chased us. I don't know if they called the cops. I don't know how you feel about this, and I don't care. I am who I am.

The rape victim, meanwhile, was cracking up. She put herself out when she told her story to the FBI. A lot of us did. Three years in, with another set of agents on the case, she was becoming paranoid. She insisted we go to the sheriff in Delaware County and involve them in the investigation. I told her it was a bad idea. I knew those guys. I had gone to them multiple times. They had always turned away from the Family's abuse.

She insisted. All I can compare it to was the experience of watching three or four straight hours of Table Topics. The pressure became so intense, I felt like I was ripping out of my skin. That was what happened to her, except the pressure built slowly, month by month, until I couldn't stop her, no matter what I said. So I went with her.

As expected, the deputies immediately blew us off. *It's old. The school is closed. Who cares?* They weren't going to interview her, even though we had an appointment. I had to throw my dick on the table: *I'm a former federal employee. I'm a former police instructor. I know our rights.*

"Wait a second. You're not her lawyer?"

She was wearing warm-up pants; I was in a business suit. Always dress for the occasion. "No," I said, "I'm a friend. I'm here for moral support."

They divided us immediately and took us into separate interrogation rooms. And these were interrogations, not interviews. They didn't treat us like victims; they treated us like criminals.

After the interrogation, they went to the Pedophile's house and interviewed him for an hour and a half. They didn't record the interview. They didn't take notes. They treated it like a social call. When they left, he lawyered up.

I blasted the sheriff's office for that. I blasted them when they claimed they didn't have recordings of our interrogations. I have a right to a copy of my interrogation; they denied me that right. I wasn't lying down on that. Sorry, you can't be satisfied with your job performance when you aggressively attack rape victims, tip off a pedophile, and "lose" the case files. The undersheriff wanted to arrest me for threatening him. He was serious. I was facing jail time, because they don't fuck around upstate, and I was a "known troublemaker" in Delaware County. A cop friend had to call and tell the sheriff, who was new to the job, *She's good people; she means well; she's just . . . an overzealous advocate.* Thank God I have friends who are cops.

Soon after, I got hold of Agent Smith's cell number. Not through Savage, through my usual methods. I went to the Newburgh FBI office and threw a shit fit until they let me talk to the director. After I came out, I casually went to a secretary and said I was supposed to get Agent Smith's number. She had just seen me in the director's office for half an hour; she gave it to me.

When Savage showed up that afternoon, Cindy, my favorite receptionist, told her, "Your confidential informant was in here this morning making a scene."

"What confidential informant?" Savage wasn't using any confidential informants.

"Liz. Your CI."

"She's not my CI. She's one of my victims." Sigh. "What did she do?"

I called Agent Smith on his cell phone every morning. He never answered, of course, so I left him a friendly message.

"Hi, Smith, this is Liz. Let's catch those rapists today."

"Hi, Smith, this is Liz. Any news on the rapists?"

I've had blowback on this strategy. People think it's self-defeating to harass an FBI agent. But this is how I do it. I am not a polite person. I am the squeaky wheel screaming from under the ten-ton cart of manure. I'm not going to ask you to look, because I know you won't, but I will damn sure try to force you.

Yeah, my parents hate it. Some online survivors hate it. Random people I lose my shit on hate it, and they should; I hate myself for losing control. But I helped shut down the Family. I helped force an exposé on the Family into the *New York Times*. I'm writing this book. I've done as much as anyone to bring down the TTI, even if it's not nearly enough.

I'm an overzealous advocate. Don't try to change me. I can only be who I am.

And don't worry, I'm tight with Agent Smith. I respect the hell out of the guy. I don't know if I should tell you this—sorry, Smith, if it gets you in trouble—but I caught him once when he was having a particularly terrible night. He was working a heinous case of child sexual abuse. He'd had to sit across from the perpetrator in the interrogation room for hours. And the man wasn't ashamed, and he wasn't sorry.

There are times, when you work in law enforcement, when the evil you witness cuts your soul.

Smith and I talked about his feelings that night—I'm a therapist, I know how—and I got to know him a little. He has a family. He's a good man. He hurts, because he cares. He cared about the Family, and some of that was because he knew me, and I was a pain in his ass.

His passion didn't matter, though, any more than Savage's passion mattered. In child rape cases, the statute of limitations is king. It wasn't more than six months later that Smith sent my Family book back to me. They couldn't make the case. The file was open, he said, but I knew it was back-burnered at best.

I was devastated. All this work. All this pain. Evil must be punished, right, or evil will breed. There had to be karma. There had to be goodness in the universe.

But all this time, I had been fighting reality, and that's hard to do. Correct me if I'm wrong, but how many priests went to prison in the Catholic scandal? How many Boy Scout leaders are serving time for rape? I believe the answer is none.

Nobody was charged at the Seed. Nobody was convicted at Straight. The only reason the founder of Synanon was criminally charged was that he tried to murder a lawyer by having his followers put a rattlesnake in his mailbox. It almost worked. The snake bit the lawyer, but a neighbor happened to be outside and called 911 in time.

But civil cases like the one being pursued by Ralph DeSimone? They had closed churches. They had bankrupted the Boy Scouts. And there was a hero who, in the early 2000s, had shown the way to take on programs in the TTI.

His name is Phil Elberg.

20

Agents of Bad-Ass

PHIL ELBERG WAS a partner in a small, two-partner medical malpractice firm. In 1999, he won a $4.5 million settlement against KIDS of Bergen County, a Troubled Teen Program founded by a Straight, Inc., executive after that program fell into disrepute.

That lawsuit, and the press it generated, essentially ended KIDS, but Phil Elberg didn't stop. In his research for the trial, survivors of KIDS kept telling him, "You need to talk to Lulu Corter. What happened to me was bad, but it was nothing compared to Lulu Corter."

Lulu Corter was sent to KIDS because she wore a skirt that KIDS told her mother was too black and too revealing and thus a sign of an emerging "druggie" lifestyle. She was thirteen. She was picked on, tormented, and tortured for the next thirteen years, with almost all of it paid for by the government. By the end, Lulu Corter was eating herself. During Table Topics (they were called something else in KIDS, but same concept), she would bite chunks out of her arms. This happens to rodents in cages and victims of torture, like prisoners of war, who have lost hope. It's the only thing that gives them a sense of control. Lulu said to keep from hurting others, she had to hurt herself. KIDS had made her think she was a dangerous animal, incapable of being set free. Her grandmother finally rescued her at twenty-six.

Phil Elberg took a new approach with Lulu's case. Other lawyers had gone after TTI programs like Straight for injury, emotional distress, or loss of earnings potential. Phil Elberg went after KIDS for medical malpractice. In a medical malpractice case, it doesn't matter if the person offering the treatment thinks it works; they have to prove it conforms to accepted medical practice. Troubled Teen Programs had always pointed to other Troubled Teen Programs to claim their treatments were mainstream, even when those programs had been shut down for abuse. Phil Elberg brought in actual doctors and therapists to say, no, starvation, hard labor, beatings, psychological torture, and prolonged confinement were not accepted medical practices. It seems obvious, but no one had approached the industry that way: as a medical service provider. And yes, the "therapy" and "addiction treatment" places like the Family and KIDS claim to provide are medical services.

Phil Elberg won a huge settlement for Lulu Corter, although KIDS didn't admit wrongdoing (because they never do, do they?). That victory is important, because Lulu deserved every penny and more for what she endured.

He also set the template. He showed how the industry could be beaten. I don't know if Ralph DeSimone knew Phil Elberg, but I bet he studied that case when he was preparing his suit against the Family.

He's our champion now. Whether he knows it or not, Ralph DeSimone is carrying our torch. He's the new Phil Elberg, and that's my highest compliment, because I know Phil Elberg. He has advised me on personal legal matters. He spent hours talking with Jon about the Truth Campaign, explaining how to stay on the right side of the law. He asked nothing of us. No money. No favors. Nothing. Instead, he repeatedly told us, *You're doing good work. I'm proud to help you. Don't stop.*

I invited him to visit the tree. Crazy, I know. Why would a man like Phil Elberg care about our tree? Why would he drive hours to spend time with a small group of survivors he'd never represented?

He said, "Liz, I would like nothing more than to spend Yom Kippur with you and the other Family survivors."

Yom Kippur. The day of atonement, the holiest day in the Jewish year. Yom Kippur, a day to repent, to pray, but also to remember. I'm sure Phil Elberg had a community to celebrate, blessings to receive, loved ones to cherish and commemorate. He chose to be with us.

He broke the TTI. He smashed the foundation of their tower of shit. They built it back. They plastered over it with the help of government agencies, negligent police departments, and media outlets unwilling to see and acknowledge the truth. And yes, sometimes it feels like the victories don't matter. That their tower will stand forever, no matter what we do.

But they aren't gods, and they aren't good. They are small and evil men and women. They are abusers of vulnerable children. Everything they do is an illusion, a sleight-of-hand unsupported by science or common sense. Every crack weakens them. Every patch in their facade is another entry point to pull them down.

Ralph DeSimone picked up Phil Elberg's sledgehammer and smashed the bastards. He settled his case against the Family on his terms. I don't know the details, and I don't need to. Ralph DeSimone has the goods. He proved everything. He's got the Family by the balls. He gave me the opportunity to do this. To tell my story without fear or compromise.

He contacted me in the fall of 2018. He said, "They're going to pass the Child Victims Act, you know. It's going to happen."

The CVA lifted the statute of limitations on civil suits for childhood sexual abuse for one year. Ralph had been skeptical it would pass, but like I said, Larry Nassar changed everything, even, for a hot minute, the government of the state of New York.

"Liz," Ralph said, "you will qualify."

I said, "Seriously, Ralph? You think I don't know that?"

New York's Child Victims Act was signed into law on February 14, 2019. Ralph DeSimone filed my suit against the Family exactly six months later, at 4:28 p.m. on August 14, 2019, the first day filings were accepted. I was the first woman to file against an institution under the law in the state of New York.

And then, as always, the world made me wait. The gears ground slowly, in some secret place I couldn't see or understand. So I dove back into my comfort zone: Survivorland. Every second I wasn't with my sons, I was lurking, posting, scheming, consoling.

"'Lo," a voice said one afternoon when I picked up the phone. "Hello? Anyone there?" I didn't recognize his voice, but I knew he was in trouble. He was slurring. I heard traffic.

"Where are you?"

"Highway." He was in the middle, by the concrete barrier that divided the lanes going opposite directions.

"Where is the highway?"

"I don't know."

"What's your name?

"Jordan."

"Do you have a contact?"

"My mom."

He gave me the number. I called her on my second phone. I always have a second phone. "Your son is in trouble."

"Who is this?"

"Jordan is in trouble. He's on a highway. Do you know where he might be?"

I switched between them until we figured out his location. They were in Florida.

"Stay on the line," I told his mother. "I'm going to call 911, but I'll come right back."

I clicked over to 911 and relayed the information, then stayed on both lines, keeping the young man and his mother calm, until I heard them through each other's phones, talking in person, and the ambulance arrived.

A couple days later, I received another call. It was Jordan's father, Warren. He wanted to thank me. I had realized during the call that this probably wasn't a drug incident, and I was right. Jordan was having a stroke. But he was okay. They had gotten him to the hospital in time, and he was okay.

Warren wanted to understand who I was and why his son called me. I had no idea until I realized Jordan had gone to the Family. I didn't know him, but he knew me. Somehow, he had my number, even though I'd taken it offline the year before.

Warren hesitated. I heard him breathe deep. "What happened there?" he asked.

It was the question I wanted every parent to ask. It was the question I wanted my parents to ask. They never did. But here was a father, desperate to listen. Jordan had struggled, Warren told me. He was doing well, holding down a job, but it hadn't been easy since the Family.

"What did they do to him?" he asked.

So I explained the Family. I explained the torture, the damaged lives. I explained what I did for survivors and why I felt I had to do it. It was a good conversation. I wish I was having it with my father, but it was a good conversation.

I want to hate our parents. I blame them, sometimes. They pay the TTI. They make it thrive. They are, too often, unable to acknowledge what they did to us. I resent my parents for exactly those things. But then I speak to a father like Warren who listens.

Who is horrified not just by what happened to his son but by what he did to his son by sending him to the Family.

I speak to Harry's mother. We lost Harry years ago, and she's devastated. I wish I could hug her, but she doesn't live near me, and I can't hug. I'm physically incapable. Even the thought makes me queasy. So we talk, mostly about Harry.

Jay hated his father, although I've met Jay's father in recent years, and he's a good man; he's devastated by his mistakes. Jon hated his father. Marisa hated her father. I hate my father. I know why: when a parent you love and trust betrays you, the pain goes deep, and it never goes away.

But I love Harry's mother. And I love Warren, who after our conversation did the most important thing a parent of a TTI survivor can do: He apologized. At one point, Jordan escaped the Family. He made it to a McDonald's in Philly. Warren met him there but wouldn't listen. When Warren said he was sending him back to the Family, Jordan threw his drink across the room. Warren considered it a sign of his son's immaturity. A sign he needed to go back. He knew better now. He apologized.

"It's okay," Jordan told him. "There's no way you could have known."

I will never forget the day I got the call: "Hello, Liz. It's your mother."

I was stunned. "No," I said, "it's not."

She laughed. "It's Jacqueline, Heather's mom. She told me you were looking for a mother."

Heather was my most important friend from Survivorland. The other people I met there, like M— and Jodi and Natalie, helped me with my outreach; Heather helped me with my life. We talked every day. That girl has listened to me cry so many tears at four in the morning, I can never repay her. A lot of those conversations were about my mother. My parents don't know this, but every time we argued, or they chastised and dismissed me, I broke down. But only after they were gone. Only with Heather, one of the few people I trust. I guess Heather told her mother about those conversations.

"I'm here, Liz," she said, "if you need a mom."

"Okay," I said. "But what do I have to do?"

Jacqueline still laughs about that. You don't have to earn a mother, I guess. You just have one. But it was never like that for me.

I knew Jacqueline was doing this out of guilt. Everyone who knew her in Survivorland loved Jacqueline. She was the parent we all wanted. But it was harder for Heather. Sending her to the Family and then not believing her for eight years left scars. And Jacqueline is overprotective. Heather overdosed twice; even though she has been clean for years, Jacqueline still panics whenever her thirty-something daughter doesn't return her call. She once called the cops for a welfare check just because Heather didn't call her back the same day. Heather resents being treated like a child.

But that's the bargain, parents, so listen up: apologizing doesn't magically make it right. It's a beginning, not an end. Your child will not forgive you overnight. They will not trust you overnight. Your relationship will never be as good as it would have been without the TTI, no matter how hard you work, and that's alright. Do the work. Things will improve.

Your child will never be as he or she would have been. And that's alright, too. We are partly the people who influenced us over the years, and you gave away your right to guide us when you gave us away to someone else.

The greatest influence in my life—the person I have modeled myself after more than any other—is Robin Ducey. I can't escape Robin Ducey. She is in my DNA. She is in my soul. She was the mother I never had. I hated her. I rebelled against her every day. And yet she was my role model by default. I didn't realize it for a long time, but everything I knew about being a strong woman, I learned from her.

And it hurt me. Robin taught me that to be a strong woman, you must be cruel.

I think about her whenever I think of the darkness in Survivorland, like our feuds over *The Doctors* or #ISeeYouSurvivor or Paris Hilton. I was one of twenty survivors interviewed by Paris for her documentary. (None of that footage has ever been seen.) It did not go well, and I let Survivorland know I thought she was a phony, using our trauma to promote herself—or, in this case, her new song about her boyfriend. I still think that's true!

But so what? It was a chance for the world to see us. It was more exposure than we'd received in a long time, if not ever. And we blew it. The group Paris teamed up with were the popular-kid survivors, the ones who bullied me over #ISeeYouSurvivor and the *New York Times*, and they used their moment in the sun to bully Survivorland. Then they turned on each other and ended up in litigation. We squandered our chance, in other words, with infighting and arguments. That's the Robin Ducey in us, because Robin hurt a lot of girls. We learned cruelty from her, or other staffers like her at other programs, and we learned it well. When we feel threatened, when we disagree, we become rolling balls of razor blades.

We're still chained, too many of us, to the pole.

But I'm trying. I'm watching Phil Elberg's kindness. Ralph DeSimone's dedication. Mike Wilson's hunger for the truth. Warren's and Jacqueline's ability to change, and its power.

I'm embracing a new model for womanhood, and it's . . . who do you think? . . . Agent Savage, of course. She's not a mother to me. She has her own grown daughters. But I've watched her more than she knows, and she's taught me to slow down. To think. To (try) not to lose control, no matter what happens. To figure out what is right, and why it is right, and to pursue it with passion and grace. She answers my calls. She takes me to lunch, and she asks about my life. She gives me advice. She shakes her head at my foolish mistakes; I know she finds me wild. She talks me through better options. But she has never said I was a bad person or a problem. She has never told me I have to change.

She says, "You are a good person, Liz. You are a strong person. You are the strongest person I know for surviving this."

She sees me. And she doesn't hate me.

She takes my hand, every time, and tells me, "I believe in you."

She has no idea how much those words have meant to me. I guess she'll find out from this book.

She was a social worker before she was an FBI agent. I discovered that recently, and it makes sense. She has a social worker's gift for putting those in pain and peril first and knowing what they need.

No one is coming, I thought in the blanket. *No one is ever coming.*

But Jon came with a glass of milk. Mike O'Donnell came with a cool smile. My children came to teach me what love means. Kay showed me I'm not alone and then passed me on to Connie and my beloved therapist Dorothy when she retired. Heather talked me through my sadness. Jacqueline and Warren modeled contrition. Phil Elberg gave us a sledgehammer. Ralph DeSimone gave us the muscle to swing it. Savage didn't nail the Pedophile—I know you're out there, Savage, don't worry, I'm still working, I will find your nexus—but she showed me what strong women are really like.

You don't have to be cruel to be powerful. You don't have to hurt others to help yourself. Diana Savage cared: for her daughters, her community, her FBI, and her victims. She saw us as people to help, not problems to solve. She was hard as nails. The woman is basically unbreakable. I couldn't crack her, and you know me, I pushed the envelope a thousand times. Savage just kept smiling. She just kept saying, "Don't worry, Liiiz, I'm with you. I believe in you."

Her kindness didn't make her weak. It was the opposite. Her love was her superpower. Diana is Wonder Woman's name, you know. Diana Savage, who loves Wonder Woman, and collects Wonder Woman tchotchkes in her off-duty life, was a hero for the same reason Wonder Woman was a hero: she was good. She used her powers, always, to help others in need.

They exist, that's what I'm telling you, survivor. The world is full of negligence and small-mindedness and half-assed excuses, but it also contains good people who love us and want to help.

So reach out. Believe in goodness. You are not alone. They will come.

I was hospitalized in late 2019 for a colon resection surgery. Physically, I'm a wreck. I have degenerate ligaments. I have fibromyalgia. I have spinal problems. I've had my gallbladder removed and my left knee reconstructed. It's the emotional stress of my teen years and the physical stress of insufficient nutrition and rest during puberty. Those are important developmental years, and my body was not allowed to develop properly. Even in our thirties and forties, a lot of female Family survivors are physically breaking down.

A resection is for a condition called floppy colon. I got a floppy colon because I held my poop too much. That started when my adult relative started raping me, but it got worse at the Family. We didn't have privacy, and I'm not a public pooper. The open toilet gave me anxiety. And psychologically, I needed something to control. That's me: *See me, world! Embrace me, world!* I have eating disorders. I have sleep disorders. I can't even poop right.

Savage and her partner came to my townhouse after the surgery. They sat on my bed as I lay recovering. They are the only outsiders I have let into my bedroom since I've lived alone, another fact I doubt they know.

They said, "You're doing good, Liz. You're going to be okay."

And I believed them, because they were strong women, and good women, and I was trying hard to be like them, and even though I failed at that, every day, they still believed in me. They believed in me more than I believed in myself. And that created a positive spiral. It lifted me up when for so long, so many people around me had been determined to bring me down.

A month later, when the pandemic hit, I was only two days off my colostomy bag.

21

Please

FOR SOMEONE LIKE me, who spent most of her time inside and online, the daily effect of the pandemic was minimal. My boyfriend moved in, but we had been seeing each other for months, and I was ready. Bubby's father and I had to change our custody schedule, but it was more a matter of lengthening stays than subtracting days. The psychological effect, though, as I watched people die by the hundreds, then thousands, was immense. It felt like the only thing to do was hunker down and wait for the virus to find us, and you know me, that's not what I do.

I had social work degrees, with an expertise in trauma. I was trained as an EMT. I was . . . mostly recovered from major surgery. I went on the government job sites and signed on for duty. I had to leave my children with my ex-husbands because of the risk of infection. But the money was great; it would help me give them things I hadn't been able to over the last several years. And the need was greater. I couldn't sit and do nothing when people were in trouble and I was trained to help. It's not the Survivorland way.

I was assigned to Billie Jean King stadium in Flushing, Queens, for three months. This was during the first wave in the spring of

2020; we worked mostly in Elmhurst. The carnage there was legendary: sick people dying in hospital halls, refrigeration trucks as morgues. Doctors and nurses were collapsing from exhaustion and sorrow. It was a jolt to America, to our sense of safety and self.

To me, it was a jolt of electricity. My duty tour in Queens made me feel useful and alive. I often forget I am at my best in a crisis. Not a personal crisis, because I get too aggressive. That's what the authorities tell me. They are put off by my "overzealous advocacy," as a judge in a custody case characterized it. But when someone else is in crisis, when a stranger or friend needs me, I tap the fire that always burns inside me. I can go twelve hours without tiring. I can stay in the zone, walking the line between taking control and being there, emotionally, for those in need.

I'm not saying my heart wasn't breaking. I sat with hundreds of people whose loved ones were dying twenty feet away, and they weren't allowed to see them or hold their hand. Of course I was devastated. I spent the day in a hazmat suit; I had to be disinfected at the end of every shift. I talked to my children on the phone every night, but it was more a reminder of how much we were losing than a comfort.

After Queens, I signed up for another duty tour, because they needed people like me. This time, I went to McAllen, Texas, near the Mexican border. America thinks Elmhurst was horrific. Elmhurst was merely a war zone. South Texas was hell.

There was no hospital. We worked out of a converted community center with intermittent air conditioning. It was 104 degrees and muggy. A hurricane had dumped a flood, and all the snakes and spiders and poisonous lizards were out of their lairs. We had amazing food service from Christina and Steve, two local heroes, but we had to hump our equipment a quarter mile from the employee parking area. The pack weighed fifty pounds, and we carried it most of the day. There were twice as many dying as in Elmhurst, and one-tenth the beds. All day long, I saw mothers and fathers, sisters and brothers, with a loved one dying in the seat beside them, driving right past our triage center and on into the desert.

Finally, I found a huge piece of cardboard, asked someone to help me with basic Spanish, and stuck a sign by our entrance that said, in Spanish: WE ARE NOT ICE. Other social workers laughed at my foolishness, but cars started stopping. And yet, for most, there was nothing we could do. What was the death rate? Seventy percent? Maybe 75 percent? The people were too sick, the field hospital too rudimentary. I sat with three or four generations of tight-knit families and told them their abuela, abuelo, hija, or hijo had died behind the curtain, just out of sight. I sat with four or five siblings, the oldest maybe ten, the youngest barely out of diapers, and told them their father had died. Then, five minutes later, I told them their mother had died, too. I did that every day for three months.

And every day, when I drove the thirty miles to the crappy motel two towns over where the government was putting me up, I passed a billboard that said the coronavirus was a hoax.

One week, they gave me a room on the Texas coast. Every day, I went from working my ass off in that hellscape to a resort where everybody was drunk and nobody was wearing a mask.

You want me to bring this back to the Family? Fine, how about this: we're too selfish, as a people, to see past our own fat tits. We don't care what's happening around the corner as long as it's not happening to us. We, the Family survivors, have lived that reality for decades. Shut up about your trauma, complainers, and hand me a margarita.

By the time I left Texas, I was broken. My energy was gone. My sense of purpose was buried under my physical and emotional exhaustion. I hadn't slept in weeks. I'd lost seventeen pounds. I just wanted to climb into my bed, in my black bedroom, in my air conditioning, and curl into a ball for the rest of the year.

But I hadn't seen Bubby in three months, and I needed to be a mother to him. He needed to spend time with his brothers, Patrick and Brenden, so Mike brought them over. One of my great joys is that Mike and I get along. We were too young when we married, but we grew up, and we figured out the coparenting thing. Our boys are incredible young men. They were good to Bubby.

Ralph called. New York had anticipated two thousand claims under the Child Victims Act. They blew past that number in a month. They exceeded ten thousand lawsuits, even before they extended the filing period by a year. Ten thousand victims of child sexual abuse in one state, all living with no chance of justice because of the statute of limitations. Just think about that.

It's slow, Ralph kept telling me. *But we'll get there. We're moving.*

Now my suit had been lumped with three others and was going forward. We were known as the Zurich Four, because the Family's insurance policies had been chopped up among companies, and our four were owned by Zurich Insurance Group, a company that had apparently made an extremely poor risk assessment. They probably had to pay their fancy lawyer more than they made on our policies. But hey, you do business with the devil, you eat his turds.

The first step, Ralph told me, was a deposition. I'd have to tell my story to a hostile lawyer. I wasn't afraid. I was excited. That was a captive audience. But knowing the deposition was coming forced me to confront my past. It forced me to think through, in more detail than ever before, what had happened to me, and that sent me to a darker place than my bedroom. It's funny—not funny ha-ha but funny WTF—that no matter how many times I confront my trauma, it rolls back on me in a different form.

I worked through my fears with art. I had for years drawn a comic called *Annie Effit* about a girl who just didn't give a fuck but always came out ahead. I posted them online. Annie had fans in Survivorland, but she was mostly for me. That winter, I used the same style to make quick line drawings of my experiences at the Family. Several appear in this book. As you can see, they are not realistic. They are quick sketches, two steps above stick figures. It was my emotions I captured in those drawings, and because those feelings were so common among survivors, I decided to post them to my Facebook page.

My deposition was scheduled for March 2021. In January, I was hit with an emergency custody order. My ex-husband's girlfriend had seen my drawings online; my ex-husband wrote to the court in a hand-scrawled complaint that "the postings are so disturbing they caused me to be alarmed and fear for mine and my four year old son's safety." He said my past experiences of abuse made me unstable and dangerous. The court granted his motion. I lost custody of Bubby. Over drawings.

The judge gave us a court date in early March. My husband would argue for permanent custody. I had to prove I wasn't an unfit mother. Over drawings.

You think I'm not terrified of the truths in this book?

I went to a dark place when I lost my son. I went into my garage and pulled out my hammer. Then I saw the tattoo on my left ribs where Robin had kicked me, the one I'd put there as a reminder of my strength before Jon, Mike, and even Marisa died. It said:

> *The horrors in*
> *her heart lit*
> *the flames in ours*
> *and she was always willing*
> *to burn for everything*
> *she has ever loved.*

It had never stopped me from self-harm before, but now, after years of fighting, I was stronger. I put down the hammer.

"This is going to be tough, Liz," Ralph told me. "The lawyer will try to break you. That's his goal, to break you. You don't understand how tough this is going to be."

He was trying to strengthen me; he knew I was struggling without my Bubby. Honestly, if I hadn't gotten my custody back at the hearing, I wouldn't have survived my deposition. I might not have been able to start it. Years of work would have been destroyed.

But I did it. I got my custody restored.

A week later, on the morning of my deposition, my boyfriend dumped me. "I've lost you to Survivorland," he said.

I was a wreck on my drive to New York City: abandoned, hurt, overwhelmed. Mikaela Shwer had sent a crew to film me; they were in the car, asking me questions, and that didn't help. The deposition was over Zoom because of the pandemic, but I was doing it in Ralph's trying-too-hard orange-and-green office on Fifth Avenue. (Ralph knows his decor sucks; we've talked about it.) I got lost on the way to the parking deck despite my GPS. I didn't want to wear my nice clothes while driving, so I changed into my witchy dress in the parking garage. Specifically, it was a Wednesday Addams Halloween costume I had found at the Goodwill.

"How does it look?" I asked the cameraman.

"I'm not supposed to comment. Pretend I'm not here."

Ralph had given me a detailed map from the parking lot to his office, even though it was only a block away. Ralph's clients were not the most capable, I gathered. Apparently, I fit right in, because I took a wrong turn and panicked, even though all the streets were numbered. The woman directing the shoot had to step in and help me. She left me at the door to the building because she wasn't allowed to film inside.

"Hey, Liz," she said, "you look good."

"Thanks," I said.

"Good luck."

Please.

Ralph had drilled me before the deposition, like a nervous dad before prom. "He will trick you, Liz. He will dominate the conversation. He will cut you off and not let you say what you want." *He's going to fuck you, Liz. That's what all these boys want. They want to fuck you.*

Please.

I had convinced Ralph to give me the name of Zurich's attorney: Howard Mankoff, from New Jersey, licensed for this case in the state of New York. I studied Howie on social media. Howie had a nice big house. Howie had a nice family. Howie tootled into New York in his Mercedes, probably listening to Mozart or the Eagles or something bougie like that. Howie was soft.

I had been waiting for this opportunity for twenty years. Do you really think I was going to let a man like Howie dominate me? Do you really think I wasn't going to say what I came there to say?

Please.

Howie never knew what hit him.

22

Alive

ABOUT A MONTH after my deposition, I went into the hospital for back surgery. I don't have definitive medical proof, but I know my back problems started in the blanket. I was never right afterward. I was in constant pain. The Family finally told my parents to take me to a doctor, and they never sent anyone to a doctor.

I remember him muttering, "That's unusual," when he looked at my X-ray, but I didn't answer his questions. The Family would know. Somehow, if I told him about the torture, Robin would know.

Apparently, I had a bulging disk. My father wrote a note to the Family asking them to hold me out of physical activities, but I didn't know that. And they didn't care. I carried cinder blocks, moved rocks, dug graves, and performed hard manual labor in excruciating pain. Knowing those bastards, they probably made me do more physical Sanctions because of the note. They exploited every weakness, even injuries.

This was my sixth back surgery. X-rays of my spine looked like a toolbox, it had so many screws in it. The screws started near the bottom, and they were working their way up. Eventually, I'll need a full spine replacement.

Just kidding. They can't do that. They will probably just fuse my back into a rod and prop me in a corner, but I have five, maybe six more good years.

My surgery went terribly wrong. The operation was fine. I had pain, but I thought it was normal. A few weeks later, it was worse. I tried to muscle through it like I always do. I had been in my bed, we think, for three days when Savage found me delirious, bone pale, and dangerously dehydrated.

I was rushed back to the hospital for a cleanup of my surgical area. The surgeon opened my back and scraped away the infection with a knife. When I got home, things weren't right. I felt like I was going to pass out. My brain was having trouble processing. I was hallucinating but didn't realize it. I decided to lie down for a nap. Then I changed my mind, thank God, and stepped onto my porch for fresh air.

That was when I got a call from the lab. They had finally read my medical tests, taken before the surgery, and realized I had *E. coli*/staph/osteomyelitis. I couldn't follow what they were saying because the infection was shutting down my brain.

"Call an ambulance," they said. "Call. An. Ambulance. You need to get to the emergency room right now."

I called my mother.

She picked me up and, oh, my God, did she drive fast. I was delirious, but I could tell she was driving fast. My mother earned her angel wings that day because her driving saved my life. By the time we arrived, I was coding. They rushed me to the first room in the ER. I knew from my EMT days that was bad. The first room was reserved for life-and-death.

And that was what happened. I died. I was flatlined, out of my body, looking down from the ceiling, as the nurses rushed to wrap me in bright white blankets. All that was missing was the duct tape.

That's my Alive Day: June 30, 2021.

I woke up a week later in a hospital bed, full of tubes. It was a long and grueling struggle back to health. I lost so much weight, my cheeks sank into my face. The medicine to fight the infection was so strong, my back teeth turned chalky and disintegrated in my mouth. My hair fell out. My beautiful hair. I have a love-hate relationship with my hair. Like eating, like sleeping, like pooping, the Family took an ordinary thing and turned it into anxiety. I had worn my hair short over the years. I had worn it long. But being bald terrified me. Being skeletal terrified me. When I looked in the mirror, it wasn't me.

I was alone because of COVID restrictions. I was agitated and paranoid, with periodic medicine- and infection-based hallucinations. I didn't trust the food, because I have paranoia around eating. I recoiled from being touched. I formed a trauma bond between the hospital and the Family, my therapist later told me. I thought Robin was finishing the job she had started in the blanket: the destruction of my soul. And I hated it. I hated that I was dying. And I hated that the Family was winning. I posted a "last" video one day, sure this was the end.

Remember me, I said to Survivorland. *Remember that I tried.*

Not that I won, because how could I win if the Family killed me? That I fought. That I tried.

But guess what? The Family didn't finish me. I am, in fact, currently alive. I rolled out of the hospital in a wheelchair about three months after my Alive Day, barely able to walk across a room.

The next week, Ralph called. Zurich had settled.

We won. We freaking won.

Ralph DeSimone did that for me. For us. He saw the potential—no, he saw an injustice that had to be righted—and I can't thank him enough. Ralph was the first man, aside from Jon, who was supersmart and still liked me. He was protective in a way no man had been since Jon. He gave me advice I will always cherish: "If you want to live a good life, Liz, always do the right thing."

I wish I could say our victory made everything right. That the recognition of their abuse, and the money that came with that recognition, soothed the pain. That it made up for the losses.

It wasn't like that.

An insurance company paid the settlement. The Family paid nothing. They admitted no wrongdoing. No staff member was punished. As with the Truth Campaign, the sadists skated. A faceless corporation was left holding the bag.

But it's a crack. It's another crack in the foundation of their tower of shit. It's proof, again, that they are wrong, their practices are evil, and catastrophically so. And one day, with enough cracks, their tower will fall. I promise you that. One day, the TTI will collapse, and the right people will pay.

I wish I could say the money made it right in my personal life, but I guess this is where I admit that my father let me down there, too. When I was twelve, I nailed dead frogs to the house, hoping to get his attention. I'd been that frog my whole life, strung up in front of him, turned inside out, desperate for him to see my pain. He was a personal injury attorney; he had been staring at a perfect case for decades. Phil Elberg, after all, had won his clients $10 million from KIDS. But my father couldn't see the abuse when it was happening to his own daughter. He couldn't see the abuse *because* it was happening to his own daughter. He couldn't see me, even though his life was dedicated to helping people like me.

Once Ralph showed the way, though, he wanted in. So I let my father clear my settlement checks through his accounts. He said it would make things easier, and I wanted to believe him. I have always wanted to believe in him. But after the checks cleared, he wouldn't give me the money.

When I pressed him on it, he demanded my brother and sister and I join him on a Zoom call. He told my siblings I had won a settlement, which was private and privileged information. He said I had accused him of trying to steal it, but I was the one who had stolen from them. My behavior had ruined their vacations. The expense of my actions had cheated them of their rightful shares. He was going to give me my money, he said, but I had caused my mother and father so many problems, including having to cash out some of their retirement savings, that I owed them. He said I owed them for the mortgage they had taken out on my townhouse.

That's when I discovered I didn't own my own place. My parents hadn't helped me buy out my ex-husband; they had bought the property themselves. I was their tenant. I wasn't paying off my mortgage every month, like I thought; I was paying my parents rent. You probably think I'm stupid for not knowing that. I signed the papers. I sent the payments. But I'm not stupid. I fell for it because I wanted it. I have always wanted my parents to be there for me.

It was humiliating. My siblings being told my private business, my father claiming I'd screwed up my family's lives, not realizing I didn't own my townhouse: every second of that Zoom call was humiliating. My father took my triumph—which I had suffered for, and hustled for, and my friends had died for—and turned it into shame.

When he came to me a few days later, he had a different reason for withholding money. He mentioned things my parents had done for me over the years. They'd given me their old Subaru, for instance, because I lost my car in the divorce—it was in my husband's name—and they weren't using it anymore. I bought the title for a dollar, or so I thought. Nope. They were charging me for a four-month loan—and I'd spent almost every day of those four months in the hospital.

"I have an itemized bill," my father said.

He tried to hand it to me. It was literally a piece of paper with a price for every kindness my parents had ever done for me.

"I don't want it," I said. Who would want such a thing?

We must have argued, because I remember the last thing my father said to me as he walked out the door: "You're just lucky we aren't charging you for our pain and suffering."

I don't know how much my parents took. I can't know. It would kill me. It's killing me now, admitting that nothing they ever did for me was out of love. Everything had a price.

And the rest of the money . . . it helped. It really helped my kids. I bought a new car for the first time. (So long, "rented" Subaru.) I bought groceries. I sent them to summer camps. I adopted my dog, Tails. He's mild mannered but up for anything. He's loyal. He may be blind and deaf, but Tails is the perfect dog, and I adore him.

But I hated the money. I thought the money had ruined our family.

It took me a long time to realize the money hadn't changed anything. It had only showed me who we were and what we really meant to each other.

23

Love in the Wild

ONE OF THE people who stayed in touch with me in the hospital was Mike Wilson, the reporter from the *New York Times*. Like Agent Savage, like Ralph DeSimone, like Phil Elberg, he had seen too much. He couldn't look away.

He thought I was dying. He interviewed me for an article, thinking that if I died from my old Family injuries, it might be a story. But guess what: no article. I am currently alive!

When we won the settlement, though, the *Times* published Mike's article about our victory. "Survivor993 Is Not Alone," the headline read. I cried when I saw it. I called the headline writer to thank him. It put into words what I wanted from my efforts in Survivorland: to honor my pack, to save my fellow survivors, to be less alone. This time, Mike didn't pull his punches on what had happened at the Family. He didn't use a euphemism like "groped." He said I'd been "sodomized." I hated that word. It was accurate, but it felt like a violation.

My parents hated the article.

But a professional writer in Georgia must have loved it, because he found me, even though I'm hidden. He wrote me a long email. He wanted to help me tell our story. He thought it could save lives. I trusted him. I could tell he was like Mike, like Savage, like Ralph: doing the right thing for the right reasons. He saw us. He was for us. That's how this book came about. It found me.

I cried when a publisher offered to publish our story. Not my story—our story, all of us who've lived the abuse. Then I got scared. This was real. It was happening. I had an opportunity, and a responsibility, to speak for Jon, for Mike, for Marisa and Jay and Heather and M— and everyone alive and dead who had been hurt by the TTI. I had a chance to knock down their tower of shit. Me. A nobody. A woman cursed and hated her whole life.

The writer wanted to come to my house. He wanted me to show him the sights. I hate it when they come in person. Why do they always want to come in person?

I hated the thought of a stranger coming into my house, into my life, rifling through my head. Who was this guy?

Turns out, he was a dork. Just a regular old dork. He came to my house. We sat in my office for days, just talking. Tails kept trying to sit on his lap, but Tails is a big old boy. That's when you know someone is okay, when your blind-deaf dog adores him.

We went out for dinner on the seventh night. On the eighth morning, he came in laughing. "We ate out together last night."

"So?"

"When I got here, you made me eat by myself. Then we ordered pizza. Last night, you ate in public. In a crowded restaurant. With another person."

He knew my disorders. We had talked about them, of course.

"Your posture is different," he said. "Your clothes are different." I wore nothing but black the first few days. Now I was wearing a white T-shirt that said, "Mama Tried." I didn't know it was Merle Haggard. Mike had posted those words the day before he died.

"You know what else?" he said.

"What?"

"You're not wearing your wig."

I had worn wigs since leaving the hospital. They were long and red, like my old hair. But it was hot in my office. That's what I told myself, anyway, when I took it off. I was hot. It felt better with my new, natural, goose-down hair.

When we went out for dinner for the second time, I didn't wear my wig. I brought it with me, I carried it a few steps out of the car, then turned around and put it back. We went to the same restaurant as the night before. I had eaten with Agent Savage at this restaurant. That was why I knew it and felt comfortable. When I walked in, the owner didn't recognize me. She was a friend. I had been ordering from her restaurant for more than a year.

But I was different now, and it wasn't just my hair. I was different because I had unburdened myself by telling my story—by having someone listen.

To speak. To be heard. It's what I want for everyone, especially you.

"We can go to Hancock tomorrow," I said.

He had been pressuring me to take him to Hancock and the old Family property, but I kept making excuses. Now I went home to pack the necessities: blanket, duct tape, extra clothes, food and water, flashlight.

That's when I realized this was my last trip to Hancock. I had driven there a thousand times since running away from the Family. I had haunted that place, like it had haunted me. But I knew, suddenly, that I didn't need to go there anymore. One last time, to say goodbye, and I was free.

We drove to the tree. We met Neil there, since he was coming from a different direction. It was early spring. The snow was two feet deep. I brushed it away from the stones. The first stone I uncovered, not knowing who I was digging toward, was Mike. Then Jon. Then everyone else, pausing over each name to remember.

My soft Georgia writer wasn't prepared for upstate New York. He was wearing Skechers in the snow. So we went through the back door of the one-room church. Neil and the writer sat in a pew to talk. I went up to the balcony and started futzing around, putting my nose into everything.

I wasn't eavesdropping, but I stopped when I heard Neil mention the blanket. He and I had never discussed it. I had never talked about it with anyone from the Family except Jon. Not only was Neil telling the story, I realized, but he was telling a slightly different story than the one I remembered.

I was nearly unconscious during that confrontation. The accusations from the staff in the downstairs office were so emotionally devastating, and so long-winded, I was barely hanging on. But I remembered being abused and destroyed by my fellow teens. I remembered the hatred in their eyes as they thrashed me at the pole. I remember it being a typical Table Topic, same as any other day.

Neil was saying it wasn't like that. A couple boys took the bait, trashing and slut-shaming me, but after a few minutes, they sensed the mood, and the room grew quiet. The staff laid into me; they goaded my fellow teens to lay into me; but no one else attacked me, even though it put them at risk.

After the girls wrapped me in the blanket and dragged me away, it was dinnertime. We had to sing before dinner. But that night, nobody sang. When I heard Neil say that, my brain exploded all over that church. To not sing at the Family. It was unheard-of. It was unspeakable.

I thought of the scene in *The Handmaid's Tale* when the handmaids dropped the rocks. I had thought of myself as June, the handmaid who dropped the first rock in defiance of the sadistic

Aunt Lydia, or as one of the bad bitches who followed her. I had imagined myself strutting down the street to my doom with my head held high.

But I was Janine, the abused and frightened girl they were supposed to stone to death. I was the reason the kids at the Family dropped their rocks. If I was a leader of the resistance—and I don't think I was—it wasn't because of anything I did; it was because of something *everyone else did for me*. That's why the Family kept me in the blanket so long. That's why Robin worked so hard to get me to "confess my lies." Because the one time the kids at the Family rose up, in defiance, it was on my behalf, to protest their treatment of my rape.

I know those kids didn't love me. Most didn't even like me. There are a handful who would spit in my face right now if I walked through the door. But I found love in the wild that afternoon when I heard what they had done. I felt it flowing through the church windows, through the pews, through the stones and the rocks, our tree and the forests nearby. Through the snow, through the grass beneath, through the roads and the fields, the graves and the pond, and back through my feet on the warm wood floor of that cold country church. It was a love that bound us, a love that flowed so strongly even the Family could never stop it or take it away.

This story was never about them. They are weak. They are bent. They are nothing.

It's not about our allies, as important as they are.

This story is about us. It's about what we can do for each other. It's about our strength. It's about our talent. It's about our perseverance. We don't need justice, and we don't need revenge. We just need to live, and live well.

I see you, survivor. And you see me. And that is enough.

There was a rope hanging at the back of the balcony. It was tied like a noose, but I knew it was something more. It was too high to reach, so I climbed onto the back of a pew, and I jumped, and when I grabbed it, I rang the steeple bell. I jumped again, and I rang the bell. I rang it until it rang out loud and clear, past our tree and our stones, the fields and the ponds.

I rang the bell because I had found love in the wild, I had found love in the world, and I knew that I was free.

Resources

First and most importantly: *do not kill yourself.* I cannot stress that enough. It doesn't help; it only hurts others. FACT: Talking to someone about suicide does not make anyone more likely to do it. If you ever encounter a stranger about to jump—stand back, move slowly, keep an open stance, use a calm voice, listen, find out their name, and keep them talking until the men and women in blue and red roll in. But if you must, preserve life by any means necessary. You might get punched, but you'll both live.

If you are actively contemplating suicide, call 988 or 911 immediately. Be honest. I have been on the other end of hundreds of such calls: We cherish your honesty. We are there only for you, so let us help you. You are not alone.

If you need mental health help but are not actively in crisis, contact the Suicide & Crisis Lifeline: 988. It is nationwide, established, and guaranteed to have someone on the other end to answer at all times.

For information on specific mental health issues:

988 Suicide & Crisis Lifeline: 988lifeline.org

American Psychological Association (APA): apa.org

NAMI (National Alliance on Mental Illness): 1-800-950-6264

These organizations will help you find the right resources in your area.

If you are in a domestic violence situation, call 911 and *order a pizza*. The operator may not catch on, but keep trying. It sometimes takes a few "orders," but they are trained for this.

If the domestic situation is actively violent, order a pizza *with pepperoni*. Never hang up, even if you have to drop the phone. Dispatchers hope you do so they can hear what's going on.

Most bars have a safe word—a drink you can order to let the bartender know you need help, including a ride home. It's often referred to as an angel shot. If you are worried for any reason, ask a bartender (preferably female) for the safe word when you arrive. And know this: every establishment with a kitchen is required to have an exit door. Use it if you have to. Don't worry. It's fine. I've done it dozens of times.

Survivors of Institutional Abuse (SIA) is the best resource for learning about and entering Survivorland. I don't recommend any others.

If you want to explore Survivorland on your own, start by googling "Troubled Teen Industry." It's a big ocean out there, with lots of islands. Happy sailing!

The International Cultic Studies Association (ICSA), www.icsa home.com, is academic and requires a membership, but you can find good information if you poke around.

For books:

The Boy Who Was Raised as a Dog and Other Stories from a Child Psychiatrist's Notebook by Dr. Bruce Perry (with Maia Szalavitz) explains the long-term effects of trauma. Read it, then give it to your mom.

The Girls in the Wild Fig Tree: How I Fought to Save Myself, My Sister, and Thousands of Girls Worldwide by Nice Leng'ete inspired me when I was writing this book. Nice (who is from Kenya) ran from genital mutilation—that means getting your clitoris cut off, girls—when she was nine years old, then came back as a grown-up ass-kicker on behalf of other women. Whenever I wanted to give up, I thought, *Did Nice give up?* Hell, no!

Help at Any Cost: How the Troubled-Teen Industry Cons Parents and Hurts Kids by Maia Szalavitz is a must-read if you care about the TTI. What are you waiting for? Google her name for her excellent articles as well; there ain't many Maia Szalavitzes out there, so the hunting is easy.

The Immortal Life of Henrietta Lacks by Rebecca Skloot is about abuse in medicine, but it made me feel like every woman can make a difference, even if she doesn't know how right now.

Institutionalized Persuasion: The Technology of Reformation in Straight Incorporated and the Residential Teen Treatment Industry by Marcus Chatfield is dry—it was the author's thesis—but the stats he compiled are earthshaking. I wish so much that more professionals would read this book.

Unbroken Brain: A Revolutionary New Way of Understanding Addiction by Maia Szalavitz is an incredible book about addiction and recovery. If you are struggling with addiction, start here.

If you want to read the articles mentioned in this book:

Tyler Kingkade and Hannah Rappleye, "The Brief Life of Cornelius Frederick: Warning Signs Missed Before Teen's Fatal Restraint," NBC News, July 23, 2020, https://www.nbcnews.com/news/us -news/brief-life-cornelius-frederick-warning-signs-missed-teen-s -fatal-n1234660.

Cathy Krebs, "Five Facts About the Troubled Teen Industry," American Bar Association, October 22, 2021, https://www .americanbar.org/groups/litigation/committees/childrens-right s/practice/2021/5-facts-about-the-troubled-teen-industry/.

Michael Wilson, "An Addict Dies in a School Restroom. He Was a Teacher," *New York Times*, January 26, 2018, https://www .nytimes.com/2018/01/26/nyregion/heroin-opioids-death-teacher -bronx-azimi-addict.

Michael Wilson, "'It's Like, Who's Next?': A Troubled School's Alarming Death Rate," *New York Times*, September 2, 2018, https://

www.nytimes.com/2018/09/02/nyregion/suicide-school-overdose-deaths-ny-family-foundation.html.

Michael Wilson, "Survivor993 Is Not Alone: Lawsuits Show Abuse at School for At-Risk Teens," *New York Times*, January 14, 2022, https://www.nytimes.com/2022/01/14/nyregion/family-foundation-school-abuse-lawsuits.html.

I wish I could recommend a therapist, but I can't. I don't know of any lists of or organizations for TTI-conversant therapists, although I hope that will change. My best advice: make sure, in your first session, that your therapist is *trauma-informed*. Make sure they understand *complex PTSD*. Make sure they are comfortable talking calmly about *suicidal ideation*, and you are comfortable talking with them about it. If I had asked these questions at my first session, I would have known immediately that Kay was right for me instead of waiting seven years (out of fear) to open up to her.

You should not have to explain your TTI experience for more than one session. If they are like "Oh, my God, I can't believe that happened," find a new therapist. They are not trauma-informed.

If you leave feeling empty, that is not therapy. If you leave feeling unheard, that is not therapy. If you feel unsafe in a session, that is not therapy. Don't bail because things get uncomfortable; discomfort is part of the experience—it means you are being honest. But don't be afraid to find a new therapist if you sense they are not right for you. As long as you feel safe and heard, you are in good hands.

You need a battle buddy—someone who will be there when you need them, no questions asked. They don't have to be a friend, just someone who understands. So reach out to other survivors; it's the best way.

And you need to be a battle buddy, too. If someone says something worrisome, or their personality changes in their socials, reach out. Don't be shy. I wish I had reached out when Jon and Mike texted, "I have to get out of New York." I wish it every day. Please don't make my mistake.

Acknowledgments

It's hard AF to shout out everyone who impacted my life, but this is my dream chance to lay it all out. For good. Remember, it's been a long run.

To my OG Wolf Pack, who left this earth but are still here. Jay Lavelle, JMC, MOD, Marisa, and all of you—I'm sorry I couldn't stop you from leaving, but I would like to think I was part of why you held on so long. I'm still pissed you went out like that; you should be here. We all tried to stop the pain in our own way, and this is mine. Not that I'm better than you—I died, too. I stayed alive enough to tell our story, and let's face it, I'm a redhead and more angry than all you shitheads combined. I will always wish you were here.

If you're reading this, I hope you fell in love with my friends. They were amazing people. I hope your friends are, too. If you don't think you have friends, then you haven't heard me when I said, "You are not alone."

To the amazing influencers in my life, in my usual random order:

The Gravy Master, Bret Witter, writer, mentor, genius, you freeze in the New York "winter," but you can add the warmth of the pen to the coldest page.

Agent Savage, mother, warrior, bad-ass, rebel, survivor.

Agent X, small but mighty, her looks can kill you or fool you—your call. It's always a party. Thanks for being you.

Agent Smith, like a dad but way cooler. I hope you now know how much I actually care.

Agent Cash, love the all-black thing you got going on. It suits you.

Those two male agents, sorry about the ruckus. I heard you are actually cool. But I went that day to Roscoe, and no, I did not die.

Ralph DeSimone, Esq., the classy Dapper Don. Human, father, Catholic AF, and you always try to do the right thing. He unsuspectingly took in a group of totally fucked-up Family kids, and trust me, he went on a ride with us, but he always went to war. Ralph, I hope the therapy helps. Not yet sure on the church.

Phil Elberg, the OG attorney who broke through the icebergs with bloody knuckles.

The Goldbergs, for shelter from the storm. You are the warm blanket in a cold world.

Carrie, three doors down.

Dawna Day, you, girl, inspired a strong woman to follow through on a heartfelt oath she took many years ago. Your tears were her tears, too. This book is testimony to that lasting sisterhood and trusted friendship. RIP.

Steve and Christina, thanks for feeding me and looking after me in 104-degree weather during the height of COVID. That shit was wild.

Howie, I hope all that shit I had to tell you was chilling. I hope it haunts you in your sleep.

Maia Szalavitz, for being exactly who you are, and wicked smart. You kind of started a revolution. Your book saved my life.

Dr. Bruce Perry, the smartest mental health professional I've ever come across.

Dear Watson, for being ride or die. Django!

Mike Wilson, you helped me crash through walls against all odds from a desk in Manhattan and a cold, bleak trip to Hancock.

The Cali, Canadian, and Bayou Bitches; the ladies in the Deep South and the Coastal Northwest; the Cholas in the boogie down Bronx; the allies; the LGBTQ+ community, supporters, and helpers, I salute you. Survivors everywhere, I salute you.

Mikaela Shwer, for accidentally saving my life and rolling the tapes. My favorite season is always autumn.

The devil's lettuce. Peace.

My compassionate and patient therapists, Paula, Connie, and my beloved Dorothy.

My tribe, the Bad Bitches, Empresses of Survivorland, survivors whisper your names into the wind to summon your storm.

Neil, my longest-living friend, you have never let me down. It's over now; lay that sword down, be happy, but leave the handle up, just in case.

Matt, my rock, the king of all friends.

Bernadette, the Beast-Godzilla of family court.

David Beke, Esq., smartest city slicker out there, the real deal, the verbal ninja. Ouch.

My Mike, Patrick and Brenden's dad, you are the most stand-up man and father, combat veteran, LEO, and backup I could have in my life. We made incredible children. You and your beautiful wife, Kristen, and her girls, the Brady Bunch, are the most loving, accepting family I have ever known.

My only niece, I love you. My tribe screams so girls coming up like you don't have to.

My dog Tails, best relationship I've ever had.

To ALL the families that loved everyone enough to get us this far, and for the time your family lent to mine. It did not go unnoticed. To the people who raised and mentored my favorite people: well done.

M—, you gave me a voice. Our sisterhood will never die. *But you shoulda put your name in this book!*

Natalie, stay wild, girl. You gave me wings to fly.

The Verb, thanks for listening to me on that loud-ass Florida highway.

Pastor Jeremy, I'm still not sure on skydaddy, but thanks for being a voice for real-life stuff, not just Jesus and his boy band. Thanks for hooking me up with the "no lightning strike upon entering" experience.

Kevin Scutt, you always do the right thing. I'm glad I broke you out. You are the kindest soul, but you'll always be little Kevin to me.

Hey, Pedophile, hope you enjoyed the high-test coffee. I told you when you got all sweaty and pale I was coming for ya, and I wasn't going to help if you dropped dead. I meant it. Hate all you want, your dumb ass underestimated me. As usual. Oh, and MOD pissed on your bed; it wasn't you. Great talk, BTW.

Robin, I wish I'd thrown you in that grave that afternoon. I showed up at your headstone with a sledgehammer, but I decided you weren't worth it.

Bob, I drooled in your dead face because I couldn't fight you at five foot six.

Linda, trick's on you, bitch. I hope you don't have that house in Vermont.

Mikey, your dad wasn't wrong when he told us you were a fat, weak, gluttonous man full of insecurities and impurities.

To any kids I housed or beat on or said horrible things to, I wish I could rewind the tapes. And to anyone who ate those pancakes, I'm sorry. I wasn't trying to hurt you. It was all for them.

Patrick and Bren, my boys, now almost men, Mama tries so hard. You are half me, half your father. Make it count. Stay wild and free. Always do what's right, not the right thing. Know the difference. Nana and Papa shipped me off for less than the crazy shit you both have pulled, so rock on. Never fear. Keep going. Live well.

Sweet Bubby, I think about you every minute of every day. I never meant to bring you into such chaos, and I hope you know I went to war for you. I had no idea when I kissed you goodbye at the park it was the last time. You are always missed and so, so loved.

To the abusers and losers and wannabe troopers (and that one ex-cop who crawled out of that sewer in New Rochelle) who were terroristic menaces or shady wannabe mouthpieces in my life, don't watch too hard for that big-ass karma bus, I heard she's on quite a bender, making wide turns and short stops. Brake check!! You might even get Waffled. Duck and weave.

To my online haters and bullies, blah blahers, fake asses, and posers hiding behind their computers, you embarrassed the fuck out of yourselves trying to throw shade on me and my crew. Show some respect. Rent is due. Try liking me. It's not so bad. The high road wins, bitches.

If you're upset about something I wrote about you, let's talk, but only after you reread what I wrote, think about your feelings and actions, and keep it classy.

To the Family and the pathetic life member loser club that took a dirty dollar from you or even did you a podunk favor, there's blood on your hands, and I hope all your nightmares come true. I am releasing you now.

Ms. Brown, worst guidance counselor of 1993, way to go.

To the VERY broken system that failed my son, I hope you realize now you chose poorly.

Dr. M., you incompetent and unethical psychiatrist, that shit was not therapy. It was fuckery, and I believe you know it. PS, I never took those meds.

To every 911 patient who landed in my arms or my ambulance, I hope I made you feel safe in your most harrowing hour. I did everything I could. To the twin girls, five in 1999 when your father had a heart attack waiting for your bus, it was great to see all three of you months later with cupcakes. To the baby boy I delivered going ninety-five at mile marker 44.5 on the Taconic, I hope your mom doesn't still hate me for fucking up her birth plan.

To the medical colleagues and contractors who deployed with me on the Rapid Response Strike Team all the way from Queens to Texas, well done. Except for Misty.

To the elderly lady in the green dress who told me, at twelve, at my grandparents' fiftieth anniversary, that I was destined to do something big in my life, thank you. You were right.

Dr. Appleby, RIP; you taught me things about college and never told anyone I struggled. You made me better.

To the midnight cop I found in your black truck that night, I remember. I still care. I'm glad you decided to hand me your gun.

To the soldiers, veterans, and LEOs I proudly served, I hope I served you well. I will never forget standing graveside at Arlington National Cemetery to bury our KIA. The marines did good that day.

KT, fall off a cliff. Take Gramps with you.

To everyone in publishing who made this dream possible. Daniel Greenberg, my agent, who took me in. Lauren Marino, my editor, who believed. Niyati Patel, you kept everything on the level. Thank you.

Quinn Fariel in marketing and Sharon Kunz in publicity, I haven't met you yet, because it's like nine months before the book comes out (I had no idea it was like this!), but I hear you kick ass, so thanks in advance.

Amanda Kain and Mark Harris, who designed and illustrated the jacket, you nailed it. Peace. I'm sorry I cried three times during the process.

Sean Moreau, amazingly patient managing editor, I'm sorry my cowriter screwed up the tech three times.

Jeff Williams, interior designer, thank you for making this book look so great inside.

Connie Oehring, thanks for the copyedit. I still don't know what you mean by my voice, but I appreciate it.

Annie Chatham and Kay Mariea, thank you both for your additional sets of eyes while proofreading my words.

To all my former grad students, the coolest kids. I was proud to go to Fordham and pay it forward to you. I'd love to know what you are up to!

Brandi Carlile, for writing songs my soul could hear.

Heather, we've weathered high seas and low tides; my love for you never ends. Eh? See you at hockey.

Damarys, stay hood 4 life.

The Punishers, I appreciate you. Always.

To the Sea and She Captains who lit lighthouses to show me the way . . . to the girls like Megan, Emily, and Amber, who cheered me every time I rolled in . . . and the boys like Maverick and Iceman who stared.

My email is iseeyousurvivor993@gmail. I'll write you back. I can't be your therapist. I've retired for my health. But I can be your friend.

The only lives that don't matter are pedophiles, child predators, and molesters. Karma will spray you with high-test sticky napalm, and when she does, think of me. Think of your victims. Think of their families. Then check under your bed.

To my parents, if you read this far, none of this was meant to hurt you, I'm just trying to save some lives including, maybe, my own. I love you both in a unique, borderline-unhealthy way, but it's my way, so . . . be glad you have me. A lot of parents wish they had their children to hold, but the Family took them. Be proud I survived and relieved I don't hate you. Celebrate me. It's not your fault I'm "different"; it's the world's fault for teaching you not to love that part of me. Unlearn that shit. Times have changed. I'm ready. I'll rip off the rearview mirror if you do, because I don't want to be at war with you. We have suffered too long, so let's release each other from the tragedy and trauma our family has endured. I never said you were totally wrong.

To my siblings, we've racked up quite a tab in life being ourselves. We certainly put the FUN in dysFUNctional, and we always love to crash a good funeral or wedding. We're assholes to each other, but we laugh and we cry, together. I'm sorry my life impacted yours in a way that caused harm.

To those lost, gone, or left behind, I see you. We all do. You were never alone; you just didn't know how loved you were—and are.

All I ask is to be remembered respectfully as the Lioness of Survivorland: cycle breaker, agitator, educator, warrior, mother, guardian, and, if you insist, a leader of the "silent" resistance. But please just call me Liz. Turns out, I was never quiet, even in my silence. The rest is up to you. Look after each other, heal together, and never stop raging against the machine. We've got lives to save; let's get to it. We always ride at dawn.

And lastly, YOU, the reader, I hope you don't linger on my struggles as much as you revel in the way I illuminated my scars, my trauma, my trials, and my triumphs against unfathomable odds.

Thank you for listening.

—Survivor993